MICHEL ROUX
Desserts
A Lifelong Passion

MICHEL ROUX
Desserts
A Lifelong Passion

TRANSLATED AND EDITED BY KATE WHITEMAN

PHOTOGRAPHS BY MARTIN BRIGDALE

CONRAN OCTOPUS

AUTHOR'S ACKNOWLEDGEMENTS

I am very grateful to the following people who have contributed so much to this book: Chris Sellors, sous-chef at The Waterside Inn and Laurent Corcaud, my pâtissier, who skilfully tested all the recipes; M.O.R.A. for generously supplying some of the specialist equipment and Valrhona for providing the chocolate used in my recipes; Martin Brigdale, who photographed them so artistically and Helen Trent, who styled them; Mary Evans for her art direction; Alison Barrett for the attractive illustrations; Kate Whiteman for editing and translating the book: the rapport we have established over the past twelve years and five books has ensured that this has been done just as I would wish; John Huber, Principal Lecturer at Thames Valley University, who meticulously read and checked the recipes; Claude Grant for typing the manuscript and coping with my ego from time to time; and of course, Robyn, who continues to support me throughout the creative process.

First published in 1994 by
Conran Octopus Limited
37 Shelton Street
London WC2H 9HN

Text copyright © Michel Roux 1994
Photography copyright © Martin Brigdale 1994
Illustrations copyright © Alison Barrett 1994
Design and layout © Conran Octopus Ltd 1994

Art director: Mary Evans
Design: Peter Butler
Project editor: Anne Furniss
Translation and editing: Kate Whiteman
Illustrations: Alison Barrett
Styling: Helen Trent
Production: Jill Macey

British Library Cataloguing in Publication Data
A catalogue record for this book is available from the British Library
ISBN 1 85029 553 0

Typeset by Servis Filmsetting
Colour reproduction by H.B.M. Print Pte Ltd, Singapore
Printed and bound by Kim Hup Lee, Singapore

CONTENTS

Page 2: Banana and Caramel Mousse Gâteau; Title page: White Chocolate Dome; Page 5: French Meringues; Page 6: Lucien Peletier; Page 7: Love Nest with a choux pastry heart; Page 8: Michel Roux

MY SECRET OBSESSION

I catch myself smiling at her, a discreet furtive smile which I have secretly harboured for longer than I can remember. I felt its first feeble flickerings in adolescence; over the years it has heated into an incandescent furnace.

Ours is a faithful relationship, pure and bottomless, which cannot easily be expressed in words. It has deepened over many years through the senses: touch, sight, smell and even hearing. I rarely speak to her, but communicate only by vague movements of my lips, almost like the first outline of a kiss.

I reinvent and recreate her every day, using simple ingredients. Inspired by my thoughts, my fingers model and caress her, gently dress her, apply a hint of makeup with the touch of a piping cone, and ornament her hair with a sugar rose. Her beauty takes my breath away; she thrills me and fills me with admiration.

MICHEL ROUX

INTRODUCTION

MY CHOSEN CAREER I am a pâtissier at heart and always shall be. The creation of a dessert is my passion. During my career, I have passed through various stages. When I first started, I aimed to emulate my teachers and peers and to match their skill. Then I was drawn to the artistic aspect of pâtisserie and successfully took part in many professional competitions.

Nearly all my desserts, both hot and cold, are served individually assembled on the plate. They are put together in the kitchen only when ordered and as a result, they are always wonderfully fresh, delicate and refined. Many years ago, I abandoned the free-for-all of dessert trolley, which all too often looks like a battlefield.

As in all cooking, I dislike mixing flavours, especially those which are diametrically opposed, on the same plate. The look and taste of the basic ingredient must be paramount. The only accompaniments which do not dominate a dessert are coulis, sponge biscuits, fruit,

mousses or ice creams. As you will see, my desserts range from simple to elaborate.

MY APPRENTICESHIP My apprentice master was Monsieur Camille Loyal. Originally from Alsace, he was a man of about fifty, huge, churlish yet modest, with a small greying moustache. He instilled in me a passion for cakes, chocolates and ice cream — but only if they were well made. As he said: 'It takes no longer to make something well than badly'. This simple logic stuck in the mind of more than one apprentice. Another favourite saying of his was: 'We don't eat sugar flowers, pastillage or elaborate decorations, but we do eat desserts'; hence his insistence on using the very best quality ingredients and the simplest techniques for his desserts.

A MATTER OF TASTE All tastes are to be found in nature and it is up to us to discover and develop them. Personal taste should be respected, but we can share, examine and study it in order to modify it. Those who do not develop their own tastebuds or accept the taste of others deprive themselves of the opportunity to discover the constantly changing beauty of taste.

In France it is customary when visiting friends or relations to present your host with a cake or dessert, especially on festive occasions. France is full of pastry shops and professional pâtissiers who bring happiness to thousands of customers every day, for pâtisserie adds a little luxury to our lives. Sharing is a gesture of friendship, so why not make a dessert to offer as a gift?

HOW PATISSERIE HAS EVOLVED Like French cooking, pâtisserie has evolved in a significant way. Nowadays, many more desserts are based on fruits, be they fresh, frozen or tinned, which are refreshing and introduce a note of healthy eating. Nearly all are lighter and contain far less butter, eggs and cream than formerly. They are also less sugary. Plain cooking chocolate and couverture range from bitter to extra-bitter, which allows us to savour the taste of the chocolate without being overwhelmed by its sweetness.

It is my pleasure to invite you to enter my magical world, the world of my favourite desserts. I do urge you to read and digest the Practical Advice section before embarking on the recipes; then with simple, clear instructions I shall help and guide you through the preparations to the final delicious result.

PRACTICAL ADVICE

These pages contain a reminder of certain basic rules and guidelines which you should follow when making the recipes. They are second nature to me, and I am sure you will find them helpful when you come to prepare the desserts in this book. I trust that they will answer some of the questions which may already have come to mind.

Silpat: Fine conical strainer: Palette knife for spreading: Round cooling rack: Cornet cone: Cardboard cake base: Fluted nozzle: Cake rack: Cannelé moulds: Madeleine tray: Spiral dipping tool for chocolate and sugarwork: 2-pronged dipping fork for chocolate and sugarwork:

THE GOLDEN RULES The three vital rules to remember before embarking on the preparation of a dessert are:

1. Have all the equipment needed for the recipe ready to hand.

2. Weigh out and measure all the ingredients before you begin and keep them in separate containers.

3. Preheat the oven to the necessary temperature.

By following these golden rules, you will produce successful and delicious desserts every time.

Rodoïde plastic: Bombe mould: Hemispherical mould: Decorating comb: Copper sugar pan: Pointed sculpting tool: Hemispherical mould: Aluminium baking beans: Pyramid mould: Fluted pastry cutters: Fluted modelling tool: Right-angled palette knife.

✽ MAKING THINGS SIMPLE Many of the more elaborate recipes in the book contain a number of elements which can be prepared several hours, or even a day or two in advance. An asterisk ✽ beside the Ingredients list indicates that the greater part of the dessert can be prepared beforehand.

WEIGHTS AND MEASURES All my recipes have been tested using metric measurements. For perfect results, it is worth investing in a set of metric measuring spoons, jug and scales. If you must use imperial measurements, remember that they are not as precise as metric and of necessity are rounded up or down as appropriate to the nearest half-ounce. On no account mix metric and imperial measurements.

SPECIAL EQUIPMENT The suggested sizes of special equipment are the ideals. However, if you do not possess, for example, a dessert ring or mould of the precise dimensions given in a recipe, use the nearest equivalent.

Rodoïde plastic: This flexible clear plastic is invaluable for giving chocolate work a high gloss. For suppliers, see page 190. Acetate, available at stationers, makes an acceptable substitute.

Silicone paper: This is also known as baking parchment. Since it is non-stick, it is useful for baking.

Silpat: Silpat is a recently developed baking medium which is exceptionally versatile and useful for baking sponge bases, pulling sugar etc. It can be reused many times. The equally effective Bake-o-Glide is more readily available in the U.K. For stockists, see page 190.

OVEN TEMPERATURES These can vary from oven to oven, so for perfect results, use an oven thermometer.

All the recipes in this book have been tested using a circotherm or convection oven. If you have a conventional oven, in every case you should increase the suggested temperature by 20°C (eg: 180°C/350°F/gas 4 should be increased to 200°C/400°F/gas 5 for a conventional oven).

SERVING TEMPERATURES It is important to serve desserts and gâteaux at the temperature which best suits their composition and flavour. Chocolate-based desserts (filled with ganache, mousse etc.) should be served at 6°–8°C/42.8°–46.4°F. Those based on fruit mousses, such as charlottes, at 8°–12°C/42.8°–53.6°F. Warm desserts (tarts and some feuilletés) at 35°–45°C/95°–113°F, and hot desserts (principally soufflés) at 70°–80°C/158°–176°F.

CHOOSING THE BASIC INGREDIENTS   To achieve a gastronomically and visually perfect dessert, it is essential to use only extremely fresh, top-quality ingredients. Eggs must be extra fresh and come from a reliable source; if you cannot guarantee this, use pasteurized eggs.

Fresh cream can go off quickly, so buy only the best quality. Cream should always be pasteurized to prevent the spread of any bacteria.

STORAGE   Recommended storage times are for foods kept in airtight containers or tightly wrapped or covered with clingfilm.
COLD STORAGE Technological advances have opened up new horizons which make for more efficiency in the field of pâtisserie.
Domestic fridges: 5°C/41°F.
Holding freezers: −18°C/0°F.
Deep freezes: −25°C/−13°F.
Blast freezers: −35°C/−31°F (ideally all foods should be frozen at this temperature for 30 minutes before being transferred to the holding freezer).

HYGIENE   You are strongly advised not to wear a watch or jewellery when baking. They can cause allergies and are unhygienic, as ingredients such as flour and icing sugar may get trapped inside.

SOME ADVICE ON INGREDIENTS AND CULINARY TECHNIQUES
Almonds and hazelnuts: Before using these to prepare a dessert, dry them in an airing cupboard or low oven, otherwise the moisture they contain could adversely affect the cooking.
Flaked almonds: Sprinkle with icing sugar and toast lightly in a hot oven or with a salamander. They are delicious scattered over a mousse or cream just before serving.
Butter, sugar and flour: Unless otherwise specified, always use unsalted butter, caster sugar and sifted plain flour for these recipes.

EGGS: *Beating egg whites:* To ensure that egg whites rise perfectly, use scrupulously clean utensils rinsed in cold water and thoroughly dried. Make sure that the whites contain no trace of yolk. If they are very fresh, add a pinch of salt to break them down. Begin by beating at medium speed to incorporate as much air as possible until the whites become frothy, then beat at the highest speed to firm them up. As soon as flecks of beaten egg appear around the edge of the bowl, add a little sugar to prevent them from becoming grainy. They will be firmer and more resistant, and therefore easier to mix and handle. This is most important when you are preparing both sweet and savoury soufflés.

Unbeaten egg whites can be kept frozen in an airtight container for several weeks.

Egg yolks: To freeze, whisk lightly with 5–10% sugar, then freeze at −25°C/−13°F for no more than four weeks.

Egg yolks 'burn' on contact with sugar or salt, so they must be beaten immediately with a whisk or spatula until completely homogeneous, otherwise they will form into hard little granules, which are impossible to break up.

A cornucopia of glossy, ripe fruit. I always demand the highest quality from fresh ingredients.

Weighing eggs: A medium-sized egg weighing about 60 g/2 oz is made up of 30 g/1 oz white, 20 g/⅔ oz yolk and 10 g/⅓ oz shell. 20 whole eggs, 32 egg whites, or 52 egg yolks = 1 litre/1¾ pints.

It is essential to note that I always use 60 g/2 oz eggs in my recipes. If a recipe calls for six eggs of 60 g/2 oz each, that makes a total weight of 360 g/12 oz. If you use 50 g/1¾ oz or 70 g/2¼ oz eggs, you will be using one-sixth less or more egg, which is not acceptable to achieve a perfect result.

Fondant: One of the classic icings for glazing choux puffs, éclairs etc. Take care not to heat it above 37°C/100°F or it will craze and lose its gloss when cold. If it is too thick, thin it with a little sorbet syrup.

Gelatine: One gelatine leaf weighs 3 g/⅒ oz. It can be replaced by an equal weight of powdered gelatine.

Glazing with eggwash: For a beautiful shiny finish, brush on two light coats of eggwash. A single, heavier coat is more likely to run.

Greasing: Use softened, clarified or melted butter as appropriate. When greasing moulds, tins, rings and baking sheets, it is important to use the precise quantity of butter specified in the recipe. Too much may crinkle the pastry, too little may cause it to stick to the mould. Spray-on silicone coating can be used instead of butter.

Kiwi fruit: To peel, place in the freezer for about 10 minutes, drop into boiling water, then into iced water, as if skinning a tomato. The skin can then be peeled off very easily without spoiling the oblong shape of the fruit, to give attractive, neat slices.

Marzipan or almond paste: If it is too crumbly or too firm, mix with fondant or liquid glucose to soften it.

PASTRY: *Frozen pastry* should be left to thaw gradually in the fridge at 5°C/41°F until malleable.

Kneading leavened dough or puff pastry: The dough is sufficiently kneaded when all the ingredients are well incorporated and it comes away cleanly from the sides of the bowl or work surface. All the protein in the flour will be hydrated to make the dough very elastic.

Kneading and proving yeast-based dough: When kneading dough in a warm room, chill the liquid ingredients (milk, water and eggs) in the fridge beforehand. After kneading, the temperature of the dough should not exceed 24°C/75°F.

After proving in a warm place, leave live yeast-based doughs (eg: brioches, Viennese pastries) at room temperature for a further 15 minutes before baking to obtain maximum volume during cooking.

Puff pastry: Transfer the rolled-out pastry to a baking sheet dampened with water. This prevents the pastry from slipping when you glaze it, and from shrinking during baking and thus spoiling the shape.

Refrigerating puff pastry: Puff pastry must be brought to room temperature before using so that the butter softens. Take it out of the fridge 3–5 minutes before rolling out to ensure that the layers of fat do not break and prevent the pastry from rising fully.

Rolled-out pastry and marzipan: To move it without spoiling the shape or breaking it, roll it loosely around a pastry rolling pin, then unroll it onto the mould or baking sheet.

Removing desserts from their rings: To retain a perfect edge, place the gâteau in its dessert ring on an object about 10 cm/4 in high (eg: a tin) and push the ring downwards to release the gâteau. This is a delicate operation, but it gives perfect results.

Scales: Small electronic scales are very precise, and are useful for pâtisserie where only a few grams of certain ingredients may be required.

Sifting: This eliminates foreign bodies and lumps from ingredients such as flour, baking powder, ground almonds and cocoa etc. It also aerates and homogenizes. Flour should always be sifted.

Staggered rows: Always arrange small pastries, macaroons, tartlet tins, brioches etc. in staggered rows on the baking sheet to ensure more even cooking.

Syrup: If it contains impurities, clarify it by adding some beaten egg white and bubbling over low heat for a few minutes. Pass gently through a conical strainer and use as required. A 30° Beaumé sorbet syrup (1.2624 density) will keep in an airtight container in the fridge for two weeks.

CHAPTER ONE

PASTRY AND DOUGH

In pastry workshops, the *tourrier* is responsible for making all the dough and pastry, so basically almost all desserts begin with him. The precise weighing and measuring of the ingredients is vital; if the pastry is too salty, too soft or too dry, the quality of the entire dessert will be compromised when it is baked.

Raw pastry has an agreeable smell which titillates the tastebuds. I find it a very sensual food; I love working it with my fingertips, kneading it carefully so that it remains firm but supple. I dust it with flour, then roll it out quickly and evenly to avoid bruising it. If I do not want to use it immediately, I can wrap it in clingfilm and freeze it for future use.

BRIOCHE

THIS RICH, BUTTERY YEAST BREAD IS DELICIOUS SERVED FOR
BREAKFAST OR TEA.

INGREDIENTS:

15 g/½ oz fresh yeast

70 ml/3 fl oz warm milk

15 g/½ oz salt

500 g/1 lb 2 oz flour, plus
   extra for dusting

6 eggs

350 g/12 oz softened butter

30 g/1 oz sugar

Eggwash (1 egg yolk beaten
   with 1 soup spoon milk
   and a pinch of salt)

Makes 1.2 kg/2¾ lbs
   dough, enough for 1 large
   brioche to serve 20, or
   16–20 individual
   brioches

Preparation time: 20
   minutes in an electric
   mixer, or 35 minutes by
   hand, plus resting and
   proving

Cooking time: 40–45
   minutes for a large
   brioche, 8 minutes for
   small brioches

MIXING THE DOUGH: Put the yeast and milk in a mixing bowl, whisk lightly, then add the salt. Add the flour and eggs and knead the dough with the dough hook of an electric mixer or by hand until it becomes smooth and elastic (this will take about 10 minutes in a mixer, 20 minutes by hand).

Beat the softened butter and sugar together, then, at low speed, add them to the dough a little at a time, making sure that they are completely amalgamated before adding more. Continue to mix for 5 minutes in a mixer or 15 minutes by hand, until the dough is perfectly smooth, shiny and fairly elastic.

Cover the bowl with clingfilm and leave at about 24°C/75°F for 2 hours, until the dough has doubled in volume.

KNOCKING BACK THE DOUGH: Flip the dough over with your fingertips a couple of times to knock it back. Cover with clingfilm and refrigerate for several hours, but not more than 24 hours.

MOULDING THE BRIOCHE: Place the dough on a lightly floured surface and shape into a large ball. If you are using a saucepan, line it with buttered greaseproof paper twice the height of the pan before putting in the dough. To make the brioche in a mould, cut off one-third of the dough to make the 'head'. Roll the larger piece into a ball and place in the mould. Make an indentation in the centre with your fingertips. Holding your hand at an angle, roll the 'head' into an elongated oval. Lightly flour your fingertips and gently press the narrow end of the oval into the indentation in the large ball.

Lightly brush the top of the brioche with eggwash, working from the outside inwards and taking care not to let it run into the cracks in the dough or onto the edges of the mould, or the dough will not rise properly.

PROVING: Leave the brioche to prove in a warm, draught-free place until it has almost doubled in bulk (about 20 minutes for the small brioches and 1½ hours for a large one).

BAKING: Preheat the oven to 220°C/425°F/gas 7.

Lightly brush the top of the brioche again with eggwash. Slash the edge of the large brioche at intervals with scissors or a razor blade dipped in cold water. Do not slash the small brioches. Bake immediately in the hot oven for 40–45 minutes for the large brioche, 8 minutes for the small ones. Unmould the brioche immediately onto a wire rack and leave to cool.

SPECIAL EQUIPMENT:

1 large brioche mould,
   24 cm/10 diam. at the
   top, 11 cm/4 in at the
   base, or an 18 cm/7 in
   copper saucepan, or 20
   small brioche moulds,
   8 cm/3¼ in diam. at the
   top, 4 cm/1½ in at the
   base

NOTES:

Brioche dough can also be plaited or shaped into a crown. Serve it sliced, sprinkled with icing sugar and glazed under a hot grill, or warm with Chocolate Sauce (page 55).

The dough can be frozen, wrapped in clingfilm, after the knocking back stage. Defrost gradually in the fridge for at least 4 hours, or overnight, before moulding, proving and baking.

SHORTCRUST
Pâte brisée

A LIGHT, CRUMBLY PASTRY WHICH IS USED AS A CLASSIC BASE FOR MANY
TARTS AND FLANS.

INGREDIENTS:
250 g/9 oz flour
150 g/5 oz butter, slightly
   softened
1 egg
A pinch of sugar
¾ teaspoon salt
1 tablespoon milk

Makes about 450 g/1 lb
Preparation time: 15
   minutes

Sift the flour onto the work surface and make a well in the centre. Cut the butter into small pieces and put them in the well with the egg, sugar and salt. Mix all these ingredients with the fingertips of your left hand, then use your right hand to draw in the flour a little at a time. When everything is almost amalgamated, add the milk to make a paste. Knead with the heel of your hand two or three times until it is completely homogeneous. Wrap in clingfilm and refrigerate for several hours before using.

NOTE:
The shortcrust can be kept for a few days in the fridge, or frozen for several weeks.

SWEET SHORT PASTRY
Pâte sucrée

THIS PASTRY IS MOSTLY USED FOR FRUIT TARTS. AS IT IS NOT TOO FRAGILE,
IT IS SUITABLE FOR PICNIC DESSERTS.

INGREDIENTS:
250 g/9 oz flour
100 g/4 oz butter, diced
100 g/4 oz icing sugar,
   sifted
A small pinch of salt
2 eggs, at room temperature

Makes about 520 g/
   1 lb 2 oz
Preparation time: 15
   minutes

Sift the flour onto the work surface and make a well in the centre. Put in the butter and work it with your fingertips until very soft. Add the icing sugar and salt, mix well, then add the eggs and mix again. Gradually draw the flour into the mixture to make a homogeneous paste. Knead the paste two or three times with the heel of your hand until very smooth. Roll it into a ball, flatten the top slightly, wrap in clingfilm and refrigerate for several hours before using.

NOTE:
This dough keeps well in the fridge for several days or in the freezer for 1 week.

SHORTBREAD PASTRY: RECIPE 1
Pâte sablée 1

THIS PASTRY IS EXTREMELY DELICATE, SO YOU MUST WORK VERY FAST AND
MUST NOT OVERHANDLE IT, AS IT SOFTENS VERY QUICKLY.

INGREDIENTS:
250 g/9 oz flour
200 g/7 oz butter, diced
100 g/4 oz icing sugar,
 sifted
A pinch of salt
2 egg yolks
Lemon or vanilla essence
 (optional)

Makes about 650 g/1 lb 6 oz
Preparation time: 15
 minutes

Sift the flour onto the work surface and make a well in the centre. Put
in the butter and work it with your fingertips until very soft. Sprinkle
the icing sugar and salt onto the butter and work in. Add the egg yolks
and mix thoroughly. Gradually draw in the flour, mixing until
completely amalgamated, but taking care not to overwork the pastry,
or it will become too elastic. Add a drop of lemon or vanilla essence
and knead the pastry two or three times with the heel of your hand.
Roll the pastry into a ball and flatten it slightly. Wrap it in clingfilm
and refrigerate for several hours before using.

SHORTBREAD PASTRY: RECIPE 2
Pâte sablée 2

THIS RECIPE CONTAINS LESS BUTTER THAN RECIPE 1, WHICH MAKES IT
EASIER TO PREPARE AND HANDLE, BUT LESS CRUMBLY AND RICH-TASTING.

INGREDIENTS:
30 g/1 oz ground almonds
250 g/9 oz flour
140 g/4¾ oz butter, diced
100 g/3½ oz icing sugar,
 sifted
A pinch of salt
1 egg
Lemon or vanilla essence
 (optional)

Makes 600 g/1¼ lbs
Preparation time: 15
 minutes

Sift the ground almonds and flour together onto the work surface and
make a well in the centre. Continue as for Recipe 1.

NOTE:
Both recipes will keep well in
the fridge for several days or
in the freezer for one week.

FLAN OR LINING PASTRY
Pâte à foncer

ANOTHER PASTRY FOR FLANS AND TARTS.

INGREDIENTS:
250 g/9 oz flour
125 g/4½ oz butter,
   softened
1 egg
1½ teaspoons caster sugar
¾ teaspoon salt
40 ml/1½ fl oz water

Makes about 450 g/1 lb
Preparation time: 15
   minutes

Sift the flour onto the work surface and make a well in the centre. Cut the butter into small pieces and put them in the well with the egg, sugar and salt. Mix these ingredients with the fingertips of your right hand, then use your left hand to draw in the flour a little at a time. When the dough is well mixed but still a little crumbly and not quite homogeneous, add the water. Knead the pastry two or three times with the heel of your hand until completely smooth. Wrap in clingfilm and refrigerate for several hours before using.

NOTE:
This pastry will keep well for several days in the fridge or for several weeks in the freezer.

1. Large tart case
2. Tartlet case
3. Barquette or boat cases
4. Fluted tartlet cases
5. Mini-tartlet cases
6. Small brioches
7. Sliced brioche loaf
8. Unsliced brioche plait
9. Plaited brioche basket
10. Sliced brioche plait

JEAN MILLET'S PUFF PASTRY

Feuilletage Jean Millet

MAKING PUFF PASTRY SHOULD HOLD NO TERRORS FOR THE HOME COOK.
TRUE, IT IS A LENGTHY PROCESS, BUT IF YOU FOLLOW JEAN MILLET'S
RECIPE, IT REALLY IS NOT AT ALL DIFFICULT.

INGREDIENTS:

500 g / 1 lb 2 oz flour, plus
    extra for turning
200 ml / 7 fl oz water
1¾ teaspoons salt
25 ml / 1 fl oz white wine
    vinegar
50 g / 2 oz melted butter
400 g / 14 oz well-chilled
    butter

Makes 1.2 kg / 2¾ lbs
Preparation time: 1 hour 10
    minutes, plus 5 hours
    resting

MIXING THE PASTRY: Sift the flour
onto the work surface or into a
mixing bowl and make a well in
the centre. Put in the water, salt,
vinegar and melted butter and
work the mixture with the
fingertips of your right hand (1).
Use your left hand to draw in the
flour little by little, and mix well.

NOTES:

If you plan to store puff
pastry, give it only 4 turns,
then complete the 2 final
turns and chill again for 30
minutes when you want to
use it. It will keep for up to
3 days in the fridge, or for
several weeks in the freezer.

Work the pastry with the heel of
your hand until it becomes
completely homogeneous but
not too firm (2). Roll it into a
ball and cut a cross in the top to
break the elasticity (3). Wrap in
clingfilm and refrigerate for 2–3
hours.

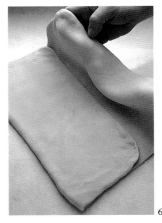

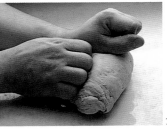

INCORPORATING THE BUTTER: On a
lightly floured surface, roll the
edges of the pastry ball in four
different places to form four
'ears' around a small, round
'head' (4). Beat the chilled butter
several times with a rolling pin
until supple but still firm and
very cold. Lay the butter on top of the 'head' to cover it without
overhanging. Fold the four 'ears' over the butter to enclose it
completely (5). Refrigerate for 20–30
minutes to bring the pastry and butter to
the same temperature and therefore the
same consistency. This process is vital.

TURNING THE PUFF PASTRY: On the lightly
floured surface, roll the pastry away from
you gently and gradually, to make a 70 × 40
cm / 27 × 16 in rectangle. Fold in the ends
to make 3 layers (6). This is the first turn.
    Rotate the pastry through 90 degrees
and gradually roll it out again into a
70 × 40 cm / 27 × 16 in rectangle.

Fold in the ends to make 3 layers. This is the second turn. Wrap the pastry in clingfilm and refrigerate for 30 minutes to rest and firm up.

Make two more turns as above and, after the fourth turn, wrap the pastry in clingfilm again and refrigerate for another 30–60 minutes. Make two final turns, making a total of six. The puff pastry is now ready to roll and cut into shape. After cutting the pastry into your desired shape, refrigerate it for at least 30 minutes before baking, or it will shrink and distort the shape.

QUICK PUFF PASTRY
Feuilletage minute

THIS PASTRY WILL RISE ABOUT 30 PER CENT LESS THAN CLASSIC PUFF PASTRY, BUT IT HAS THE GREAT ADVANTAGE OF BEING VERY QUICK AND SIMPLE TO PREPARE.

INGREDIENTS:
500 g/1 lb 2 oz flour, plus extra for turning
500 g/1 lb 2 oz firm but not too hard butter (remove from the fridge 1 hour before using)
1 teaspoon salt
250 ml/9 fl oz iced water

Makes 1.2 kg/2¾ lbs
Preparation time: 20 minutes, plus 50 minutes chilling

Sift the flour onto the work surface or into a mixing bowl and make a well in the centre. Cut the butter into small cubes and put it in the well with the salt. Using the fingertips of your right hand, work the ingredients together, gradually drawing in the flour with your left hand.

When the cubes of butter have become very small and the mixture is turning grainy, pour in the iced water and work it gradually into the pastry without kneading. Stop working the pastry as soon as it becomes almost homogeneous but still contains some small flakes of butter.

On the lightly floured surface, roll the pastry away from you into a 40 × 20 cm/16 × 8 in rectangle. Fold in the ends to make three layers. Rotate the pastry through 90 degrees and roll it out again into a 40 × 20 cm/16 × 8 in rectangle. Fold again into three. These are the first two turns. Wrap the pastry in clingfilm and refrigerate for 30 minutes.

Make two more turns. The pastry is now ready to use. Wrap it in clingfilm and store, or roll it into the desired shape, place on a dampened baking sheet and refrigerate for 20 minutes before using.

NOTE:
Quick puff pastry will keep for only 2 days in the fridge or 1 week in the freezer.

CHOUX PASTE AND PUFFS
Pâte à choux

THIS VERSATILE PASTE FORMS THE BASIS OF MANY DESSERTS, INCLUDING MY
BLACK AND WHITE SAINT-HONORÉ (PAGE 106).

INGREDIENTS:

125 ml/4½ fl oz water

125 ml/4½ fl oz milk

100 g/4 oz butter, finely
    diced

½ teaspoon fine salt

¾ teaspoon sugar

150 g/5 oz flour, sifted

4 eggs

Eggwash (1 egg yolk mixed
    with 1 soup spoon milk
    and a pinch of salt)
    (optional)

Makes 22–25 small choux
    puffs or éclairs

Preparation time: 20
    minutes

Cooking time: 10–20
    minutes, depending on the
    size and shape of the puffs

MIXING THE CHOUX PASTE: Combine the water, milk, butter, salt and sugar in a saucepan and boil over high heat for 1 minute (1). If any visible pieces of butter are left, boil for a few seconds more. Take the pan off the heat and quickly tip in the flour, stirring continuously to make a very smooth paste.

Return the pan to the heat and stir the paste with a spatula for 1 minute (2). This 'drying out' process is vitally important for making a good choux paste. By now, some of the water will have evaporated. Take care not to let the paste dry out too much, or it will crack during cooking and spoil your choux puffs. Transfer the paste to a bowl and immediately use a spatula to beat in the eggs one by one (3). Beat until the paste is very smooth. It is now ready to use. If you do not wish to use it immediately, spread a little eggwash over the surface to prevent a crust from forming.

NOTE

Choux paste will keep in an airtight container for 3 days in the fridge or 1 week in the freezer.

PIPING OUT THE CHOUX PASTE: Using a piping bag with an appropriate nozzle, pipe the paste into your desired shapes or a flat base onto a baking sheet lined with silicone or buttered greaseproof paper (4). Brush with eggwash and press the top of the shapes lightly with the back of a fork, dipping it into the eggwash each time. This ensures that the choux puffs develop and rise evenly.

BAKING THE CHOUX PUFFS: Preheat the oven to 220°C/425°F/gas 7. Bake the choux puffs for 4–5 minutes, then open the oven door a crack and leave it ajar. Continue to bake for another 5–15 minutes, depending on the size of the choux puffs.

Baked choux puffs on a Saint-Honoré base

PANCAKES
Crêpes

I USE PANCAKES IN MY COULIBIAC OF WINTER FRUITS (PAGE 98) AND SOUFFLEED CHOCOLATE PANCAKES (PAGE 90).

INGREDIENTS:
250 g/9 oz flour
30 g/1 oz caster sugar
A pinch of salt
4 eggs
650 ml/22 fl oz milk,
   boiled and cooled
200 ml/7 fl oz double
   cream
Flavouring of your choice
   (eg: vanilla, Grand
   Marnier, orange flower
   water, lemon zest)
30 g/1 oz clarified butter

Serves 10
Preparation time: 10
   minutes, plus resting
Cooking time: 1 minute per
   pancake

MAKING THE BATTER: Combine the flour, sugar and salt in a bowl, then add the eggs, two at a time, mixing well with a balloon whisk. Stir in 200 ml/7 fl oz milk to make a smooth batter. Add the cream and the rest of the milk, then leave the batter to rest in a cool place for at least 1 hour before using.

COOKING THE PANCAKES: Stir the batter and add your chosen flavouring. Brush a 30 cm/12 in frying pan with clarified butter and heat. Ladle in a little batter and cook the pancake for about 1 minute on each side, tossing it or turning it with a palette knife.

SERVING: Roll or fold the pancakes and eat at once, either plain or sprinkled with sugar. They are also delicious filled with Apricot Jam with Almonds (page 58) or Apple Jelly (page 59).

NOTE:
Layer the cooked pancakes with bands of greaseproof paper to prevent them from sticking together.

TULIP PASTE FOR BASKETS AND RIBBONS
Pâte à tulipe/ruban/caissette

THIS PASTE IS USED TO MAKE 'CIGARETTES' FOR PETITS FOURS, AND LITTLE BASKETS WHICH YOU CAN FILL WITH ICE CREAM, SORBETS OR FRESH FRUITS. SINCE IT IS VERY MALLEABLE, I ALSO USE IT TO MAKE DECORATIONS SUCH AS RIBBONS (SEE PHOTO PAGE 188) OR MULTI-COLOURED BANDS TO ENCIRCLE A GATEAU.

INGREDIENTS:
100 g/4 oz softened butter
100 g/4 oz icing sugar, sifted
100 g/4 oz egg whites, at room temperature
75 g/3 oz flour, sifted
40 g/1½ oz unsweetened cocoa powder, sifted (optional: see note opposite)

Makes 375 g/13 oz
Preparation time: 10 minutes

Put the softened butter and icing sugar in a bowl and mix with a spatula, then add the egg whites, a little at a time, and finally stir in the flour and cocoa to make a smooth, homogeneous paste. Cover the bowl with clingfilm and keep in the fridge for up to a week.

Take the paste out of the fridge several hours before using and leave it to soften at room temperature so that it becomes easier to work.

NOTES:
40 g/1½ oz cocoa is enough to colour and flavour all the paste. Like flour, it acts as a binding agent, so you will need to add an extra 20 g/¾ oz egg whites (120 g/4½ oz in total). The paste can also be flavoured with vanilla or a few drops of lemon extract or orange flower water.

Once baked, the paste is delicate and loses its texture after 24 hours, especially in humid weather.

CIGARETTE PASTE FOR STRIPED BISCUITS
Pâte à cigarette pour biscuit rayé

USE THIS PASTE TO GIVE AN ATTRACTIVE STRIPED EFFECT TO YOUR SHOWPIECE DESSERTS AND GATEAUX.

INGREDIENTS:
100 g/4 oz softened butter
100 g/4 oz icing sugar, sifted
110 g/4 oz egg whites
80 g/3 oz flour, sifted
Food colourings as appropriate (eg: green/red), or cocoa powder for chocolate brown

Makes about 400 g/14 oz
Preparation time: 15 minutes

Cream the butter in a bowl. Work in the icing sugar until smooth, then add the egg whites, little by little. Finally add and mix in the flour. When the paste is completely homogeneous, add a few drops of food colouring to achieve your desired effect. The paste is now ready to use.

Spread the paste onto Silpat or silicone paper, in stripes or extremely thin layers, using a palette knife, comb, piping cone or your fingers, depending on the desired effect. Freeze for at least 10 minutes to harden the paste, then spread on a layer of Joconde or Genoise sponge (pages 31 and 33), and bake according to the recipe.

NOTE:
Cigarette paste can be kept in an airtight container in the fridge for up to a week. Bring it back to room temperature and work with a spatula to make it flexible and malleable before using.

SPICED CAKE
Pain d'épices

THIS RECIPE WAS GIVEN TO ME BY MY FRIEND DENIS RUFFEL OF THE PATISSERIE MILLET IN PARIS. I USE IT AS A BASE FOR MY LIQUORICE GATEAU WITH A PEAR FAN (PAGE 116).

INGREDIENTS:
250 g/9 oz highly perfumed honey
125 g/4½ oz strong rye flour and 125 g/4½ oz plain flour, sieved together
20 g/¾ oz baking powder
125 ml/4½ fl oz milk
3 eggs
50 g/2 oz caster sugar
1 teaspoon ground cinnamon
A pinch of grated nutmeg
A pinch of aniseed, crushed
30 g/1 oz candied orange and lemon peel, finely chopped
A few drops of vanilla or lemon essence

Serves 8
Preparation time: 20 minutes
Cooking time: about 1 hour, depending on the size

THE CAKE MIXTURE: In a saucepan, warm the honey over low heat until completely liquid. Take off the heat and cool to about 25°C/77°F.

Put the sieved flours and baking powder in a bowl. Pour on the melted honey, then the milk, eggs and sugar, whisking to obtain a smooth, creamy paste. Finally, add the cinnamon, nutmeg, aniseed, candied peel and your chosen essence. The paste should be supple, smooth and slightly elastic.

Preheat the oven to 160°C/320°F/gas 2–3.

BAKING THE CAKE: Pour the mixture into the prepared cake tin, place on a baking sheet and bake in the preheated oven for 30 minutes. Slide a second baking sheet underneath the first after this time and bake the cake for a further 30 minutes. Leave the cooked cake to cool in the tin for 15 minutes, then unmould it onto a cooling rack and leave at room temperature.

PRESENTATION: Peel off the paper from the cold cake, slice it and serve plain. I adore it served with a cup of tea or hot chocolate.

SPECIAL EQUIPMENT:
1 cake tin, 24 × 10 × 8 cm/ 10 × 4 × 3¼ in, lined with silicone paper and greased
2 baking sheets

NOTES:
If you like, ice the cake when it comes out of the oven with a thin coating of apricot jam, then one of lemon icing (see Little Lemon Cakes, page 179).

This spiced cake keeps for up to a week if stored in an airtight container at room temperature.

CHAPTER TWO

SPONGE
AND MERINGUE BASES

These sweet bases are of prime importance in the craft of pâtisserie. How elegantly they drape and support gâteaux, individual desserts and small cakes! Soft, light or crunchy, they range from the palest pastel blonde to golden brown. Their silken beauty can be enhanced by decoration, either applied by hand or piped.

They can be filled, covered, masked, enrobed in mousse, cream or ganache to delight the eye and palate. Remember, too, that they are delicious served on their own for a teatime treat.

These bases will keep well for two or three days if wrapped in clingfilm and kept in a cool, dry place. They can also be successfully frozen for at least a week.

Light sponge fingers (see a recipe for these on page 32)

HAZELNUT OR COCONUT DACQUOISE
Dacquoise noisette ou coco

CRUNCHY OUTSIDE, SOFT INSIDE AND VERY SUGARY, A DACQUOISE RESEMBLES A
TYPE OF MACAROON. I USE IT FOR MY COFFEE PARFAITS (PAGE 75).

INGREDIENTS:
150 g/5 oz egg whites
100 g/3½ oz caster sugar
60 g/2 oz very finely
   ground almonds
180 g/6 oz very finely
   ground hazelnuts, or
160 g/5½ oz very finely
   grated coconut
250 g/9 oz icing sugar,
   sifted

Makes one 60 × 40 cm/
   24 × 16 in sheet
Preparation time: 15
   minutes
Cooking time: 15–18
   minutes

PREPARATION: Mix the ground almonds, hazelnuts or coconut and icing sugar very thoroughly. Beat the egg whites until half-risen, then add the caster sugar and continue to beat until very firm. Sprinkle the nut and icing sugar mixture onto the egg whites, folding them in delicately with a slotted spoon until well mixed, but taking care not to overwork the mixture.

SPREADING AND COOKING THE DACQUOISE: Preheat the oven to 180°C/350°F/gas 4.

Line the baking sheet with the paper or Silpat and spread on the dacquoise mixture to a thickness of about 7 mm/⅜ in. Bake immediately for 15–18 minutes; after 15 minutes, check the cooking by gently pressing the central part of the biscuit with your fingertips. It should be fairly firm on top but still slightly soft in the middle.

Remove the dacquoise from the oven and immediately slide the paper on to a wire rack. Leave to cool at room temperature.

When the dacquoise is almost cold, peel it off the paper and use it at once.

SPECIAL EQUIPMENT:
60 × 40 cm/24 × 16 in
   baking sheet
Buttered and lightly floured
   greaseproof or silicone
   paper, or Silpat

NOTE:
The dacquoise can be
wrapped in clingfilm and
frozen for at least a week.

JOCONDE SPONGE
Biscuit joconde

THIS FINE, DELICATE SPONGE IS USED AS A BASE FOR MANY MOUSSE-BASED
DESSERTS.

INGREDIENTS:
375 g/13 oz tant pour
   tant (equal quantities of
   ground almonds and icing
   sugar sifted together)
5 eggs, plus 5 extra whites
25 g/1 oz caster sugar
40 g/1½ oz butter, melted
   and cooled
50 g/2 oz flour

Makes one 60 × 40 cm/
   24 × 16 in sheet
Preparation time: 15 minutes
Cooking time: 2–3 minutes

Preheat the oven to 250°C/500°F/gas 10.

Put the tant pour tant and whole eggs in a mixing bowl and beat at high speed to a ribbon consistency. Beat the egg whites until well-risen, then add the sugar and continue to beat at high speed until very firm. Using a skimmer, fold first the melted butter, then the flour into the whole egg mixture. Blend in one-third of the egg whites, then tip in the remainder and fold in very delicately until completely amalgamated. Take care not to overmix.

Use a palette knife to spread the mixture over the silicone paper or Silpat to a thickness of about 3 mm/⅛ in. Bake immediately for 2–3 minutes until the sponge is just firm to the touch, but still moist. Slide the cooked sponge on its paper onto a wire rack and leave to cool. Remove the paper immediately before using the sponge.

SPECIAL EQUIPMENT:
60 × 40 cm/24 × 16 in
baking sheet, lined with
silicone paper or Silpat

NOTE:
It is not easy to achieve good
results using less than the
given quantities. If only half
the quantity is required, I
suggest that you make the
whole recipe and freeze half
the sponge for later use.
Freeze it flat on the paper,
or rolled up like a Swiss roll.

SPONGE BISCUIT MIXTURE (FOR A SWISS ROLL)
Biscuits à la cuillère

USE THESE BISCUITS AS THE BASE FOR A CHARLOTTE, OR SANDWICH THEM
TOGETHER WITH CHANTILLY CREAM (PAGE 42).

INGREDIENTS:
4 eggs, plus 3 extra yolks
85 g/3 oz caster sugar
35 g/1¼ oz flour
40 g/1½ oz potato flour

Makes one 60 × 40 cm/
  24 × 16 in sheet
Preparation time: 20
  minutes
Cooking time: about 6
  minutes, depending on the
  size of the sponge

THE BASIC MIXTURE: Separate the whole eggs and put the whites in one mixing bowl and all the yolks in another. Beat the yolks with two-thirds of the sugar to a ribbon consistency. Beat the whites until well-risen, then add the remaining sugar and continue to beat at high speed for 1 minute until very firm.

Using a skimmer, fold one-third of the egg whites into the yolks and blend thoroughly. Tip in the remaining whites all at once and delicately fold them into the mixture. Before it becomes completely homogeneous, sift in the flour and potato flour, mixing continuously. Stop mixing as soon as the mixture becomes perfectly smooth, or it will lose its lightness.

Preheat the oven to 220°C/425°F/gas 7.

SWISS ROLL: To make a Swiss roll, spread the mixture with a palette knife onto a sheet of silicone paper or Silpat. Alternatively, use a piping bag fitted with any size nozzle from 5 mm/¼ in to 15 mm/⅝ in, depending on the desired effect.

Slide the paper onto a baking sheet and bake in the oven for about 6 minutes if you used a 5 mm/¼ in nozzle, longer for a larger nozzle. Invert the cooked sponge onto a tea towel and immediately peel off the paper. Cool, then fill and roll the sponge.

SPECIAL EQUIPMENT:
60 × 40 cm/24 × 16 in
baking sheet
A sheet of silicone paper or
Silpat.

SPONGE BISCUIT MIXTURE
(FOR SPONGE FINGERS OR DESSERT BASES)

INGREDIENTS:
6 eggs
190 g/6½ oz caster sugar
180 g/6 oz flour
30 g/1 oz icing sugar, for
  sponge fingers

Makes: about 600 g/1¼ lbs
Preparation time: 20
  minutes
Cooking time: 8 minutes for
  sponge fingers, 25 minutes
  for a dessert base

Prepare the mixture as in the recipe above. Preheat the oven to 220°C/425°F/gas 7. To make sponge fingers, use a piping bag with a plain 15 mm/⅝ in nozzle to pipe 10 cm/4 in long fingers onto a baking sheet lined with silicone paper or Silpat. Lightly dust them with icing sugar, leave to rest for 5 minutes, then dust with icing sugar again and bake in the oven for 8 minutes. Lift the fingers off the paper with a palette knife before they have cooled completely, and place on a wire rack.

DESSERT BASE: To make a dessert base, pour the mixture into a lightly greased and floured 23–25 cm/9–10 in cake tin and bake at 190°/375°F/gas 5 for 20–25 minutes, depending on the thickness of the sponge. Invert it onto a wire rack as soon as it is cooked.

SPECIAL EQUIPMENT:
Baking sheet lined with
silicone paper or Silpat, or a
23–25 cm/9–10 in diam.
cake tin.

NOTE:
Use the sponge on the day it
is made, or it will lose its
delicious delicate taste.

A hollowed-out Genoise sponge filled with cherries in syrup

PLAIN GENOISE SPONGE
Génoise nature

INGREDIENTS:
250 g/9 oz caster sugar
8 eggs
250 g/9 oz flour
50 g/2 oz warm clarified
   butter (optional)
25 g/1 oz butter and a
   pinch of flour for the cake
   tins

Makes about 1 kg/2¼ lbs
   (two 22 cm/8½ in diam.
   sponges, or one 40 cm/
   16 in square sponge)
Preparation time: about 25
   minutes
Cooking time: about 30
   minutes

Preheat the oven to 190°C/375°F/gas 5.

Whisk the sugar and eggs in an electric mixer. Stand the bowl in a bain-marie and continue to whisk until the mixture reaches 40°C/104°F. Remove the bowl from the bain-marie and whisk the mixture for 5 minutes, until well risen, then reduce the speed of the mixer and whisk for another 5 minutes, until the mixture has cooled and reached a ribbon consistency.

Sift in the flour and fold it gently into the mixture with a flat skimmer. Do not overwork it. Add the clarified butter now if you are using it. Divide the mixture between two lightly greased and floured cake tins or one large tin, and bake immediately. The 22 cm/8½ in sponges will take 30 minutes; a very large cake will need about 50 minutes. To test whether it is ready, insert a skewer into the centre; it should come out clean and dry.

As soon as the sponges are cooked, unmould onto a wire rack and leave to cool completely, giving them one quarter-turn every 15 minutes to prevent them from sticking to the rack.

CHOCOLATE GENOISE: Replace the 250 g/9 oz flour with 200 g/7 oz flour sifted with 75 g/3 oz unsweetened cocoa powder, and proceed as above.

SPECIAL EQUIPMENT:
Two 22 cm/8 in diam.
cake tins, or one 40 cm/
16 in square tin

NOTES:
It is best to bake the genoise sponges a day in advance, as they will hold their shape better when sliced. They can be wrapped in clingfilm and kept in the fridge for 3 days, or frozen for up to 2 weeks.

If you plan to serve the cake plain, the addition of clarified butter will greatly improve the flavour.

It is also delicious hollowed out and filled with fruit.

33

WALNUT SPONGE BISCUIT
Biscuit aux noix

INGREDIENTS:

MIXTURE 1

80 g/3 oz egg yolks, mixed
  with 30 g/1 oz egg
  whites and 50 g/2 oz
  runny honey

MERINGUE

150 g/5 oz egg whites
50 g/2 oz caster sugar

MIXTURE 2

50 g/2 oz walnut kernels,
  finely chopped with a
  knife, mixed with
  10 g/⅓ oz instant coffee
  and 60 g/2 oz flour

MIXTURE 1: Preheat the oven to 180°C/350°F/gas 4. In an electric mixer, beat Mixture 1 to a ribbon consistency, then transfer to a wide-mouthed bowl.

THE MERINGUE: Beat the 150 g/5 oz egg whites in the electric mixer until half-risen, then add the sugar and continue to beat until stiff.

MIXING THE BISCUIT: Immediately sprinkle Mixture 2 onto Mixture 1, then delicately fold in the meringue without overworking the mixture, stopping as soon as it becomes homogeneous.

SPREADING AND BAKING THE BISCUIT: Use a palette knife to spread the biscuit over the whole surface of the paper or Silpat, and bake in the preheated oven for 10 minutes.

Immediately slide the paper onto a cooling rack and leave at room temperature to cool completely.

SPECIAL EQUIPMENT:
60 × 40 cm/24 × 16 in
  baking sheet lined with
  lightly buttered and
  floured greaseproof or
  silicone paper, or Silpat

NOTES:
Use the biscuit immediately
after it has cooled, or remove
the paper, wrap the biscuit
in clingfilm, roll up like a
Swiss roll and freeze; it will
keep for at least a week.

Makes one 60 × 40 cm/
  24 × 16 in sheet
Preparation time: 10
  minutes
Cooking time: 10 minutes

CHOCOLATE SPONGE
Biscuit chocolat

INGREDIENTS:

240 g/9 oz bitter couverture
  or best quality cooking
  chocolate, chopped
50 g/2 oz butter, diced
60 g/2 oz egg yolks
250 g/9 oz egg whites
90 g/3 oz caster sugar

Makes one 60 × 40 cm/
  24 × 16 in sheet, or a
  24 cm/10 in round
  sponge
Preparation time: 15
  minutes
Cooking time: 8 minutes for
  a sheet, 35 minutes for a
  round sponge

THE SPONGE MIXTURE: Put the chocolate in a bowl, stand it in a bain-marie over medium heat and melt it at 40°C/104°F. Add the diced butter and mix with a spatula.

Preheat the oven to 180°C/350°F/gas 4.

Put the egg yolks in a bowl and cream with 20 g/¾ oz sugar until just pale. Beat the egg whites until semi-firm, then add the remaining sugar and beat until very firm, shiny and smooth. Add the yolks, fold in delicately with a spatula, then gently mix in the chocolate.

BAKING THE SPONGE: Immediately, use a palette knife to spread the mixture onto the Silpat or silicone paper to a thickness of 5 mm/¼ in, or pour it into the prepared ring. Bake the sheet in the preheated oven for 8 minutes, or the cake for 35 minutes. Place the cooked sponge on a cooling rack and use when cold.

SPECIAL EQUIPMENT:
Silpat or silicone paper, or a
  lightly greased dessert
  ring, 24 cm/10 in
  diam., 5 cm/2 in deep

NOTE:
This light sponge base
contains no flour, which
makes it extremely fragile
and delicate.

Meringue Topping made with Egg Yolks
Meringage aux jaunes d'oeuf

This topping is often used to coat gateaux or ice creams, then glazed for 30 seconds under a salamander or with a blowtorch. I use it in my recipe for Souffleed Oranges with Caramel Sauce (page 84).

INGREDIENTS:
5 egg yolks, plus 50 g/2 oz icing sugar
5 egg whites, plus 100 g/ 4 oz icing sugar

Makes 400 g/14 oz
Preparation time: 15 minutes

With an electric mixer or by hand, whisk the egg yolks with 50 g/ 2 oz sugar to a ribbon consistency, then keep at room temperature.

As soon as you have whisked the yolks, beat the whites with the 100 g/4 oz sugar until very smooth and firm (this can be done in an electric mixer or by hand). Using a spatula, delicately fold the two mixtures together. The meringue is now ready and must be used immediately, or it will lose its lightness and volume.

NOTE:
The egg yolks for this meringue can be flavoured with a little vanilla or a hint of instant coffee or cocoa powder.

Meringue Topping made with Egg Whites
Meringage aux blancs d'oeuf

Like the topping made with egg yolks, this is used to glaze patisserie and desserts, but its texture is less rich and soft. Use whichever type you choose; it is purely a matter of taste.

INGREDIENTS:
5 egg whites
250 g/9 oz caster sugar

Makes 400 g/14 oz
Preparation time: 7 minutes

With an electric mixer or by hand, beat the egg whites with half the sugar until risen and semi-firm. Add the remaining sugar and beat to a very firm, smooth and shiny consistency. Use this meringue immediately.

NOTE:
The meringue topping is often piped onto the dessert with a decorative or plain nozzle to give an attractive finish.

ITALIAN MERINGUE
Meringue italienne

I USE THIS MERINGUE IN ALL MY MOUSSES AND IN CHIBOUST CREAM
(PAGE 39) AND BUTTERCREAM (PAGE 41).

INGREDIENTS:
80 ml/3 fl oz water
360 g/12 oz caster sugar
30 g/1 oz liquid glucose
   (optional)
6 egg whites

Makes about 650 g/1½ lbs
Preparation time: 7 minutes
Cooking time: 15–20
   minutes

Pour the water into the pan and add the sugar and glucose. Bring to the boil over medium heat, stirring with a skimmer. Skim the surface and wash down the inside of the pan with a pastry brush dipped in cold water. Increase the heat and put in the sugar thermometer.

When the sugar reaches 110°C/230°F, begin beating the egg whites in an electric mixer until firm. Keep an eye on the sugar and stop cooking as soon as it reaches 121°C/248°F.

When the egg whites are firm, set the mixer to its lowest speed and pour in the cooked sugar in a thin, steady stream, keeping it clear of the beaters. Continue to beat at low speed for about 15 minutes, until the mixture becomes tepid (about 30°C/86°F). The meringue is now ready to use.

SPECIAL EQUIPMENT:
Heavy-based sugar pan
Sugar thermometer

NOTES:
Glucose prevents the formation of sugar crystals, but is not essential.

It is not really possible to make a successful Italian meringue using smaller quantities, but the mixture will keep in an airtight container in the fridge for several days

FRENCH MERINGUE
Meringue française

I USE THIS RECIPE IN MY MERINGUE PILLOWS WITH MARRONS GLACÉS (PAGE
74) AND IN VACHERINS OF ICE CREAM OR SORBETS.

INGREDIENTS:
100 g/4 oz egg whites
170 g/6½ oz icing sugar,
   sifted

Makes 9 double meringues
   (about 275 g/10 oz)
Preparation time: 15
   minutes
Cooking time: 1 hour 50
   minutes

A stack of crisp French meringues

THE MERINGUE MIXTURE: Using an electric mixer or a bowl and whisk, beat the egg whites with half the icing sugar until semi-firm. Add the remaining sugar and beat to obtain a firm, shiny, homogeneous mixture.

Preheat the oven to 100°C/200°F/gas ½.

PIPING THE MERINGUE: Pipe the meringue onto the paper or Silpat, using the fluted nozzle to make eighteen 8 cm/3¼ in long meringues, or the plain nozzle to pipe eighteen 5 cm/2 in diam. balls.

COOKING THE MERINGUES: Slide the paper or Silpat onto a baking sheet and cook the meringues in the oven for 1 hour 50 minutes. Leave to cool on the paper at room temperature, then peel off the meringues, place on a wire rack and leave in a dry place.

CHOCOLATE MERINGUES: Use only 150 g/5 oz icing sugar and add 30 g/1 oz unsweetened cocoa powder for the last minute of whisking.

SPECIAL EQUIPMENT:
Piping bag with a fluted
   14 mm/⅝ in nozzle or a
   plain 12 mm/½ in nozzle
Greaseproof or silicone paper,
   or Silpat

NOTES:
The meringues will keep for several days in an airtight container well away from any humidity.

A convection oven is best for making French meringues, which will emerge light and crisp on the outside and soft in the middle.

CHAPTER THREE

CREAMS, MOUSSES, BAVAROIS AND PARFAITS

These creamy confections, with their glowing or pastel colours, are used to garnish, fill or mask cakes, gâteaux and desserts. CREAMS are always used in fruit tarts. Often, different creams are mixed together (pastry cream with almond cream, for example). They are delicious and not too rich in calories. Most of my MOUSSES AND BAVAROIS are made from fruit, lightly whipped cream and Italian meringue, with a little gelatine to keep their shape and consistency. Go easy on the gelatine; it is only there to hold the lightness between making the dessert and eating it. Too much will give the dessert an unpleasant rubbery texture. PARFAITS should always be served iced. A creamy marriage of mousses and ice creams, they are very rich, so are best served in small portions.

Creams, mousses, bavarois and parfaits cannot successfully be made in small quantities, or they will lose their lightness and texture. They do, however, freeze very well.

Piping Chiboust Cream onto Princess Tart with Bilberries (see recipe page 132)

PASTRY CREAM
Crème pâtissière

INGREDIENTS:
6 egg yolks
125 g/4 oz caster sugar
40 g/1½ oz flour
500 ml/18 fl oz milk
1 vanilla pod, split
A little butter or icing sugar,
    for cooling

Makes about 750 g/
    1 lb 10 oz
Preparation time: 15
    minutes

In a bowl, whisk the egg yolks with about one-third of the sugar until pale and of a light ribbon consistency. Sift in the flour and mix it in thoroughly.

In a saucepan, bring the milk to the boil with the remaining sugar and the vanilla pod. As soon as it begins to bubble, pour about one-third onto the egg mixture, stirring continuously. Pour this custard back into the pan and bring to the boil over very gentle heat, stirring continuously. Bubble for 2 minutes, then transfer to a bowl. Dot the surface with a few flakes of butter or dust lightly with icing sugar to prevent a skin from forming as the pastry cream cools. To cool it more quickly, pour the pastry cream onto a marble work surface and keep turning it back onto itself with a palette knife for 2 minutes.

COFFEE OR CHOCOLATE PASTRY CREAM: Substitute a little instant coffee or cocoa powder for the vanilla. If you use cocoa, use a touch less flour and a little extra sugar.

NOTE:
Pastry cream can be stored in the fridge at 5°C/41°F for 36 hours.

CHIBOUST CREAM
Crème Chiboust

I USE THIS DELICATE CREAM FOR MY LOVE NESTS WIH REDCURRANT PEARLS
(PAGE 80) AND PRINCESS TART WITH BILBERRIES (PAGE 132)

INGREDIENTS:
6 egg yolks
80 g/3 oz caster sugar
30 g/1 oz custard powder
350 ml/12 fl oz milk
½ vanilla pod, split
1 quantity freshly-made
    Italian Meringue (page
    37), cooled to tepid
2 gelatine leaves, soaked in
    cold water and well
    drained
50 ml/2 fl oz Curaçao,
    Grand Marnier or rum
A little butter, for cooling

Makes 1.3 kg/2 lbs 14 oz
Preparation time: 25
    minutes

THE PASTRY CREAM: In a bowl, whisk the egg yolks with one-third of the sugar until pale and of a light ribbon consistency. Sift in the custard powder and mix well. In a saucepan, bring the milk to the boil with the remaining sugar and the vanilla. As soon as it starts to bubble, pour about one-third onto the egg mixture, stirring continuously. Pour the mixture back into the pan and bring to the boil over low heat, stirring all the time. Bubble for 2 minutes, then take the pan off the heat. Warm the alcohol, dissolve the gelatine in it and stir into the pastry cream. Transfer to a bowl, remove the vanilla pod, dot the surface with butter and leave to cool until tepid (it should be at the same temperature as the meringue).

THE CHIBOUST CREAM: Using a whisk, fold one-third of the tepid meringue into the tepid pastry cream, then use a spatula to fold in the rest delicately until the cream is completely homogeneous. Do not overmix the cream or it will lose its lightness.

CHOCOLATE CHIBOUST CREAM: Add 75 g/3 oz melted plain couverture or cooking chocolate to the cooked pastry cream and use only 20 g/¾ oz custard powder.

NOTE:
Chiboust cream must be used as soon as you have mixed in the meringue, so have the base for your dessert ready before finishing the cream. The finished dessert can be frozen for 3–4 days.

Creme Anglaise

SERVE THIS DELICIOUS CUSTARD WELL CHILLED AS AN ACCOMPANIMENT TO
CAKES OR BERRY FRUITS.

INGREDIENTS:
12 egg yolks
250 g/9 oz caster sugar
1 litre/1¾ pints milk
1 vanilla pod, split

Makes about 1.5 litres/
    2½ pints
Preparation time: 15
    minutes

In a bowl, whisk the egg yolks with one-third of the sugar to a ribbon consistency. Bring the milk to the boil with the remaining sugar and the vanilla and pour it onto the egg mixture, whisking continuously. Return the mixture to the pan and gently heat, stirring continuously, to 80°C/175°F, until the custard is just thick enough to coat the spoon. Do not let it boil.

Pass the custard through a conical strainer into a bowl and leave in a cool place until completely cold. Stir occasionally to prevent a skin from forming.

COFFEE OR CHOCOLATE CREME ANGLAISE: Replace the vanilla pod with 3 tablespoons instant coffee powder or 100 g/4 oz melted plain chocolate or couverture.

NOTES:
For a less rich custard, you can reduce the number of egg yolks, but you will need a minimum of 8 per litre/1¾ pints milk.

The crème anglaise can be stored in the fridge at 5°C/41°F for 48 hours. Pass it again through a conical strainer before using.

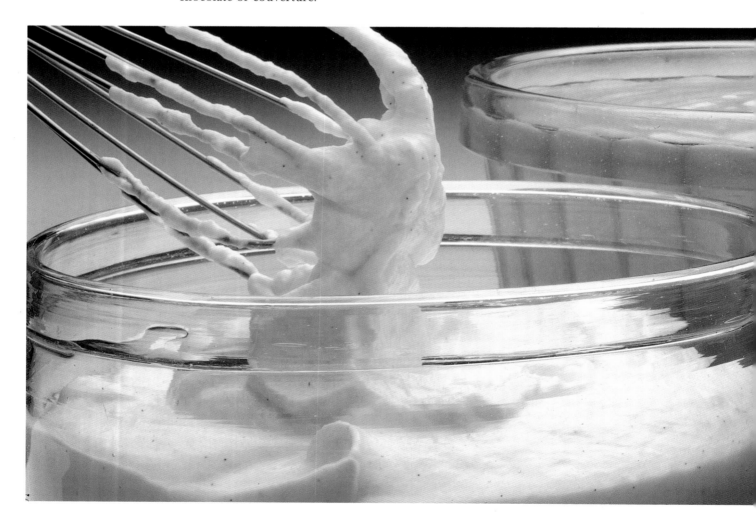

BUTTERCREAM
Crème au beurre

MY VERSION OF BUTTERCREAM IS NOT TOO RICH OR SICKLY, WHICH MAKES
IT EASILY DIGESTIBLE.

INGREDIENTS:
175 ml/6 fl oz water
450 g/1 lb caster sugar
40 g/1½ oz liquid glucose
 (optional)
6 egg whites
700 g/1½ lbs butter, diced,
 at room temperature

Makes about 1.6 kg/3½ lbs
Preparation time: 20
 minutes

THE ITALIAN MERINGUE: First make an Italian meringue, following the method on page 37, and using all the ingredients except the butter. Leave in the mixer until almost cold.

THE BUTTERCREAM: Add the butter to the cooled meringue, a little at a time. Beat for 5 minutes until the buttercream is very smooth and homogeneous.

COFFEE BUTTERCREAM: Add instant coffee powder to taste, dissolved in a very little water.

NOTE:
Buttercream can be stored in an airtight container in the fridge for a week. Leave at room temperature for 1 hour before using, then stir well until smooth.

Left to right: Vanilla Chantilly cream; Caramel mousse; Dark chocolate mousse

MOUSSELINE CREAM
Crème mousseline

I USE THIS LIGHT CREAM AS A FILLING FOR TARTS AND TARTLETS, AND IN MY
MARZIPAN FIGS (PAGE 68).

INGREDIENTS:
PASTRY CREAM
4 eggs, plus 2 extra yolks
220 g/8 oz caster sugar
50 g/2 oz flour
500 ml/18 fl oz milk

250 g/9 oz butter, finely
    diced, at room temperature
Flavouring of your choice
    (eg: caramel, chocolate,
    coffee, Grand Marnier)

Makes about 1.3 kg/2 lbs
    14 oz
Preparation time: 30
    minutes

THE PASTRY CREAM: Follow the method on page 39 using all the ingredients except the butter and flavouring.

THE MOUSSELINE CREAM: As soon as the pastry cream is cooked, take the pan off the heat and beat in one-third of the diced butter. Transfer to a bowl and keep in a cool place, stirring occasionally to prevent a skin from forming and to cool the cream more quickly.

In an electric mixer, beat the remaining butter at low speed for about 3 minutes, until fairly pale. Increase the speed to medium and add the cooled pastry cream, a little at a time. Beat for 5 minutes, until the mousseline is perfectly light and creamy. Use it plain, or add your chosen flavouring.

NOTE:
Mousseline cream keeps well in the fridge for up to 4 days. Store in an airtight container or a bowl covered with clingfilm.

CHANTILLY CREAM
Crème Chantilly

I USE CHOCOLATE AND VANILLA FLAVOURED CHANTILLY CREAMS IN MY
BLACK AND WHITE SAINT-HONORÉ (PAGE 106).

INGREDIENTS:
500 ml/18 fl oz well-
    chilled whipping cream, or
    425 ml/15 fl oz chilled
    double cream mixed with
    75 ml/3 fl oz very cold
    milk
50 g/2 oz icing sugar, or
    50 ml/2 fl oz Sorbet
    Syrup (page 144)
Vanilla powder or extract
    (optional)

Makes about 600 g/1¼ lbs
Preparation time: 8 minutes

Put the chilled cream, sugar or syrup and vanilla in a chilled mixing bowl and whip at medium speed for 1–2 minutes. Increase the speed and whip for another 3–4 minutes, until the cream begins to thicken. It should be a little firmer than a ribbon consistency. Do not overbeat, or it may turn into butter.

CHOCOLATE CHANTILLY: Melt 150 g/5 oz plain couverture or best quality chocolate in a bain-marie to 45°C/113°F, stirring continuously. Off the heat, whisk the melted chocolate into the Chantilly cream, without beating over-vigorously.

COFFEE CHANTILLY: Dissolve 2 tablespoons instant coffee powder in 1 tablespoon hot milk and add it when you whip the cream, or use 1 tablespoon coffee extract.

SPECIAL EQUIPMENT:
Chocolate thermometer

NOTE:
Chantilly cream is best used as soon as it is made, but can be kept in the fridge at 5°C/41°F for 24 hours.

FRANGIPANE OR ALMOND CREAM
Crème d'amandes

I USE THIS LOVELY ALMOND CREAM IN MY WALNUT PITHIVIERS (PAGE 100).

INGREDIENTS:
250 g/9 oz butter, at room temperature
500 g/1 lb 2 oz tant pour tant (equal quantities of ground almonds and icing sugar sifted together)
50 g/2 oz flour
5 eggs
50 ml/2 fl oz rum (optional)

Makes 1.15 kg/2 lbs 10 oz
Preparation time: 15 minutes

Beat the butter until very soft. Still beating, add the tant pour tant and flour, then the eggs, one at a time, beating well between each addition until the frangipane is light and homogeneous. Finally stir in the rum.

NOTES:
Frangipane can be kept in the fridge at 5°C/41°F for up to a week. Store in an airtight container or a bowl covered with clingfilm and remove from the fridge 30 minutes before using.

For a moister frangipane, stir in 20–30% extra pastry cream just before using.

Frangipane-filled Walnut Pithiviers

CHESTNUT BAVAROIS
Bavaroise aux marrons

THIS MOUSSE MARRIES BRILLIANTLY WITH MERINGUES AND CHOCOLATE.

INGREDIENTS:
300 ml/11 fl oz milk
5 egg yolks
50 g/2 oz caster sugar
4 gelatine leaves, soaked in cold water and well drained
400 g/14 oz tinned sweetened chestnut purée
500 ml/18 fl oz whipping cream, whipped to a ribbon consistency
30 ml/2 fl oz rum (optional)

Makes about 1.3 kg/ 2 lbs 14 oz
Preparation time: 10 minutes

THE CHESTNUT CUSTARD: In a saucepan, bring the milk to the boil. Put the egg yolks and sugar in a bowl and whisk until pale and of a ribbon consistency. Pour the boiling milk onto the mixture, whisking continuously, then pour the custard back into the pan and gently heat, stirring continuously with a wooden spatula until the custard is thick enough to coat it. Do not let it boil.

When the custard is ready, take the pan off the heat, stir in the gelatine and chestnut purée, then rub the mixture through a fine strainer into a bowl. Leave at room temperature, whisking from time to time until the mixture is barely tepid.

MIXING THE BAVAROIS: Using a spatula, fold the cooled chestnut custard into the whipped cream without overworking the mixture, then stir in the rum. The bavarois is now ready to use, before the gelatine sets.

LIQUORICE BAVAROIS
Bavaroise à la réglisse

I USE THIS BAVAROIS IN MY LIQUORICE GATEAU WITH A PEAR FAN (PAGE 116). THE FLAVOUR OF LIQUORICE ALSO GOES WELL WITH LIGHTLY CARAMELIZED APPLES AND PEARS.

INGREDIENTS:
300 ml/11 fl oz milk
50 g/2 oz caster sugar
5 egg yolks
3 gelatine leaves, soaked in cold water and well drained
25 g/1 oz liquorice extract, or 50 g/2 oz liquorice stick, cut into small pieces
200 g/7 oz freshly-made Italian Meringue (page 37), cooled to tepid
150 ml/5 fl oz whipping cream, whipped to a ribbon consistency
50 ml/2 fl oz Armagnac (optional)

Makes about 570 g/1¼ lbs
Preparation time: 15 minutes

THE LIQUORICE CUSTARD: Combine the milk and half the sugar in a saucepan and bring to the boil. If you are using a liquorice stick, add the pieces now to dissolve them in the hot milk.

Meanwhile, in a bowl, whisk the egg yolks with the remaining sugar until pale and of a light ribbon consistency. Pour the boiling milk onto the mixture, whisking continuously, then return the custard to the pan and heat gently, stirring with a wooden spatula, until the custard is thick enough to coat it. Do not let it boil.

When the custard is ready, take the pan off the heat, stir in the gelatine and liquorice extract and pass through a fine strainer into a bowl. Leave at room temperature, whisking from time to time, until barely tepid.

MIXING THE BAVAROIS: Pour the cooled custard onto the still tepid Italian meringue and mix it in delicately with a balloon whisk. Using a spatula, fold in the whipped cream (to which you have added the Armagnac) without overworking the mixture. The bavarois is now ready to use, before the gelatine sets.

APPLE BAVAROIS
Bavaroise aux pommes

I USE THIS DELICIOUSLY LIGHT BAVAROIS IN MY APPLE CHARLOTTE WITH APPLE CRISPS (PAGE 113).

INGREDIENTS:
350 ml/12 fl oz apple juice
5 egg yolks
35 g/1¼ oz caster sugar, plus 100 g/4 oz for cooking the apples
4 gelatine leaves, soaked in cold water and well drained
2 apples, total weight about 300 g/11 oz

THE APPLE CUSTARD: Pour the apple juice into a saucepan and boil to reduce by one-third. Meanwhile, in a bowl, whisk the egg yolks with 35 g/1¼ oz sugar until pale and of a ribbon consistency. Pour the boiling apple juice onto the mixure, whisking continuously. Pour the custard back into the pan and heat over low heat, stirring gently with a wooden spatula, until the custard is thick enough to coat it. Do not let it boil.

When the custard is ready, take the pan off the heat, stir in the gelatine, then pass it through a fine strainer into a bowl. Leave at room temperature until almost completely cold.

THE APPLES: Peel, core and cut into small dice and mix with the lemon

Juice of ½ lemon
50 g/2 oz butter
100 ml/4 fl oz Calvados
100 g/4 oz apple purée
200 g/7 oz freshly-made
 Italian Meringue (page
 37), cooled to tepid
500 ml/18 fl oz whipping
 cream, whipped to a
 ribbon consistency

Makes about 1.65 kg/
 3½ lbs
Preparation time: 30
 minutes

juice. Heat the butter in a frying pan, toss in the diced apples and cook over high heat for 2 minutes. Add the 100 g/4 oz sugar and cook briskly for another 2 minutes, stirring continuously. Pour in the half the Calvados and flame it, then immediately transfer the apples to a bowl and keep in a cool place.

MIXING THE BAVAROIS: Mix the cooled diced apples, apple purée and the remaining Calvados into the almost cold, half-set custard. Using a spatula, delicately fold in the tepid Italian meringue and finally the whipped cream. Stop working the mixture as soon as it becomes smooth. The bavarois is now ready to use, before the gelatine sets.

PEAR BAVAROIS
Bavaroise aux poires

FOR A LOVELY LIGHT DESSERT, FOLD SOME DICED PEARS POACHED IN SYRUP INTO THE MOUSSE AND SANDWICH IT BETWEEN ROUNDS OF GENOISE OR JOCONDE SPONGE (PAGES 33 AND 31).

INGREDIENTS:
350 ml/12 fl oz pear
 syrup, strongly flavoured
 with vanilla (from freshly
 poached pears, or from
 tinned pears in syrup)
35 g/1¼ oz powdered milk
10 egg yolks
60 g/2 oz caster sugar
3 gelatine leaves, softened in
 cold water and well
 drained
100 g/4 oz freshly-made
 Italian Meringue (page
 37), cooled to tepid
60 ml/2 fl oz pear
 eau-de-vie
400 ml/14 fl oz whipping
 cream, lightly whipped to
 a ribbon consistency

Makes 950 g/2 lbs
Preparation time: 15
 minutes

THE CUSTARD: Combine the syrup and powdered milk in a saucepan and, over a low heat, bring to the boil, whisking continuously.

 Put the egg yolks and sugar in a bowl and whisk to a pale, light ribbon consistency. Pour the boiling syrup mixture onto the egg yolks and, whisking continuously, pour the mixture into the pan and poach over low heat, stirring with a wooden spatula, taking care not to let it boil. When the custard is thick enough to coat the spatula, take the pan off the heat, stir in the gelatine and pass the custard through a conical strainer into a bowl. Leave it to cool at room temperature until barely tepid, whisking from time to time.

MIXING THE BAVAROIS: Pour the pear custard over the tepid meringue, folding it in lightly with a balloon whisk, then add the pear eau-de-vie. Use a spatula to fold in the whipped cream, without overworking the mixture. The bavarois is now ready to use, before the gelatine sets.

NOTES:
This recipe makes enough bavarois to fill twenty-two 6 cm/2⅜ in diam., 3 cm/1¼ in deep dessert rings; serve on individual plates garnished with poached pear and a ribbon of coulis around the edge.

 The bavarois can be kept frozen in the rings for at least a week.

CARAMEL MOUSSE
Mousse au caramel

I USE THIS RECIPE, WITH ITS RICH CARAMEL FLAVOUR AND UNCTUOUS CREAMINESS, IN MANY CAKES AND DESSERTS, INCLUDING BANANA AND CARAMEL MOUSSE GATEAU (PAGE 110).

INGREDIENTS:

CARAMEL CREAM
400 ml/14 fl oz whipping cream
150 g/5 oz liquid glucose
1 split vanilla pod
200 g/7 oz caster sugar
50 g/2 oz butter

BOMBE MIXTURE
80 ml/3 fl oz water
60 g/2 oz caster sugar
30 g/1 oz liquid glucose
200 g/7 oz egg yolks
5 gelatine leaves, soaked in cold water and well drained
220 ml/8 fl oz whipping cream, whipped to a ribbon consistency

Makes about 900 g/2 lbs
Preparation time: 50 minutes

THE CARAMEL CREAM: Combine the cream, glucose and vanilla in a saucepan and bring to the boil. Meanwhile, dissolve the sugar in a heavy casserole over low heat, stirring continuously with a spatula, until it turns to a nutty brown caramel. Do not let it become too dark, or it will taste bitter. Take the pan off the heat and pour the boiling cream mixture into the casserole to prevent the caramel from cooking further. Return the casserole to the heat and let the mixture bubble gently for 2 minutes. Take the pan off the heat again and whisk in the butter, then pass the caramel cream through a conical strainer into a bowl and leave to cool to about 24°C/75°F.

THE BOMBE MIXTURE: Put the water, sugar and glucose in a saucepan and bring to the boil over low heat. Boil for 2 minutes, skimming the surface of the sugar to remove any impurities, and washing down the inside of the pan with a pastry brush dipped in cold water.

After 2 minutes, put the egg yolks in the bowl of an electric mixer and gently pour in the boiled sugar, whisking it in by hand. Stand the base of the bowl in a bain-marie of boiling water, set over medium heat and poach the egg mixture, whisking continuously until it reaches a temperature of about 70°C/158°F. Now beat the mixture with the electric mixer on low speed until it cools to about 24°C/75°F.

THE MOUSSE: Dissolve the gelatine in 2 tablespoons of hot water and mix it into the caramel cream. With the caramel cream and the bombe mixture at the same temperature, mix the two together. Delicately fold in the whipped cream, then use the resulting caramel mousse immediately.

SPECIAL EQUIPMENT:
Sugar thermometer

NOTES:
The quantities in this recipe will fill eighteen 6 cm/2⅜ in diam., 3 cm/1¼ in deep dessert rings; use a Walnut Sponge Biscuit base (page 34).

This easily prepared dessert is particularly good in winter and can be frozen for up to a week.

LIME MOUSSE
Mousse au citron vert

A MOUSSE FOR ALL SEASONS, WHICH IS SO REFRESHING THAT YOU WILL
NEVER TIRE OF IT. I USE IT IN MY JEWELLED FRUIT GATEAU (PAGE 114),
BUT YOU COULD ALSO SERVE IT IN SMALL RAMEKINS, TOPPED WITH A FEW
WILD STRAWBERRIES OR RASPBERRIES.

INGREDIENTS:
300 ml/11 fl oz lime juice
50 g/2 oz sugar
4 gelatine leaves, soaked in
  cold water and well
  drained
30 g/1 oz lime zests, finely
  sliced and blanched
300 g/11 oz freshly-made
  Italian Meringue (page
  37), cooled to tepid
500 ml/18 fl oz whipping
  cream, whipped to a
  ribbon consistency

Makes 1.25 kg/2¾ lbs
  (enough for 2 desserts for
  8 people)
Preparation time: 10
  minutes

PREPARATION: In a small saucepan, heat about one-third of the lime
juice with the sugar. As soon as the juice is warm and the sugar has
dissolved, take the pan off the heat, stir in the gelatine to dissolve it,
then add the remaining lime juice and the zests.

MIXING THE MOUSSE: Pour the lime juice mixture onto the meringue,
folding it in with a balloon whisk, without overworking it. With a
spatula, delicately fold in the whipped cream. Use the mousse at
once, before the gelatine begins to set.

SPECIAL EQUIPMENT:
2 dessert rings, 22 cm/
  8½ in diam., 5 cm/2 in
  deep

NOTES:
To make individual desserts,
fill twenty-eight 6 cm/
2⅜ in diam., 3 cm/1¼ in
deep dessert rings with the
mousse and decorate the
plates with a border of wild
strawberries and raspberries.
Serve this delectable dessert
with or without a fruit
coulis.
  The mousses can be kept
frozen in the rings for at
least a week.

Top to bottom:
Mint mousse
Raspberry parfait
Pear mousse
Dark chocolate mousse
Coffee parfait mousse
White chocolate mousse

BANANA MOUSSE

Mousse à la banane

INGREDIENTS:

250 g/9 oz very ripe
  bananas
Juice of 2 lemons
Juice of 1 orange
125 g/4 oz caster sugar
 2 tablespoons kirsch
  (optional), or 2
  tablespoons water
3 gelatine leaves, soaked in
  cold water and well
  drained
350 ml/12 fl oz whipping
  cream, whipped to a
  ribbon consistency

Makes about 820 g/1¾ lbs
Preparation time: 20
  minutes

Peel the bananas and cut them into chunks. Place in a blender with the lemon and orange juices and the sugar, and purée until very smooth, then transfer to a bowl. Warm the kirsch or water, then, off the heat, stir in and dissolve the gelatine and add it to the banana purée. Using a spatula, gradually and delicately fold the cream into the purée, without overworking the mixture. Use the mousse as soon as it becomes homogeneous, before the gelatine sets.

NOTES:
To make individual desserts, fill eighteen 6 cm/2⅜ in diam., 3 cm/1¼ in deep dessert rings with the mousse and serve on separate plates. The bottom of the rings can be lined with a Coconut Daquoise (page 31) for a wonderful marriage of flavours.

Like all mousses, this one freezes very well for up to a week

MINT MOUSSE

Mousse à la menthe

INGREDIENTS:

250 ml/9 fl oz milk
100 g/4 oz caster sugar
25 g/1 oz mint leaves
  (preferably spearmint),
  washed, drained and
  snipped
2 gelatine leaves, soaked in
  cold water and well
  drained
250 ml/9 fl oz whipping
  cream, whipped to a
  ribbon consistency
1 tablespoon green
  peppermint eau-de-vie

Makes about 650 g/1½ lbs
Preparation time: 30
  minutes

In a saucepan, bring the milk and sugar to the boil, whisking all the time. As soon as it bubbles, toss in the snipped mint leaves, whisking continuously, then take the pan off the heat and put on the lid. Leave to infuse for 20 minutes.

Dissolve the gelatine in the infused milk, then pass through a conical strainer into a bowl. Leave at room temperature and, as soon as the mixture is cold (but before the gelatine begins to set), stir in the whipped cream and eau-de-vie. Use the mousse immediately, before it sets.

GINGER MOUSSE
Mousse au gingembre

THIS FINE-FLAVOURED MOUSSE IS PARTICULARLY DELICIOUS IN WINTER, AND IS SIMPLE TO PREPARE. I USE IT IN MY NOUGATINE BASKETS WITH YELLOW PEACHES (PAGE 76) AND MILLE-FEUILLE OF GINGER MOUSSE WITH CRUNCHY QUINCES (PAGE 118).

INGREDIENTS:
BOMBE MIXTURE
50 ml/2 fl oz water
50 g/2 oz caster sugar
4 egg yolks

4 gelatine leaves, soaked in
   cold water and well drained
250 g/9 oz freshly made
   Italian Meringue (page
   37), cooled to tepid
400 ml/14 fl oz whipping
   cream, whipped to a
   ribbon consistency
80 g/3 oz preserved ginger,
   finely diced
50 ml/2 fl oz ginger
   eau-de-vie
40 g/1½ oz slivers of
   Candied Grapefruit Peel
   (page 168), finely diced
   (optional)

Makes 900 g/2 lbs
Preparation time: 50
   minutes

THE BOMBE MIXTURE: Pour the water into a small saucepan, add the sugar and bring to the boil over low heat. Boil the syrup for 2 minutes, washing down the inside of the pan with a pastry brush dipped in cold water.

Meanwhile, put the egg yolks in a bowl and break them up with a whisk, then gently pour on the syrup, whisking continuously. Stand the base of the bowl in a bain-marie, set over medium heat and whisk until the mixture reaches a ribbon consistency and a temperature of about 75°C/167°F. Take the bowl out of the bain-marie and continue to whisk until the temperature of the mixture reduces to about 24°C/75°F.

MAKING THE MOUSSE: Place the gelatine in a bowl and dissolve it in 2 soup spoons of hot water, then pour it into the bombe mixture, whisking continuously. Using a slotted spoon, fold the mixture into the tepid Italian meringue. Finally, delicately fold in the whipped cream, ginger, eau-de-vie and the candied grapefruit peel. The mousse is now ready to use, before the gelatine begins to set.

SPECIAL EQUIPMENT:
Sugar thermometer

NOTES:
To make individual desserts, fill twenty 6 cm/2⅜ in diam., 3 cm/1¼ in deep dessert rings with the mousse, using a Coconut Daquoise (page 31) for the base.

The mousse will freeze well for up to a week.

CHAPTER FOUR

COULIS, SAUCES, JELLIES AND JAMS

COULIS: The choice of fruit is important when making a coulis to accompany a dessert. If the flavour is too strong, it will dominate the dessert, which it should not do. As a general rule, coulis should be light, with a pure flavour and not too much sweetness. Pour only a small amount onto the plate or in a ribbon around the dessert, but it may be wise to serve a little extra coulis separately in a sauceboat for greedy gourmets!

SAUCES: Sauces are always popular. They are richer and creamier than coulis and can be served hot or cold, depending on their composition and how they are intended to enhance and enrich the dessert.

JELLIES AND JAMS: The recipes in this chapter are amongst my favourites, particularly Apricot and Almond Jam. I adore this spread on pancakes or toast. A favourite childhood memory is of my mother buying the ripest fruits in season at the market and making them into jams. Each jar was meticulously labelled with the date of its creation, for jams are best eaten whilst still young and fresh.

Apricot Jam with Almonds
(*see recipe page 58*)

FRUIT COULIS
Coulis de fruits

YOU CAN MAKE A COULIS WITH ALMOST ANY SINGLE TYPE OF FRUIT,
DEPENDING ON THE DESSERT IT IS INTENDED TO ACCOMPANY, BUT DO NOT
USE A MIXTURE OF DIFFERENT FRUITS.

INGREDIENTS:
800 g / 1¾ lbs fresh fruit
   (eg: berry fruits,
   pineapple, apricots,
   peaches, kiwis etc.)
Juice of 1 lemon
250 ml / 9 fl oz Sorbet
   Syrup (page 144)

Makes 800 g–1 kg /
   1¾–2¼ lbs, depending on
   the texture and density of
   the fruit
Preparation time: 15
   minutes

Wash and drain, hull, peel or core the fruit as appropriate. Purée in a blender or food processor with the lemon juice and syrup until smooth. Pass through a conical strainer and keep in the fridge until ready to use.

NOTES:
Fruit coulis can be made with tinned or bottled fruits. Use only 125 ml / 4 fl oz sorbet syrup and dilute it with the same quantity of water.

   All fruit coulis will keep in an airtight container in the fridge for several days. They also freeze well. Defrost and beat vigourously before serving.

STRAWBERRY JUICE
Jus de fraises

CHILDREN ADORE THIS LIGHT COULIS (YOU CAN ALSO USE OTHER RED FRUITS, SUCH AS
RASPBERRIES, WILD STRAWBERRIES, REDCURRANTS AND CHERRIES). IT CAN ALSO BE USED AS
THE BASE FOR A VERY LIGHT, FRUITY SORBET. SIMPLY CHURN IT WITHOUT ADDING SYRUP.

INGREDIENTS:
750 g / 1½ lbs best quality
   frozen strawberries
75 g / 3 oz caster sugar
½ lemon, roughly chopped

Makes about 850 ml /
   1½ pints
Preparation time: 5 minutes
Cooking time: 3 hours

Put all the ingredients in a bowl and cover very tightly with clingfilm. Stand the bowl in a bain-marie and poach at 90°–95°C / 194°–204°F for three hours, taking great care that it does not boil.

   Lay the muslin in a colander set over a bowl and pour in the poached juice and fruit pulp. Leave to drain for 30 minutes, then gather up the ends of the muslin and press lightly to extract a little more juice, but do not squeeze or the juice will become cloudy. When it is cold, pour into an airtight container and refrigerate until ready to use. It will keep for up to 2 weeks.

SPECIAL EQUIPMENT:
Muslin
Cooking thermometer

NOTES:
A spoonful of strawberry juice added to a glass of champagne or sparkling white wine makes a delicious cocktail.

Orange Sauce
Sauce à l'orange

THIS SAUCE MAKES AN EXCELLENT ACCOMPANIMENT TO MANY COLD DESSERTS
OR A CHOCOLATE MOUSSE. I USE IT WITH MY GRATINS OF REDCURRANTS
AND WILD STRAWBERRIES (PAGE 92).

INGREDIENTS:
2 eggs
150 g/5 oz caster sugar
250 ml/9 fl oz orange juice
  (preferably freshly
  squeezed)

Serves 8
Cooking time: 8 minutes

Break the eggs into a bowl, add one-third of the sugar and whisk to a ribbon consistency. In a saucepan, boil the orange juice with the remaining sugar, then pour the boiling juice onto the eggs, whisking continuously. Pour the mixture back into the pan and cook over medium heat for 2 minutes, whisking continuously. Pass the sauce through a conical strainer into a bowl and leave to cool at room temperature, whisking from time to time. When the sauce is cold, transfer it to a sealed container and refrigerate.

NOTE:
The sauce will keep in the fridge for three days.

Apple Coulis
Coulis de pommes

THIS VERSATILE COULIS MAKES A PERFECT ACCOMPANIMENT FOR MANY DESSERTS. IF IT
IS TOO THICK FOR YOUR TASTE, THIN IT WITH A LITTLE SORBET SYRUP (PAGE 144).

INGREDIENTS:
500 g/1 lb 2 oz apples,
  preferably Granny Smiths
375 ml/13 fl oz water
75 g/3 oz caster sugar
Juice of 1 lemon
1 vanilla pod, split

Makes 600 ml/1 pint
Preparation time: 10
  minutes

Wash the apples in cold water and cut each one into 6 or 8 segments. Place in a saucepan with all the other ingredients, cover and cook gently until the apples have reduced almost to a purée. Remove the vanilla pod, then purée the apples in a blender for 2 minutes, until very liquid. Pass through a fine conical strainer and leave to cool at room temperature.

NOTES:
Apple coulis keeps well in an airtight container in the fridge at 5°C/41°F for up to a week.

As with my apple sorbet, I do not peel the fruit or discard the cores, since they contain so much flavour.

SABAYON WITH RASPBERRY EAU-DE-VIE
Sabayon à l'alcool de framboises

I USE THIS SABAYON IN MANY OF MY RECIPES, INCLUDING FRESH FIGS ON A
SABAYON QUILT (PAGE 67). OR SERVE IT PLAIN IN A BOWL TO ACCOMPANY
RASPBERRIES OR WILD STRAWBERRIES OR MY HAZELNUT TUILES (PAGE 172).

INGREDIENTS:
3 egg yolks
65 g/2½ oz caster sugar
50 ml/2 fl oz water
75 ml/3 fl oz raspberry
  eau-de-vie
½ gelatine leaf (this is only
  necessary for a cold
  sabayon)

Serves 4 (makes about
  400 ml/14 fl oz)
Preparation and cooking
  time: 15–20 minutes

Fresh Figs on a Sabayon
Quilt

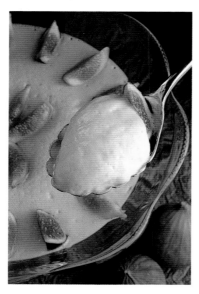

THE SABAYON: Half-fill a saucepan large enough to hold the base of a mixing bowl with warm water and heat gently to 35°–40°C/ 95°–104°F. Combine the egg yolks, sugar, water and raspberry eau-de-vie in a bowl and stand it in the saucepan (bain-marie). Whisk continuously with a balloon whisk for 10–12 minutes, making sure that the water temperature does not rise above 90°C/194°F, or the sabayon may coagulate. If necessary, turn off the heat while you whisk the sabayon. It should swell into a ribbon consistency, like half-risen beaten egg whites, and the texture should be smooth, shiny, airy and wonderfully rich, with an internal temperature of 50°C/122°F.

If you plan to eat the sabayon hot, it is best served immediately. For a cold sabayon, soak the ½ gelatine leaf in a soup spoon of warm water in a ramekin and as soon as it dissolves, whisk it into the sabayon.

PRESENTATION: Serve the sabayon in large burgundy glasses or champagne coupes, or in a glass bowl. If you plan to serve it cold, place the filled glasses or bowl for 5 minutes in the freezer, then chill in the fridge for an hour or two. Serve the sabayon cold and still trembling, not frozen.

SPECIAL EQUIPMENT:
Cooking thermometer

NOTES:
Other eaux-de-vie, such as pear or plum, can be substituted for the raspberry, or you could use a heavy sweet wine like a Banyuls or Marsala.

The sabayon can be kept in the bain-marie for 10–15 minutes before serving, but after that it will lose some of its lightness.

CHOCOLATE SAUCE
Sauce chocolat

INGREDIENTS:
200 g/7 oz best quality
    bitter cooking chocolate,
    plain chocolate drops or
    couverture
150 ml/5 fl oz milk
2 tablespoons double cream
30 g/1 oz caster sugar
30 g/1 oz butter, diced

Makes about 450 g/1 lb
Preparation time: 10
    minutes

Melt the chocolate in a bain-marie set over medium heat, stirring from time to time. In a saucepan, bring to the boil the milk, cream and sugar, stirring gently with a whisk. Pour this mixture onto the melted chocolate, stirring continuously. Return the sauce to the pan and let it bubble for 15 seconds.

Off the heat, beat in the butter, a little at a time, until the sauce is smooth and completely homogeneous. Pass through a conical strainer. and serve warm.

NOTE:
The sauce will keep in the fridge for 3 days; store in an airtight container or a bowl covered with clingfilm. Reheat gently before serving.

Warm chocolate sauce ready for pouring

CARAMEL SAUCE
Sauce caramel

INGREDIENTS:
100 g/4 oz caster sugar
80 ml/3 fl oz water
500 ml/18 fl oz double
    cream
2 egg yolks, lightly beaten
    (optional)

Makes about 700 ml /
    1¼ pints
Preparation time: 5 minutes

In a large saucepan, dissolve the sugar with the water over low heat and bring to boiling point. Wash down the inside of the pan with a pastry brush dipped in cold water to prevent crystals from forming. Cook until the sugar turns to a deep amber colour. Immediately turn off the heat and whisk in the cream.

Set the pan back over high heat and stir the sauce with the whisk. Let it bubble for 2 minutes, then turn off the heat. You can now strain the sauce and use it when cooled, or, for a richer, smoother sauce, pour a little of the caramel onto the egg yolks, then return the mixture to the pan and heat to 80°C/175°F, taking care that it does not boil. Pass the sauce through a conical strainer and keep in a cool place, stirring occasionally to prevent a skin from forming.

SPECIAL EQUIPMENT:
Cooking thermometer

NOTE:
The caramel sauce will keep in an airtight container in the fridge for 48 hours.

HONEY SAUCE
Sauce au miel

INGREDIENTS:
250 ml/9 fl oz runny honey
125 ml/4 fl oz Sorbet
    Syrup (page 144)
Juice of 3 limes

Makes 400 g/14 oz
Preparation time: 5 minutes

Mix all the ingredients with a spatula and keep the sauce in an airtight container until needed.

NOTES:
Use this very sweet sauce in small quantities. It can be flavoured with vanilla, cinnamon or cloves. For an orange or lemon honey sauce, add some thin slivers of blanched orange or lemon zest.

OLD BACHELOR'S BOTTLED FRUIT
Confiture de vieux garçon

ELDERLY GENTLEMEN LOVE SWEET THINGS AND HERE IS THE PERFECT SWEET TREAT. SOME MAY PREFER IT EVEN SWEETER, IN WHICH CASE INCREASE THE SUGAR BY 15–20%. I ADORE THIS BOTTLED FRUIT, WHICH LYN HALL KINDLY GAVE ME AS A CHRISTMAS GIFT MANY YEARS AGO AND WHICH I HAVE ENJOYED EVERY CHRISTMAS SINCE THEN. THE IDEAL TIME TO PREPARE THE FRUIT IS IN EARLY SUMMER. YOU SHOULD WAIT THREE MONTHS BEFORE EATING IT, BUT IT IMPROVES WITH KEEPING AND WILL TASTE EVEN BETTER AFTER SIX MONTHS – IF YOU CAN WAIT THAT LONG!

INGREDIENTS:
1 kg/2¼ lbs soft fruit of your choice (eg: cherries, small strawberries, raspberries, blackcurrants, redcurrants, seedless grapes)
750 g/1½ lbs granulated sugar
1 vanilla pod, split
2 small cinnamon sticks
2 small ginger roots, peeled with a potato peeler
A pinch of nutmeg
10 allspice berries (optional)
750 ml/1½ pints Cognac or white rum

Makes two 1 litre/1¾ pint jars
Preparation time: 10 minutes

PREPARING THE FRUIT: Wash, drain and dry on absorbent paper. De-stalk the blackcurrants, redcurrants and grapes. Hull the strawberries and raspberries. Trim the cherry stalks to 2 cm/¾ in.

BOTTLING THE FRUIT: Sterilize the jars with boiling water and dry thoroughly. Place the fruit in the jars, layering it at intervals with the sugar and aromatics. Pour over your chosen alcohol and close the jars. If the fruit ferments after a few days, add a little more of the same alcohol and reseal the jars. You can top up with more fruit after two weeks, when the first fruits have shrunk.

SPECIAL EQUIPMENT:
2 wide-mouthed 1 litre/ 1¾ pint kilner jars

NOTE:
Serve the fruit in a liqueur glass after dinner, to be eaten with a coffee spoon or wooden cocktail stick, then drink the juice after your coffee. What a delight!

RHUBARB COMPOTE WITH SAUTERNES
Compote de rhubarbe au Sauternes

SERVE THIS SWEET FRUITY COMPOTE WITH SLICES OF BUTTERY BRIOCHE (PAGE 19).

INGREDIENTS:
450 g/ 1 lb very tender young rhubarb, peeled
200 ml/7 fl oz Sauternes or sweet dessert wine
50 g/2 oz caster sugar
Juice of 1 lemon

Serves 4
Preparation time: 5 minutes
Cooking time: 6 minutes

PREPARATION: Wash the rhubarb and cut into 4 cm/1½ in lengths. Place in a saucepan with all the other ingredients and bring slowly to the boil. Lower the heat and poach gently for about 6 minutes, until the rhubarb is tender, leave in the poaching liquid at room temperature until cold, then refrigerate for 2 hours before serving.

PRESENTATION: Serve the compote in a glass bowl or individual dishes.

A spoonful of Old Bachelor's Bottled Fruit

APRICOT JAM WITH ALMONDS
Confiture d'abricots aux amandes

THIS JAM IS DELECTABLE SPREAD ON TOAST. I SERVE IT TO MY GUESTS AT THE WATERSIDE INN FOR BREAKFAST DURING THE SUMMER.

INGREDIENTS:

750 g / 1½ lbs very ripe apricots

75 ml / 3 fl oz water

550 g / 1¼ lbs caster sugar mixed with 1 teaspoon pectin (optional)

Juice of 1 lemon

75 g / 3 oz whole almonds, skinned and soaked in milk for 2 hours (see note)

Makes 1.2 kg / 2¾ lbs

Preparation time: 10 minutes

Wash the apricots in cold water, halve them and remove the stones.

Combine the water, sugar and pectin mixture and the lemon juice in the jam pan and gently bring to the boil over low heat. Add the apricots and cook gently, skimming the surface occasionally. Drain the almonds, rinse in cold water and add them to the pan after 45 minutes if the apricots are extremely ripe, or 1 hour if they are only just ripe, and cook for a further 3 minutes.

Leave the jam to cool in the pan and spoon into sterilized jars when it is still just warm. Cool completely, then seal the jars with cellophane covers.

SPECIAL EQUIPMENT:
Jam pan

NOTE:
When fresh almonds are in season, during June and July, substitute them for the semi-dried variety for an even better jam. It is not neccessary to soak fresh almonds in milk.

BLACKBERRY JELLY
Gelée de mûres

THIS WONDERFUL JELLY REMINDS ME VIVIDLY OF MY CHILDHOOD. FROM EARLY SEPTEMBER, I WOULD GATHER THEM FROM THE BRAMBLE HEDGES IN THE VENDEE AND TAKE MY HARVEST BACK TO MOTHER. WITHIN A FEW HOURS, THE JELLY WAS PREPARED AND IN ITS JARS. WHAT A FANTASTIC MOTHER! THE FRUIT NEVER HAD TIME TO SPOIL, AND IT WAS A DELIGHT THE NEXT DAY TO EAT PANCAKES SPREAD WITH FRESH JELLY. NOT A SINGLE JAR EVER LASTED THROUGH THE WINTER IN OUR HOUSE!

INGREDIENTS:
1 kg/2¼ lbs blackberries, preferably wild
200 ml/7 fl oz water
1 lemon, washed and cut into large pieces
Caster sugar (the same quantity as the juice from the cooked blackberries)

Makes about 750 g/1½ lbs
Preparation time: 15 minutes, plus draining the juice
Cooking time: about 7 minutes

PREPARING THE BLACKBERRIES: Wash and hull the fruit and place in a saucepan with the water and lemon. Bring to the boil over low heat, then bubble gently for 5 minutes. Remove the pieces of lemon, then rub the blackberries and juice through the mouli. Pour the pulp into the jelly bag or muslin and leave the juice to drip through gently. After 30 minutes, squeeze very gently to extract as much juice as possible. Measure the juice and pour it into the jam pan with an equal amount of sugar.

COOKING THE JELLY: Cook gently, stirring with a spatula at first to dissolve the sugar completely. Bring to the boil, then start timing the cooking; the jam will be ready in about 7 minutes. Skim the surface if necessary. Pour the blackberry jelly into sterilized jars and leave to cool before sealing with cellophane covers.

SPECIAL EQUIPMENT:
Vegetable mouli with a coarse blade
Jelly bag or muslin

NOTE:
Since the sugar and juice content of blackberries varies, it is difficult to give a precise quantity of sugar before they are cooked.

APPLE JELLY OR GLAZE
Gelée de pommes

THIS TRANSLUCENT JELLY MAKES AN EXCELLENT GLAZE FOR FRUIT TARTS AND GATEAUX.

INGREDIENTS:
500 ml/18 fl oz water
250 g/9 oz caster sugar
500 g/1 lb 2 oz dessert apples (preferably Coxes)
1 lemon
6 gelatine leaves soaked in cold water and well drained

Makes 650 ml/1¼ pints
Preparation time: 20 minutes
Cooking time: 15 minutes

In a saucepan, heat the water and sugar until the sugar has dissolved completely and the liquid begins to boil, stirring occasionally with a whisk and skimming the surface if necessary.

Wash the apples and lemon, but do not peel them. Coarsely chop the fruit, cores, pips and all, and put them into the boiling sugar syrup. Cover the pan and simmer for 10 minutes. Take the pan off the heat and push the fruit to one side to make room to put in the gelatine and dissolve it. When it has dissolved completely, pass the jelly carefully through a conical strainer or jelly bag set over a bowl. Use the jelly as a glaze when it is cold but not yet set.

SPECIAL EQUIPMENT:
Jelly bag or conical strainer

NOTE:
The jelly will keep in an airtight container in the fridge for 4 days. Reheat and leave to cool again before using.

COLD DESSERTS

For over twenty years I have served my cold desserts ready assembled on the plate. The result is visually and gastronomically incomparable. To serve your desserts at home in this way, assemble them several hours or just a few minutes before serving and spoon a little coulis or sauce on the side or around the edge. Your guest can thus enjoy a delicate, individual dessert, specially prepared, presented and served at the ideal temperature. Specialist cookshops sell stacking rings for plates, which are perfect for this; once you have assembled the dessert on individual plates, place a ring round the edge, stack the plates into one or two piles and refrigerate, all ready to serve.

Decorative feather patterns made on the plate with a combination of two or three coulis, sauces or creams look attractive. Use the tip of a knife or a toothpick to swirl circles or ovals, but keep the decoration discreet. It should not detract from the main attraction, the dessert.

Red Fruit Tulip

APPLE FANTASY
L'Assiette de pommes

I ADORE THE CONTRASTING CRUNCHY AND SMOOTH TEXTURES OF THIS
SIMPLE DESSERT. ALL THREE COMPONENTS CAN BE PREPARED IN ADVANCE AND
ASSEMBLED AT THE LAST MINUTE..

INGREDIENTS: ❊
SYRUP:
200 g/7 oz caster sugar
½ vanilla pod, split
200 ml/7 fl oz water
Juice of 1 lemon

4 apples, not too ripe, about
    200 g/7 oz each
100 g/4 oz Pastry Cream
    (page 39)
½ quantity Apple Sorbet
    (page 146)
20 g/¾ oz icing sugar
    (optional)

Serves 4
Preparation time: 25
    minutes
Cooking time: 20 minutes

THE SYRUP: Combine the caster sugar, vanilla, water and lemon juice
in a saucepan and heat gently until the syrup starts to bubble.

THE APPLE GAUFRETTES: Peel and core the fruit with an apple corer.
Adjust the rippled blade of the mandoline to a thickish setting and
cut a ridged slice from one side of an apple. Discard this first slice,
and cut 8 latticed slices (gaufrettes) from the sides of three of the apples
(discarding all the first slices), giving the fruit one-quarter turn each
time, so that they resemble latticed potato crisps. Drop the gaufrettes
at once into the boiling syrup and immediately stop the cooking.
Leave them to cool in the syrup.
   Preheat the oven to 160°C/310°F/gas 2–3.

THE LACY APPLE CRISPS: Finely dice the remaining apple. spread on a
non-stick baking sheet and cook in the preheated oven for 20
minutes. Leave to cool at room temperature.
   Increase the oven temperature to 180°C/350°F/gas 4.
   Lay the template on a non-stick baking sheet, Silpat or silicone
paper, put in a little pastry cream and smooth with a palette knife.
Move the template sideways and make 16 discs of pastry cream in this
way. Place the cooked diced apples in the centre of the pastry cream
discs and cook in the preheated oven for 3 minutes, until pale golden.
Carefully lift off the discs with a palette knife and crinkle them
slightly with your fingertips. Place the lacy apple crisps on a cooling
rack and dust with icing sugar if you wish.

PRESENTATION: Place a large scoop of apple sorbet in the middle of four
chilled deep plates. Stick four lacy apple crisps in each ball of sorbet.
Arrange the gaufrettes around the edge and spoon a little of the
poaching syrup over them. Serve at once.

SPECIAL EQUIPMENT:
Mandoline
2 non-stick baking sheets, or
    Silpat or silicone paper
6 cm/2⅜ in diam.
    template, 1 mm/¹⁄₂₄ in
    thick

RED FRUIT TULIPS

Tulipes de fruits rouges

THESE CRISP, MELT-IN-THE-MOUTH PASTRY TULIPS ADD AN EXTRA DIMENSION
TO SERVING RED FRUITS.

INGREDIENTS: ❄
1 quantity Tulip Paste
  (page 28) (to be made 24
  hours in advance)
10 g/⅓ oz cocoa powder,
  sifted
1 kg/2¼ lbs assorted berry
  fruits in season (eg:
  blackberries, cultivated
  and wild strawberries,
  redcurrants, bilberries)
150 ml/5 fl oz Peach
  Coulis (see Fruit Coulis,
  page 51), mixed with the
  juice of 1 orange and
  ½ lemon

Serves 6
Preparation time: 40
  minutes

Cooking time: about 12
  minutes

THE TULIP PASTE: Follow the recipe on page 28. When the paste is ready, place one-quarter in a bowl and mix in the cocoa to colour and flavour it.

SHAPING THE TULIPS: Lay the largest stencil on a corner of a baking sheet and spread a very thin layer of the plain tulip paste in the centre, using a palette knife to spread it flat across the template (1). Move the template along and repeat the operation five times to make six wafer-thin, very even round shapes. Use the smaller templates to make six 13 cm/5 in and six 10 cm/4 in circles.

Preheat the oven to 180°C/350°F/gas 4.

DECORATING AND COOKING THE TULIPS: Fill the decorating cone with the chocolate tulip paste. Snip off the end of the cone with scissors and decorate the pastry circles with spirals (2). Then, with the tip of a knife, lightly mark out rays, alternately starting from the centre of the spiral drawing outwards (3), then from the outside inwards to make an attractive wavy effect, like the fondant icing on a mille-feuille. Space the rays about 1.5 cm/⅝ in apart on the largest circles and a little closer on the smaller circles.

Place one baking sheet at a time in the heated oven and bake the pastry circles for 3–4 minutes, until pale nutty brown. Turn them over on the baking sheet, then roll them one at a time around the

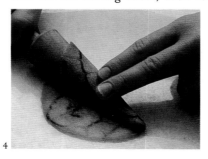

foil-covered cone, starting at the opposite side from the centre of the spiral (4). Press the tulip into shape, lightly at first, then a little more firmly, until it is stable enough to be removed from the cone. Place the shaped tulips on a cooling rack and leave in a dry place until needed.

SPECIAL EQUIPMENT:
3 wafer-thin templates,
  16 cm/6 in diam.,
  13 cm/5 in diam.,
  10 cm/4 in diam.
Paper decorating cone
Foil-covered cardboard cone,
  for shaping the cooked
  tulips
3 lightly greased 60 × 40 cm/
  24 × 16 in baking sheets

NOTE:
The tulips can be made a day in advance, but it is essential to keep them in an airtight container in a dry place.

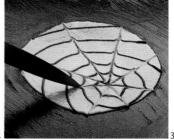

PRESENTATION: Wash all the fruits except the wild strawberries, drain well, hull and mix them together. Arrange one tulip of each size on each serving plate and delicately fill them with the fruits, allowing some to spill out seductively. Pour a ribbon of peach coulis around the tulips and a little in between them, and serve at once.

RED BERRIES WITH LIGHTLY CANDIED ORANGE BEADS

L'Assiette de baies rouges aux pustules d'oranges mi-confites

LAVENDER FLOWERS ARE HIGHLY PERFUMED. IT IS BEST TO USE THEM AS THEY FIRST COME INTO FLOWER, WHEN THEIR SCENT IS NOT TOO POWERFUL. THEY LOOK VERY PRETTY WHEN LIGHTLY CANDIED, AND ADD A FLAVOUR OF SUMMER. A FEW STALKS MARRY WELL WITH THE ORANGES, CARAMEL SAUCE AND RED BERRIES — BUT DON'T EAT THEM ALL.

INGREDIENTS: ❋

2 large, very juicy oranges

350 ml/12 fl oz Sorbet Syrup (page 144), plus an extra 150 ml/5 fl oz if you are using lavender

100 g/4 oz caster sugar

20 small stalks of lavender, newly come into flower (optional)

400 g/14 oz chilled mixed red berries, according to the season (equal quantities, or in whichever proportion you prefer), eg: small strawberries. raspberries, wild strawberries, redcurrants, blackberries, blackcurrants, blueberries

Serves 4

Preparation time: 25 minutes

Cooking time: 2½ hours (for the orange peel)

PREPARING THE ORANGES: Use the tip of a small knife to incise the orange peel into 4 quarters, then, with your thumb, carefully remove the quartered peel without damaging it. Place the peel in a saucepan, cover with cold water, bring to the boil and blanch for 2 minutes, then refresh and drain.

Pour 350 ml/12 fl oz sorbet syrup into another saucepan, bring to the boil, then drop in the orange peel and simmer over low heat for 1 hour (see photo). Leave the peel to cool in the syrup at room temperature. When it is cold, bring the syrup back to the boil and simmer for another hour. If the syrup becomes too thick, add a little cold water. When the peel is lightly candied, leave it in the syrup at room temperature until cold. Drain the peel and cut each piece into round beads with small, different-sized pastry cutters, then place in a bowl. The trimmings can be cut into large dice, rolled in sugar and served as little sweetmeats with coffee.

THE ORANGE CARAMEL SAUCE: Separate the peeled oranges into quarters, remove any pips and purée the fruit in a blender for 2–3 minutes. Pass the purée through a muslin-lined fine sieve set over a saucepan, pressing to extract as much juice as possible (you should have about 150 ml/5 fl oz). Heat the juice gently.

Put the sugar into another saucepan and dissolve it over very low heat, stirring continuously until it becomes a pale caramel. Pour on the warm orange juice, little by little, stirring all the time, then reduce the sauce over medium heat for 3 or 4 minutes. Leave it to cool at room temperature, then refrigerate.

THE LAVENDER: Bring the 150 ml/5 fl oz sorbet syrup to the boil and drop in the lavender flowers. Simmer very gently for 2 minutes, then leave the lavender to cool in the syrup at room temperature. Drain it just before serving.

PRESENTATION: Arrange your chosen well-chilled fruits in four deep plates. Dot the candied orange beads among the berries and add five sprigs of lavender to each plate. Pour on some chilled orange caramel sauce, and serve.

NOTE:

All the elements of this dessert can be prepared in advance, even the day before if you wish; you will need just 5 minutes to arrange all the ingredients on the plates when you are ready to serve.

Fresh Figs on a Sabayon Quilt
La coupe de figues sur douillet de sabayon

THIS CREAMY AND DELICIOUS AUTUMN DESSERT IS EXCEPTIONALLY EASY TO MAKE AND CAN BE PREPARED A DAY IN ADVANCE. IT IS A GREAT FAVOURITE WITH BOTH YOUNG AND OLD.

INGREDIENTS: ❄
Double quantity Sabayon (page 53), made with Marsala or Sauternes
5 or 6 very ripe figs, preferably 2 types, black and green

Serves 6–8
Preparation time: 5 minutes

THE SABAYON: Before starting, chill a glass bowl until very cold.

Follow the sabayon recipe on page 53, substituting Marsala or Sauternes for the raspberry eau-de-vie. Since the sabayon is to be served cold, you will need to add the gelatine.

Pour the sabayon into the chilled bowl and place in the freezer for 10 minutes, then in the fridge for at least 2 hours.

PRESENTATION: Just before serving, cut the figs into segments and arrange them round the edge and in the centre of the bowl, alternating the black and green segments. Serve immediately.

Pistachio Creme Brulee
Crème brûlée pistache

I ADORE PISTACHIOS AND MY FAVOURITE VERSIONS OF CREME BRULEE ARE THOSE WITH PISTACHIOS OR WILD STRAWBERRIES. A VANILLA ICE CREAM (PAGE 137) SERVED SEPARATELY IN A GLASS OR COUPE WILL FURTHER ENHANCE THE PISTACHIO FLAVOUR.

INGREDIENTS:
500 ml/18 fl oz milk
500 ml/18 fl oz whipping cream
60 g/2 oz pistachio paste
260 g/9 oz caster sugar
200 g/7 oz egg yolks
30 g/1 oz skinned pistachios

Serves 6
Preparation time: 10 minutes
Cooking time: 30 minutes

Fresh figs on a Sabayon Quilt

THE CUSTARD: Heat the milk, cream, pistachio paste and 90 g/3 oz of the sugar in a saucepan, whisking continuously at first.

In a bowl, lightly whisk the egg yolks with 60 g/2 oz sugar until slightly pale. As soon as the milk comes to the boil, pour it onto the eggs, little by little, whisking all the time.

COOKING THE CUSTARDS: Preheat the oven to 100°C/200°F/gas ½.

Ladle the custard into the gratin dishes and cook in the warm oven for 30 minutes. Remove from the oven and carefully slide the dishes onto a wire rack. Once the custards are completely cold, transfer them to the fridge.

PRESENTATION: Just before serving, sprinkle the tops of the crèmes brûlées with 70 g/2½ oz sugar and caramelize them with a blowtorch, or under a very hot grill, to make a thin, pale nut-brown topping.

Heat an empty small frying pan, then toss in the pistachios, sprinkle them with the remaining sugar and stir vigorously for 1 minute, so that they are well coated with the sugar. Tip them onto a plate, separate the pistachios with a fork and arrange about 8 pistachios on top of each crème brûlée. Serve immediately.

SPECIAL EQUIPMENT:
Six 15 cm/6 in diam. gratin dishes
Blowtorch (optional)

NOTES:
The sugar topping will soften within an hour or two, depending on the humidity, so I would recommend that you caramelize the crème brûlées only a short time before serving.

If you cannot buy commercially-made pistachio paste, make your own by pounding freshly skinned pistachios in a small mortar to make a very smooth purée.

MARZIPAN FIGS
Figues au parfum d'amandes

YOUR CHILDREN WILL BE INTRIGUED BY THE PREPARATION OF THIS SIMPLE,
IMAGINATIVE DESSERT. THEY MIGHT EVEN HELP YOU TO MAKE THE MOCK FIGS!

INGREDIENTS: ❄
½ quantity Choux Paste
  (page 26)
2 very ripe black or green
  figs
½ quantity Mousseline
  Cream (page 42)
2 tablespoons kirsch
  (optional)
500–750 g/1 lb 2 oz–
  1 lb 10 oz marzipan
  (depending on your taste
  and artistry)
Food colourings: mauve, red,
  green, yellow (depending
  on the desired effect)
50 g/2 oz icing sugar for
  dusting

Serves 6
Preparation time: 45
  minutes
Cooking time: 20 minutes

PIPING AND BAKING THE CHOUX 'FIGS': Preheat the oven to 200°C/
400°F/gas 6.

Using the piping bag with the 5 mm/¼ in nozzle, pipe about
twelve 3 cm/1¼ in diam. choux puffs onto a baking sheet. They need
not be uniformly sized; after all, not all figs are the same size. Bake
in the oven for 20 minutes, then pierce the bases of the puffs with
the tip of a sharp knife, transfer to a cooling rack and leave to cool at
room temperature.

FILLING THE CHOUX 'FIGS': Finely dice the fresh figs, mix them
delicately into the mousseline cream and add the kirsch. Using the
piping bag with the 1 cm/½ in nozzle, generously fill the choux buns
with this mixture through the incision in the bases.

PREPARING THE MARZIPAN AND WRAPPING THE FIGS: Put the marzipan on
the work surface and, using your hands, colour two-thirds with
mauve-toned colouring and the rest with greener tones. Use your
own artistic judgement to decide the precise shades.

Dust the work surface with icing sugar and roll out 50–70 g/
2–3 oz marzipan into a small disc, about 3 mm/⅛ in thick, lightly
blending the two colours to achieve a marbled effect. Lay a choux puff
on the disc and gather up the marzipan over the puff. Pinch the edges
together to form a stem and voilà! there is your 'fig'. Mark it with the
modelling tool or the back of a knife blade to resemble a real fig, and
lightly dab on a little icing sugar here and there with your fingertips
(see photo, opposite). Wrap and decorate all the choux puffs in the
same way.

PRESENTATION: Serve the marzipan figs on a china plate or, for a more
rustic effect, in the wooden crate in which the real figs were sold.

SPECIAL EQUIPMENT:
Plastic modelling tool (eg:
  for Playdoh) (optional)
Piping bag with a plain
  5 mm/¼ in nozzle
Piping bag with a plain
  1 cm/½ in nozzle

NOTE:
For a picnic, transport the
figs in their wooden crate.
They should be eaten within
24 hours, as the mousseline
cream will sour if kept for
longer.

ANGEL'S HAIR IN A LIGHT SAUTERNES JELLY

Cheveux d'ange en gelée de Sauternes mi-prise

THIS ORIGINAL, REFRESHING DESSERT IS THE PERFECT ENDING FOR AN
ELEGANT SUMMER MEAL.

INGREDIENTS: ❊

½ bottle sweet white wine,
preferably Sauternes
2 gelatine leaves, soaked in
cold water and well
drained
200 ml/7 fl oz Sorbet
Syrup (page 144)
8 egg yolks, strained
6 kumquats
1 small pomegranate

Serves 6
Preparation time: 30
minutes, plus setting
Cooking time: 10 minutes
for the kumquats

THE SAUTERNES JELLY: Heat 50 ml/2 fl oz of the Sauternes in a small
saucepan. Off the heat, add and dissolve the gelatine, then stir in the
remaining wine, without overmixing. Refrigerate for about 1 hour,
until the jelly is lightly set.

THE ANGEL'S HAIR: Heat the syrup in a deep roasting
pan. As soon as it starts to tremble, fill a paper piping
cone with 2 egg yolks, and snip off the end to make a
tiny opening. Move the cone backwards and forwards
across the roasting pan about 5 cm/2 in above the
surface of the syrup, letting the yolks escape through
the hole into the syrup (see photo, right). Poach for
about 1 minute until they form strands like angel's hair.
Remove with a flat slotted spoon and place in a bowl of
cold water. Repeat until you have used all the yolks.
Leave the angel's hair in the cold water for 5 minutes,
then drain, place in a bowl and refrigerate.

THE KUMQUATS: Blanch in a small saucepan of boiling
water, refresh and drain. Pour the poaching syrup from

NOTE:
The dessert can be prepared a
day in advance and assembled
just before serving.

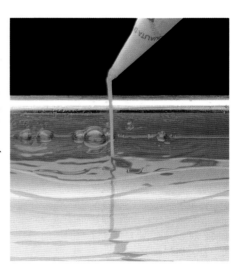

the angel's hair into the same pan and bring to the boil. Put in the kumquats and poach for 10 minutes, keeping the syrup at a gentle simmer. Leave to cool in the syrup at room temperature, then refrigerate them.

THE POMEGRANATE: Peel, scoop the seeds into a bowl and refrigerate.

PRESENTATION: Arrange the angel's hair in the centre of six balloon glasses or shallow glass bowls. Put a kumquat in the middle and the pomegranate seeds around the edge. Lightly whisk the Sauternes jelly just to loosen it, then pour it into the bowls to cover the angel's hair, kumquats and pomegranate seeds. Serve with a spoon and fork.

SPECIAL EQUIPMENT:
Paper piping cone

PALM TREES WITH EXOTIC FRUIT
Le cocotier et ses fruits éxotiques

THE PERFECT DESSERT FOR A CHILDREN'S PARTY. THEY WILL LOVE THE COMBINATION OF FRUIT AND CRISP PASTRY.

INGREDIENTS: ❋
600 g/1¼ lbs Jean Millet's
    Puff Pastry (page 24), or
    Quick Puff Pastry
    (page 25)
Flour for dusting
Eggwash (1 egg yolk mixed
    with 1 tablespoon milk
    and a pinch of salt)
Icing sugar for dusting
1 very ripe mango, about
    300 g/11 oz
70 ml/2½ fl oz Sorbet
    Syrup (page 144)
70 ml/2½ fl oz water
1 coconut

Serves 4
Preparation time: 30
    minutes
Cooking time: 10 minutes

THE PASTRY PALM TREES: On a lightly floured surface, roll out the pastry into a 60 × 14 cm/24 × 6 in rectangle, 2 mm/¹⁄₁₂ in thick. Lay the template on one side of the rectangle and, using the tip of a small sharp knife, cut the pastry into the shape of a palm tree. Invert the template, trunk upwards, leaves towards you, so as to waste as little pastry as possible. Cut out a second palm tree, then repeat the operation to make four trees in all.
  Delicately transfer the trees to a lightly dampened baking sheet, taking care not to spoil the shape. Brush with eggwash and refrigerate for 20 minutes.
  Preheat the oven to 180°C/350°F/gas 4.

BAKING THE PALM TREES: Brush the trees again with eggwash and bake in the preheated oven for 10 minutes. 1 minute before removing them from the oven, dust with icing sugar and bake for another minute to glaze them.

THE MANGO COULIS: Peel the mango, cut off the flesh from around the stone and purée in a blender with the syrup and water for 1 minute, to make a smooth coulis.

THE COCONUT: Remove the shell and break the flesh into small pieces.

PRESENTATION: Arrange the palm trees on four plates. Pour the mango coulis around each one and place little heaps of coconut at the base

SPECIAL EQUIPMENT: ❋
*Home-made cardboard
    template of a double palm
    tree, about 12 cm/5 in
    high (see page 188 for a
    photo of the pastry palm
    tree)*

NOTE:
*You can use sweet short
pastry (page 20) instead of
puff pastry. Roll it out to a
thickness of 3 mm/⅛ in and
do not glaze with icing
sugar.*

ANISEED PARFAIT WITH BLACKBERRY COULIS
Parfait à l'anis et son coulis de mûres

THE COMBINATION OF BLACKBERRIES WITH ANISEED AND THE RICHNESS OF
THE PARFAIT IS SURPRISING AND IMMENSELY POPULAR. THIS DESSERT IS A
GREAT SUMMER AND AUTUMN FAVOURITE AT THE WATERSIDE INN.

INGREDIENTS: ❋
½ quantity Joconde Sponge
  (page 31)
140 g/4½ oz Nougatine
  (page 189)

BLACKBERRY COULIS
350 g/12 oz blackberries
1 tablespoon Pastis or Ricard
120 ml/4 fl oz Sorbet
  Syrup (page 144)

BOMBE MIXTURE
100 g/4 oz caster sugar
Juice of ½ lemon
4 egg yolks
40 ml/1½ fl oz Pastis or
  Ricard
1 gelatine leaf, soaked in
  cold water and well
  drained
300 ml/11 fl oz whipping
  cream, whipped to a
  ribbon consistency

GARNISH
36 blackberries, washed and
  hulled
8 small sprigs of mint

SERVES 8
Preparation time: 45
  minutes

THE SPONGE BASES: Cut out eight sponge circles with a plain 6 cm/
2⅜ in pastry cutter. Arrange the dessert rings on a small baking sheet
and line the bases with the sponge circles, then refrigerate.

THE BLACKBERRY COULIS: Wash and hull the blackberries, and purée in
a food processor with the Pastis or Ricard and the sorbet syrup for 2
minutes. Pass the coulis through a muslin-lined conical strainer and
refrigerate.

THE NOUGATINE BASES: Roll out the nougatine until wafer-thin and cut
out eight 8 cm/3¼ in rounds. Keep in a dry place.

THE BOMBE MIXTURE: Combine 2 tablespoons water, the sugar and lemon
juice in a small, heavy-based saucepan and bring to the boil. Wash
down the inside of the pan with a pastry brush dipped in cold water.
Put the sugar thermometer in the syrup and cook gently until it reaches
115°C/240°F. Now start creaming the egg yolks in an electric mixer or
by hand. As soon as the sugar temperature reaches 121°C/250°F, stop
cooking and leave the syrup to bubble down for 1 minute.
  Start pouring the syrup onto the egg yolks in a thin stream, still
beating, but more slowly. When all the syrup is incorporated into the
yolks, continue to beat until completely cold. Warm the Pastis or
Ricard and dissolve the gelatine in it, then leave to cool for a few
minutes before folding it delicately into the whipped cream.
  Use a whisk to fold one-third of the whipped cream into the
bombe mixture, then delicately fold in the rest with a spatula.

ASSEMBLING THE PARFAITS: Fill a piping bag with the parfait mixture and
pipe it into the dessert rings. Smooth the surface with a palette knife
and place in the freezer for at least 2 hours.

PRESENTATION: Use a coffee spoon to hollow out a small 2 cm/¾ in
deep cavity in the centre of each parfait. Lift the rings off the parfaits
by heating the outsides very gently with a blowtorch, or by sliding a
knife blade dipped in hot water between the parfaits and the rings.
  Arrange each parfait on a nougatine round and place on individual
plates. Halve the 12 largest blackberries lengthways. Place three
whole blackberries in the cavity of each parfait, then arrange three
halved berries on the plate, along with a sprig of mint. Pour a little
of the light blackberry coulis onto the whole berries and a little onto
the plates, and serve at once.

SPECIAL EQUIPMENT:
Sugar thermometer
8 dessert rings, 6 cm/2⅜ in
  diam., 3 cm/1¼ in deep
Piping bag with a plain
  7 cm/2¾ in nozzle
Blowtorch (optional)

NOTE:
This iced dessert will keep
well in the freezer for at least
a week.

MERINGUE PILLOWS WITH MARRONS GLACÉS
Douillets de meringue aux marrons glacés

FOR AN EXTRA TREAT, SERVE A COULIS OR WARM CHOCOLATE SAUCE (PAGE 55) WITH
THIS DIVINE DESSERT.

INGREDIENTS: ❄

½ quantity French Meringue
(page 37)

30 g/1 oz almonds, lightly
toasted and cut into slivers

½ teaspoon poppy seeds
(optional)

200 g/7 oz Chocolate
Chantilly Cream (page
42)

⅓ quantity Chestnut
Bavarois (page 43),
prepared in advance and
refrigerated

200 g/7 oz marrons glacés,
or chestnuts in syrup
(whole or pieces)

Serves 6

Preparation time: 35
minutes, plus 1 hour for
the meringues

THE MERINGUE BASES: Preheat the oven to 100°C/200°F/gas ½. Make the meringue according to the method on page 37. Using the template, make a round of meringue on the baking sheet or Silpat, and smooth with a palette knife. Move the template along and make seventeen more meringue bases in the same way (see pictures, right). Scatter the almonds and poppy seeds over six of them. Cook the meringues for 1 hour, remove from the oven and leave on the baking sheet to cool. When they are almost cold, use a palette knife to transfer them to a wire rack. Once they are completely cold, keep in a very dry place.

ASSEMBLING THE PILLOWS: Prepare the chocolate Chantilly cream and put it into the piping bag. Pipe a border three rings high onto all the plain meringue bases, giving a height of about 1 cm/½ in. Refrigerate the pillows for 5 minutes to harden the cream.

SPECIAL EQUIPMENT:
1 template 7.5 cm/3 in
diam., 4 mm/⅙ in thick
Piping bag with a plain
3 mm/⅛ in nozzle
1 non-stick baking sheet, or
Silpat

NOTES:
Apart from the Chantilly
cream which must be made
at the last moment, all the
other elements of this dessert
can be made the day before.
The chestnut bavarois should
be firm so that it does not
soften the meringue, which
should remain crunchy
outside and a little gooey
inside.

PRESENTATION: Reserve 6 of the best marron pieces for decoration. Spoon the chestnut bavarois into the centre of the 12 pillows with borders and arrange 2 or 3 small pieces of marrons glacés on the mousse. Double up the bases by placing one on top of another and finish with an almond and poppy seed base. Use a palette knife to slide the pillows onto serving plates. Decorate each with an attractive marron piece or half and serve without delay.

COFFEE PARFAITS
Parfaits au café

KEEP THE DECORATION RESTRAINED ON THESE PARFAITS; A LIGHT CHOCOLATE COATING OR A FEW COFFEE OR CHOCOLATE BEANS ARRANGED ON TOP ARE ENOUGH TO ENHANCE THE PRESENTATION.

INGREDIENTS:
½ quantity baked Hazelnut Dacquoise (page 31)
1 tablespoon water
75 g / 3 oz caster sugar
4 egg yolks
1 gelatine leaf, soaked in cold water and well drained
2 soup spoons instant coffee, dissolved in 2 soup spoons warm water
250 ml / 9 fl oz whipping cream, whipped to a ribbon consistency

Serves 10
Preparation time: 40 minutes

THE DACQUOISE BASES: Cut out ten dacquoise circles the size of the dessert rings. Place the rings on a baking sheet, line them with the dacquoise bases and refrigerate.

THE BOMBE MIXTURE: Put the water into a small, heavy-based saucepan, add the sugar and set over low heat. Bring to the boil, washing down the inside of the pan with a pastry brush dipped in cold water. Put the thermometer into the syrup and cook until the temperature reaches 115°C/240°F. Now start whisking the egg yolks in an electric mixer or by hand. As soon as the syrup reaches 121°C/250°F, turn off the heat and leave the syrup to bubble down for 1 minute. Pour the syrup onto the yolks in a thin stream, whisking continuously but slowly. When the syrup is well amalgamated with the yolks, stir in the well-drained gelatine and whisk until the mixture is completely cold. Stir the dissolved coffee into the mixture, then using a spatula, delicately fold in the whipped cream.

ASSEMBLING THE PARFAITS: Pipe the coffee bombe mixture into the lined rings and smooth the surfaces with a palette knife. Place the parfaits in the freezer.

PRESENTATION: To remove the rings, heat the outsides very lightly with a blowtorch, or run a knife blade dipped in hot water between the parfaits and the rings and lift them off. Place each parfait on a plate and serve frozen like an ice cream. Serve them just as they are or pour a ribbon of coffee Crème Anglaise (page 40) around the edge.

SPECIAL EQUIPMENT:
Sugar thermometer
Piping bag with a plain 7 mm / ⅜ in nozzle
10 dessert rings, 6 cm / 2⅜ in diam., 3 cm / 1¼ in deep
Blowtorch (optional)

NOTES:
The parfaits keep well in the freezer for up to a week, so this recipe may make enough for two meals, depending on how many guests you are entertaining and how greedy you are.

NOUGATINE BASKETS WITH YELLOW PEACHES
La coupelle de nougatine aux pêches jaunes

AN ELEGANT AND DELICATE DESSERT FOR A GRAND OCCASION OR A CANDLELIT
DINNER, WHICH REQUIRES SOME DEXTERITY. SINCE THIS IS A WINTER DESSERT,
I USE TINNED PEACHES IN SYRUP, WHICH TASTE DELICIOUS AND WHOSE COLOUR
AND FLAVOUR GO WONDERFULLY WELL WITH THE NOUGATINE.

INGREDIENTS: ❊
840 g/1¾ lbs freshly-made
  Nougatine (page 189)
2 tablespoons groundnut oil,
  for greasing
2 tablespoons Royal Icing
  (page 181)
50 g/2 oz caster sugar
½ quantity Ginger Mousse
  (page 49), to be prepared
  at least 2 hours in advance
  and kept in the fridge
6 yellow peach halves in
  syrup (about 320 g/
  11½ oz, drained weight)
48 pine nuts, sprinkled with
  icing sugar and glazed
  under a very hot grill

Serves 6
Preparation time: 1 hour 15
  minutes

THE NOUGATINE BASES: Preheat the oven to 160°C/320°F/gas 2–3. On
a warmed but not very hot greased baking sheet or a sheet of Silpat,

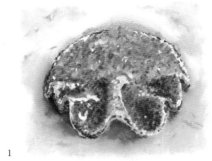

roll out half the nougatine to a
thickness of 2 mm/¹⁄₁₂ in. It
should be freshly made, and
therefore still malleable. If it is
too hard, place the baking sheet
with the nougatine in the warm
oven for a few seconds, but do
not overheat the nougatine or it
will stick to the baking sheet.

Cut out six nougatine rounds
with a plain 15 cm/6 in diam. pastry cutter, then quickly pleat each
one into five waves with your fingers. Give one wave at the front a
more pronounced shape (1). Place the bases on a wire rack.

THE NOUGATINE BASKETS: Heat the blade of a small, very sharp knife
over a gas flame. Gently warm the hemispherical mould in the oven.
Roll out the remaining nougatine in the same way as before and
cut out another six rounds.
Use the very hot knife blade
to cut an incision from the
centre of each round out to
the edge, heating the blade
again if necessary. Shape
these rounds by moulding
them one at a time round the
warmed mould. Roll over the
nougatine at the point where

you made the incision and press it into two small curls (2), taking
care that the entire shape of the basket is neatly formed. Throughout
this operation the nougatine should remain malleable but not too
soft.

Place the nougatine shapes on the wire rack and use a piping cone
to decorate the edges with royal icing.

Put 50 g/2 oz caster sugar in a small saucepan and dissolve it over
very low heat without water, stirring continuously. As soon as it
dissolves into a caramel, use a teaspoon to dab a little of the caramel
onto the bottom of one basket and immediately stick this onto a
nougatine base. Assemble all the baskets in this way.

SPECIAL EQUIPMENT:
1 hemispherical stainless
  steel dome, 4.5 cm/1¾ in
  high, 9 cm/3½ in diam.
Heavy wooden or special
  metal rolling pin for
  nougatine
Lightly greased baking sheet,
  or a sheet of Silpat
Paper piping cone
Piping bag with a plain
  15 mm/⅝ in nozzle

NOTES:
To ensure that the nougatine
is malleable when you are
rolling it out or shaping the
waves, warm it whenever
necessary for a few seconds
in a microwave oven, or for
2 or 3 minutes in a
conventional oven at
160°C/320°F/gas 2–3.

  The nougatine baskets can
be made two or three days in
advance. Keep them in a very
dry place and do not fill
with mousse more than 2
hours before the meal.

THE GINGER MOUSSE: The mousse should have been prepared at least 2 hours in advance and refrigerated, so that it has set. Put in the piping bag and pipe it into the baskets, without filling them right to the top. The baskets can now be kept in the fridge for up to 2 hours.

PRESENTATION: Drain and pat dry the peach halves. Thinly slice each half and arrange one on the mousse in each basket, fanning out the slices into a flower shape. Scatter on the pine nuts and place the nougatine baskets on plates which complement their shape. Serve cold but not chilled.

INDIVIDUAL KOUGLOFS
Kouglof à ma façon

THIS IS MY VERSION OF A WONDERFUL WINTER DESSERT. THE KOUGLOFS ARE
SLIGHTLY REMINISCENT OF BREAD AND BUTTER PUDDING, BUT MORE DELICATE AND
ATTRACTIVE. IF YOU DO NOT HAVE SMALL KOUGLOF MOULDS, MAKE ONE LARGE
DESSERT, SOAKING IT FOR LONGER AND BASTING REGULARLY WITH THE SYRUP.

INGREDIENTS:

KOUGLOF DOUGH:

12 g/½ oz fresh yeast

60 ml/2 fl oz milk, boiled
and cooled to tepid

7 g/¼ oz fine salt

250 g/9 oz flour

3 eggs

175 g/6 oz softened butter

35 g/1¼ oz caster sugar

Flour for dusting

100 g/4 oz sultanas, plus
about 50 g/2 oz for the
garnish, soaked in
50 ml/2 fl oz rum

90 blanched almonds, split
(ie: 180 halves)

1 egg white

500 ml/18 fl oz Sorbet
Syrup (page 144)

300 g/11 oz Chantilly
Cream (page 42)

15 small mint sprigs

750 ml/1½ pints Crème
Anglaise (page 40)

Makes 15 individual
kouglofs, or 1 large
kouglof

Preparation time: 50
minutes, plus 45 minutes
proving and 24 hours
resting

Cooking time: 25 minutes

THE KOUGLOF DOUGH: Follow the method for Brioche dough on page
19 and leave the dough to rest in the fridge for 24 hours.

MOULDING THE KOUGLOFS: Mix the 100 g/4 oz sultanas into the dough.
Divide it into fifteen small 50 g/2 oz pieces and, on a lightly floured
surface, use the hollow of your hand to roll these into balls, shaping
them one at a time. Press one ball into a kouglof mould, making sure
that it follows the contours of the mould. Fill the rest of the moulds
in the same way.

Moisten the flat side of the almond halves with a little egg white
and press the flat side onto the dough in each of the indentations in
the moulds. Leave the
kouglofs to prove in a
warm, draught-free place
for about 45 minutes.

Preheat the oven to
200°C/400°F/gas 6.

BAKING THE KOUGLOFS:
Bake in the preheated oven
for 25 minutes. Carefully
unmould the kouglofs,
taking care not to dislodge
the almonds. Place them
on a wire rack and leave to
cool at room temperature.

SOAKING THE KOUGLOFS: Bring the sorbet syrup to the boil with
250 ml/9 fl oz water, then leave to cool to about 40°C/104°F.
Arrange the kouglofs in one or two deep dishes and spoon over the
syrup. Leave to steep for about 20 minutes, then drain on a wire rack.

When the kouglofs are cold, pipe the Chantilly cream into the
cavities and decorate with a sprig of mint.

PRESENTATION: Place a kouglof in the centre of each plate. Pour a
ribbon of crème anglaise around the edge and sprinkle on the
reserved sultanas. Serve at room temperature.

SPECIAL EQUIPMENT:

15 small kouglof moulds,
4 cm/1½ in diam. at the
base, 9 cm/3½ in at the
top, 5 cm/2 in deep,
greased with 50 g/ 2 oz
butter

Piping bag with a fluted
1 cm/½ in nozzle

NOTE:

It is not possible to make a
smaller quantity of dough
without adversely affecting
the quality of these cakes,
but you could keep some of
the unsoaked kouglofs in an
airtight container in a dry
place for several days, or
freeze them for up to 8 days.
Soak them in syrup just
before serving.

LOVE NESTS WITH REDCURRANT PEARLS
Puits d'amour aux perles de groseille

THE PERFECT DESSERT FOR A SPECIAL OCCASION, SUCH AS A VALENTINE'S DAY CELEBRATION OR A WEDDING ANNIVERSARY. IT IS ALSO DELICIOUS SERVED WITH A RED FRUIT COULIS (PAGE 51).

INGREDIENTS: ✳
250 g/9 oz trimmings of Quick Puff Pastry (page 25) or Flan pastry (page 22)
A pinch of flour
Eggwash (1 egg yolk mixed with 1 soup spoon milk and a pinch of salt)
½ quantity Choux paste (page 26)
Butter for greasing
200 g/7 oz caster sugar
½ quantity warm Chiboust Cream (page 39), freshly made without alcohol
200 g/7 oz redcurrants, plus a few sprays for decoration

Serves 8
Preparation time: 25 minutes
Cooking time: 25 minutes

PREPARING THE BASES: On a lightly floured surface, roll out the pastry trimmings to a thickness of 3 mm/⅛ in. Cut out 8 rounds with the pastry cutter and transfer to a baking sheet, without damaging the shape. Prick several times with a fork. Refrigerate for 20 minutes.

BAKING THE NESTS: Preheat the oven to 220°C/425°F/gas 7.

Brush the inner border of each pastry circle with eggwash. Fill the piping bag fitted with the plain nozzle with choux paste and pipe a neat sausage of paste over the eggwashed area. Next pipe a spiral of choux paste in the centre of each base, holding the nozzle very close to the base, to make a coil of half-squashed and therefore thinner paste than the outer border. Brush the edges of the choux paste with eggwash and bake the nests in the hot oven for 10 minutes. Now lower the temperature to 180°C/350°F/gas 4 and bake for a further 7 or 8 minutes. Remove the nests from the oven and slide them onto a pastry rack.

THE CHOUX PASTE HEARTS: Fill a greaseproof paper cone with choux paste and snip off the pointed end with scissors to make a tiny opening. Onto a lightly greased baking sheet, pipe out eight hearts, approximately 4 × 4 cm/1½ x1½ in, and eight smaller hearts of about 2.5 × 2.5 cm/1 × 1 in. Bake these in the oven at 180°C/350°F/gas 4 for 8 minutes, then place them on the pastry rack with the nests.

THE CARAMEL: In a small saucepan, dissolve the sugar over low heat, stirring continuously to make a very pale blond caramel. Immediately take the pan off the heat. Dip the base, sides and borders of all the choux nests in the caramel, one at a time, taking care to coat only a little of the pastry and not its entire thickness with the caramel. This operation should be done by hand. Using tweezers, dip one half of each heart in the caramel, so that only half the thickness is coated. Place the hearts on a pastry rack. If during this process the caramel cools and hardens, warm it over a very low heat for 30–60 seconds to keep it liquid and not coat the choux pastry too thickly.

ASSEMBLING THE LOVE NESTS: Fill the piping bag fitted with the star nozzle with the freshly-made, warm Chiboust cream. Pipe a generous rosette of Chiboust cream into the hollow of each nest. On top of each border of choux pastry, arrange a necklace of redcurrant pearls. Place a large and a small heart in the cream, then finish each Love Nest with a small spray of redcurrants.

SPECIAL EQUIPMENT:
1 plain 10 cm/4 in pastry cutter
2 piping bags, one with a 1 cm/½ in plain nozzle, one with a 15 mm/⅝ in star nozzle
Tweezers

NOTES:
The completed Love Nests can be frozen, but it is better to decorate them with the redcurrants after they come out of the freezer.

Although you will need only a quarter quantity of Chiboust cream to fill the nests, you must make at least a half quantity for a successful recipe. Serve the remainder in glasses with some diced fruit on the following day.

CHAPTER SIX

HOT DESSERTS

Hot or warm desserts are particularly welcome in autumn and winter. They usually involve a certain amount of advance preparation, and must be cooked during or just at the end of the meal. However, if you keep the situation under control, it is not difficult to make a successful hot dessert.

As you will see from the number of hot soufflés featured in this chapter, they never fail to thrill me. There is no dessert as delicate, light, melting and tempting as a soufflé. They are the consecration of a meal, the royal seal on a missive. Soufflés are not merely for eating – they are for savouring. They are delicious served with a coulis, a very light sauce or an ice cream. The three golden rules for successful soufflés are:

1. The desire to succeed

2. Good organisation

3. Serve them the moment they are ready. As the saying goes: 'You can wait for a soufflé, but a soufflé will not wait for you'.

Pouring raspberry sauce into the centre of the soufflé

CANDIED FRUIT SOUFFLÉS
Soufflés aux fruits candis

WE HAVE SERVED THESE MELTINGLY SWEET, FRUITY SOUFFLÉS AT THE WATERSIDE INN FOR MANY YEARS AND OUR REGULAR CLIENTS NEVER SEEM TO TIRE OF THEM. A FRESHLY CHURNED HONEY ICE CREAM MAKES A DELIGHTFUL ACCOMPANIMENT, BUT IS NOT INDISPENSABLE.

INGREDIENTS:

30 g/1 oz softened butter

80 g/3 oz caster sugar, plus 30 g/1 oz for the dishes

100 g/4 oz mixed candied fruits, in equal quantities (cherries, angelica, orange or lemon, apricots)

4 tablespoons milk

1 split vanilla pod, or 1 coffee spoon vanilla essence

180 g/6 oz Pastry Cream (page 39)

20 g/¾ oz runny honey

7 egg whites

8 vanilla-flavoured macaroons (optional)

2 tablespoons icing sugar

Serves 4

Preparation time: 25 minutes

Cooking time: 6–7 minutes

SPECIAL EQUIPMENT:

4 soufflé dishes, 10 cm/ 4 in diam., 6 cm/2⅜ in deep

PREPARING THE SOUFFLÉ DISHES: Brush the insides of the dishes with the softened butter. Put 30 g/1 oz sugar into one dish and rotate it so that the inside is well coated with sugar. Tip the excess sugar into the next dish and repeat the operation to coat all the dishes.

Preheat the oven to 220°C/425°F/gas 7 and place a baking sheet in the oven to heat.

ASSEMBLING THE SOUFFLÉS: Chop the candied fruits very finely. Put the milk in a bowl and mix in the fruits with a spoon. Scrape out the inside of the vanilla pod with the tip of a knife and stir it or the vanilla essence into the mixture.

Place the pastry cream in a wide-mouthed bowl and warm it to tepid in a microwave oven, or in a bain-marie. Now add the fruit mixture and the honey.

Beat the egg whites in an electric mixer or by hand until half-risen, then add the remaining sugar and continue to beat until stiff. Use a whisk to fold one-third of the egg whites into the pastry cream, then add the rest and fold them in with a spatula. Fill the soufflé dishes up to one-third with the mixture, sprinkle two lightly crushed macaroons over each one, then fill up the dishes and smooth the surface with a palette knife. Ease the mixture away from the edge of the dishes with the tip of a knife.

COOKING THE SOUFFLÉS: Place the soufflé dishes on the hot baking sheet and bake in the hot oven for 6–7 minutes.

PRESENTATION: As soon as the soufflés come out of the oven, dust them with a light veil of icing sugar, place on individual plates lined with a paper doily and serve at once.

Souffléed Oranges with Caramel Sauce
Oranges soufflées, sauce caramel

This delicious dessert is delicate, and cannot be kept waiting. This is true of all soufflés, but particularly so in this case, since the fragile mixture contains no flour. The contrast between the warm, melting soufflé and the cold chocolate sorbet is divine.

Ingredients:

12 oranges, about 300 g / 11 oz each

75 g / 3 oz caster sugar

2 quantities freshly-made Orange Caramel Sauce (see Red Berries with Lightly Candied Orange Beads, page 64)

50 ml / 2 fl oz Grand Marnier (optional)

½ quantity Chocolate Sorbet (page 148), churned several hours in advance, and very firm

20 g / ¾ oz softened butter

48 small fresh lemon verbena or mint leaves

1 quantity Meringue Topping made with Egg Yolks (page 35)

1 vanilla pod, split

Serves 8

Preparation time: 45 minutes

Cooking time: 7–8 minutes

Special equipment:

Piping bag with a fluted 15 mm / ⅝ in nozzle

Ice cubes or coarsely crushed ice

Note:

As the ice cubes in the roasting pan will be almost completely melted, be careful not to slop water everywhere when you take the pan out of the oven.

The candied orange zests: Wash the oranges in cold water and dry them. Use a potato peeler to pare off the zests from two of the oranges. Cut the zests into thin slivers with a sharp knife. Place in a small saucepan, cover with cold water and bring to the boil over high heat. Refresh and drain. Return the zests to the pan with the caster sugar and enough cold water to cover. Cook gently until almost all the liquid has evaporated, leaving only about 1 soup spoon of syrup. Tip the candied zests into a colander and drain until needed.

The orange segments: Take four oranges, including the two from which you removed the zests. Peel them with a fine knife, removing all the pith and membrane, and cut out the segments, sliding the knife between the membrane and flesh. Reserve the segments in a bowl. Holding them over the bowl, squeeze the orange pulp and membranes with your hands to extract all the juices. Keep at room temperature.

The orange caramel sauce: Keeping the more stable end of the remaining oranges as the base, slice one-third off the tops in a zig-zag. Use a soup spoon to scoop out the pulp into a bowl, taking care not to damage the orange skins. Discard the small top parts of the orange skins.

Place the orange skin containers in the fridge. Extract the juice from the pulp in a food processor, then prepare the orange caramel sauce following the method on page 64, adding the Grand Marnier if you wish. Keep the cooked sauce at room temperature.

The orange containers: Preheat the oven to 170°C/325°F/gas 3.

Using a pastry brush, very lightly brush the edges of the zigzags with softened butter. Divide the chocolate sorbet between the orange containers. Place in the freezer for at least 20 minutes.

The serving plates: Meanwhile, prepare the serving plates. (It is essential to do this before assembling and cooking the souffléed oranges). Arrange six orange segments in a rosette on each plate, leaving a space in the centre for the souffléed orange. Place a lemon verbena or mint leaf between each segment, and pour a little sauce onto the plates.

Assembling and cooking the souffléed oranges: Make the meringue topping, following the method on page 35. Scrape out the seeds from

84

the vanilla pod with the tip of a knife to flavour the meringue.

Place the ice in a 4–5 cm/1½–2 in deep roasting pan large enough to hold all 8 oranges, and put in the sorbet-filled oranges. Pipe in the meringue to within 2 cm/¾ in of the top of the zigzags. Immediately cook in the preheated oven for 7–8 minutes.

PRESENTATION: The instant the oranges are ready, place one in the centre of each plate. Arrange the candied zests on top and serve without delay.

PASSION FRUIT SOUFFLÉS

Soufflés aux fruits de la passion

THE PERFECT DESSERT: A SHARP-FLAVOURED SOUFFLÉ WHICH IS EASY TO PREPARE.

INGREDIENTS:

30 g/1 oz softened butter

120 g/4 oz caster sugar, plus 30 g/1 oz for the dishes

250 g/9 oz Pastry Cream (page 39)

12 passion fruit (about 240 g/9 oz)

8 egg whites

Serves 4

Preparation time: 15 minutes

Cooking time: 7–8 minutes

PREPARING THE SOUFFLÉ DISHES: Brush the insides of the dishes with softened butter. Put 30 g/1 oz sugar into one dish and rotate to coat the whole surface with sugar. Tip the excess sugar into the next dish and repeat to coat all the dishes.

Preheat the oven to 190°C/375°F/gas 5 and put in a baking sheet to heat.

ASSEMBLING THE SOUFFLÉS: Put the pastry cream in a wide-mouthed bowl and reheat it to tepid in a microwave oven, or by standing the base in a bain-marie set over medium heat. Halve the passion fruit and use a teaspoon to scrape the seeds from ten of them into the goblet of a blender. Reserve the seeds from the remaining two fruits for the garnish.

Blend the seeds for several seconds to break them up slightly, then add them to the pastry cream.

In an electric mixer or by hand, beat the egg whites until half-risen. Add the remaining sugar and continue to beat into semi-firm peaks. Use the whisk to mix one-third of the egg whites into the pastry cream, then delicately fold in the rest with a spatula. Pour the mixture into the prepared dishes and smooth the surface with a palette knife. With the tip of a knife, ease the mixture away from the edge of the dishes.

SPECIAL EQUIPMENT:

4 soufflé dishes, 10 cm/ 4 in diam., 6 cm/2⅜ in deep

COOKING THE SOUFFLÉS: Place the dishes on the hot baking sheet and cook the soufflés in the preheated oven for 7–8 minutes.

PRESENTATION: As soon as the soufflés come out of the oven, spoon a few of the reserved passion fruit seeds on the top of each one and spread them gently over the centre. Place the soufflés on serving plates each lined with a paper doily and serve immediately.

CHOCOLATE SOUFFLÉS
Soufflés chocolat

THESE SOUFFLÉS ARE VERY EASY TO MAKE. IF YOU LIKE, ACCOMPANY THEM WITH A VELVETY FRESHLY-CHURNED VANILLA ICE CREAM (PAGE 137) OR SOME DOUBLE CREAM AND LET YOUR GUESTS ADD A SPOONFUL TO THEIR SOUFFLÉ.

INGREDIENTS:
30 g / 1 oz softened butter
150 g / 5 oz caster sugar, plus 30 g / 1 oz for the dishes
300 g / 11 oz Pastry Cream (page 39)
65 g / 2½ oz unsweetened cocoa powder, sifted
8 egg whites
2 soup spoons icing sugar

Serves 4
Preparation time: 20 minutes
Cooking time: 7–8 minutes

PREPARING THE SOUFFLÉ DISHES: Brush the insides of the dishes with softened butter. Put 30 g / 1 oz sugar into one dish and rotate it so that the inside is well coated with sugar. Tip the excess sugar into the next dish and repeat to coat all the dishes in this way.

Preheat the oven to 190°C/375°F/gas 5 and place a baking sheet on the middle shelf to heat.

ASSEMBLING THE SOUFFLÉS: Put the pastry cream into a wide-mouthed bowl and reheat it to tepid in a microwave oven, or stand the base of the bowl in a bain-marie set over medium heat. When the cream is warm, whisk in the cocoa.

Beat the egg whites in an electric mixer or by hand until half-risen. Add the remaining caster sugar and beat into semi-firm peaks. Still using a whisk, fold one-third of the egg whites into the chocolate pastry cream, then delicately fold in the remainder with a spatula. Pour the mixture into the dishes and smooth the surface with a palette knife. Ease the mixture away from the edge of the dishes with the tip of a knife.

COOKING THE SOUFFLÉS: Place the dishes on the hot baking sheet and cook the soufflés in the hot oven for 7–8 minutes.

PRESENTATION: As soon as the soufflés come out of the oven, dust them with icing sugar, place each one on a plate lined with a paper doily and serve at once.

SPECIAL EQUIPMENT:
4 soufflé dishes, 10 cm/ 4 in diam., 6 cm/2⅜ in deep

MARBLED PEPPERMINT AND CHOCOLATE SOUFFLÉS

Soufflés à la menthe marbré au chocolat

THESE REFRESHING SOUFFLÉS ARE REALLY OUT OF THE ORDINARY. THE MARRIAGE OF
MINT WITH THE POCKETS OF MELTED CHOCOLATE IS SURPRISING AND UNUSUAL.

INGREDIENTS:

30 g/1 oz softened butter

150 g/5 oz caster sugar, plus 30 g/1 oz for the dishes

300 g/11 oz Pastry Cream (page 39)

50 ml/2 fl oz green peppermint liqueur

8 egg whites

80 g/3 oz bitter couverture or best quality cooking chocolate, chopped

4 sprigs of mint

2 tablespoons icing sugar

Serves 4

Preparation time: 20 minutes

Cooking time: 7–8 minutes

SPECIAL EQUIPMENT:

4 soufflé dishes, 10 cm/ 4 in diam., 6 cm/2⅜ in deep

PREPARING THE SOUFFLÉ DISHES: Brush the insides of the dishes with softened butter. Put 30 g/1 oz caster sugar into one dish and rotate it to coat the surface completely with sugar. Tip the excess sugar into the next dish and repeat until all the dishes are coated.

Preheat the oven to 190°C/375°F/gas 5 and put in a baking sheet to heat.

ASSEMBLING THE SOUFFLÉS: Put the pastry cream into a wide-mouthed bowl and warm to tepid, or stand the base of the bowl, in a bain-marie set over medium heat. Stir in the peppermint liqueur.

Beat the egg whites until half-risen, then add the remaining caster sugar and beat into semi-firm peaks. Use a whisk to mix one-third of the beaten egg whites into the pastry cream, then delicately fold in the rest with a spatula. Scatter in the chopped chocolate. Pour the mixture into the prepared dishes and smooth the surface with a palette knife. Use the tip of a knife to ease the mixture away from the edge of the dishes.

COOKING THE SOUFFLÉS: Place the soufflé dishes on the hot baking sheet and cook in the hot oven for 7–8 minutes.

PRESENTATION: As soon as the soufflés come out of the oven, place a mint sprig on each one and dust with a light veil of icing sugar. Place each dish on a plate lined with a paper doily, and serve immediately.

SOUFFLÉED CHOCOLATE PANCAKES
Crêpes soufflées au chocolat

HERE TRULY IS A PUDDING FOR CHOCOHOLICS: CHOCOLATE PANCAKES,
CHOCOLATE SOUFFLÉ WITH CHOCOLATE SAUCE IF YOU FANCY THAT AS WELL,
ALL DELECTABLE AND CREAMY.

INGREDIENTS:
40 g/1½ oz unsweetened
  cocoa powder
1 tablespoon icing sugar,
  plus 2 pinches for dusting
20 g/¾ oz flour
2 extra eggs, plus 1 egg yolk
75 ml/3 fl oz whipping
  cream
115 ml/4 fl oz milk
45 g/1½ oz clarified butter
1 quantity Chocolate Soufflé
  mixture (page 87)
½ quantity Chocolate Sauce
  (page 55) (optional)

Makes 12 pancakes
  (to serve 6)
Preparation time: 20
  minutes, plus 30 minutes
  resting
Cooking time: 27 minutes

THE PANCAKE BATTER: Combine the cocoa, 1 tablespoon icing sugar, the flour, whole eggs and extra yolk and the cream in a bowl. Mix with a whisk, without overworking the mixture, then pour in the milk, stirring as you go. Cover the bowl with clingfilm and leave the batter to rest at room temperature for 30 minutes.

1

COOKING THE PANCAKES: Place the non-stick frying pan on the heat and brush the base with clarified butter. When the pan is very hot, ladle in enough batter to cover the base (1). Cook the pancake for 1 minute, then carefully turn it over with a palette knife and cook for another minute. Transfer the cooked pancake to a plate and lay a band of greaseproof paper on top to prevent the next pancake from sticking to the first and so on.

2

Cook and stack all the pancakes in this way, brushing the pan with melted butter after every two pancakes. Leave them to cool at room temperature and, when they are cold, trim each pancake into a 14 cm/5½ in circle using a sharp knife or pastry cutter (2).

SPECIAL EQUIPMENT:
Non-stick 16 cm/6½ in
  frying pan
11 narrow strips of
  greaseproof paper

NOTE:
Souffléed pancakes will tolerate waiting even less than a soufflé, so it is essential to serve them the moment they are ready.

3

BAKING AND FILLING THE PANCAKES: Preheat the oven to 200°C/400°F/gas 6 and heat six serving plates.

Lay six pancakes on a baking sheet and fill the centre of each one with 2 generous soup spoons of soufflé mixture. Fold the pancakes in half with a palette knife, without pressing them (3). Do the same with the remaining pancakes and immediately bake them in the hot oven for 3 minutes (4). As soon as they are ready, dust with icing sugar, then slide a palette knife under one pancake at a time and transfer them to heated plates, allowing two per person. Serve at once.

4

PRESENTATION: If you like, pour a little chocolate sauce around the pancakes on one side of each plate.

GRATINS OF REDCURRANTS AND WILD STRAWBERRIES
Gratins de perles de groseilles et fraises des bois

THESE MOIST, DELICATE HOT GRATINS CAN BE PREPARED SEVERAL DAYS IN
ADVANCE AND COOKED AT THE LAST MOMENT.

INGREDIENTS: ❋

Italian Meringue (page 37),
 made with 5 egg whites
 and 160 g/5 oz caster
 sugar
125 ml/4 fl oz lemon juice
125 ml/4 fl oz whipping
 cream
6 egg yolks
60 g/2 oz caster sugar
25 g/1 oz flour
2 gelatine leaves, soaked in
 cold water and well
 drained
1 tablespoon lemon zest,
 finely grated and blanched
125 g/4½ oz wild
 strawberries and 125 g/
 4½ oz redcurrants, or
 250 g/9 oz of one variety
30 g/1 oz icing sugar
½ quantity Orange Sauce,
 chilled (page 52), for
 serving

Serves 10
Preparation time: 35
 minutes, plus 2–3 hours
 freezing
Cooking time: 8 minutes

THE ITALIAN MERINGUE: Make the meringue according to the recipe on
page 37. Place in a bowl, cover with clingfilm and keep at room temperature until tepid.

THE LEMON PASTRY CREAM: Heat the lemon juice and cream in a
saucepan. Place the egg yolks and 60 g/2 oz sugar in a bowl, and
whisk to a light ribbon consistency. Add the flour and work until
smooth. Pour the boiling lemon and cream onto the eggs, whisking
continuously. Return the mixture to the pan and bubble over high
heat for 2 minutes, whisking all the time. Take the pan off the heat
and stir in the drained gelatine. Leave to cool.

THE GRATIN MIXTURE: Using a whisk, fold half the tepid Italian
meringue into the tepid pastry cream, then delicately fold in the rest
with a spatula, and shower in the lemon zest like rain. Stop working
the mixture as soon as it becomes homogeneous.

ASSEMBLING THE GRATINS: Reserve one-third of the best fruits for
decoration. Line a baking sheet with greaseproof paper and arrange
the tartlet rings on it. Using a palette knife or a piping bag
fitted with a plain 1 cm/½ in nozzle, fill the bottom of the
rings up to one-third and coat the sides with the tepid
gratin mixture. Scatter on the remaining strawberries and
redcurrants, then fill up the rings with the rest of the
gratin mixture and smooth the surface with a palette knife.
Place in the freezer for several hours.

COOKING THE GRATINS: Preheat the oven to 220°C/
425°F/gas 7.
 Remove the gratins from the freezer. Dip the tip of a small
knife in boiling water, then slide it between the inside of each
tartlet ring and the mixture, and lift off the rings. Sprinkle the
gratins generously with icing sugar. Slide a palette knife under
each gratin and place one in each buttered dish. Cook in the
hot oven for about 8 minutes, until the gratins puff up and are
lightly coloured. They should still be soft and slightly runny
in the centre (see photo, right).

PRESENTATION: As soon as the gratins come out of the oven,
pour a ribbon of orange sauce around each one. Arrange the
reserved wild strawberries on the sauce and top the gratins
with a small cluster of redcurrants. Serve at once.

SPECIAL EQUIPMENT:
10 tartlet rings, 8 cm/
 3¼ in diam., 2 cm/¾ in
 deep
10 round gratin dishes,
 14 cm/5½ in diam., very
 lightly buttered in the
 middle 8 cm/3¼ in

NOTE:
The prepared gratins can be
frozen for up to a week; just
cover with clingfilm as soon
as the mixture is frozen. You
could make several batches of
this dessert to serve at
different meals.

Citrus Ravioli with Peach Gratin
Ravioles au citrus et gratin de pêches

THIS MULTI-FACETED THREE-STAR DESSERT REQUIRES PATIENCE AND SOME DEXTERITY, SO I HAVE GIVEN YOU STEP-BY-STEP INSTRUCTIONS TO FOLLOW. I ASSURE YOU THAT IT IS WORTH THE EFFORT.

INGREDIENTS:

LEMON FILLING
40 ml/1½ fl oz lemon juice
Zest of ½ lemon
30 g/1 oz caster sugar
A large pinch of cornflour
1 egg yolk
15 g/½ oz egg white

RAVIOLI DOUGH
15 g/½ oz lard, at room temperature
75 g/3 oz plain flour, plus extra for dusting the work surface
30 ml/1 fl oz water
A tiny pinch of fine salt
Eggwash (1 egg yolk mixed with 1 soup spoon milk and a pinch of salt)
30 g/1 oz caster sugar
5 mint leaves

ORANGE AND PASSION FRUIT SAUCE
150 ml/5 fl oz orange juice
30 g/1 oz caster sugar
3 passion fruit

3 bananas
60 g/2 oz demerara sugar
½ quantity freshly made Sabayon (page 53), made with Sorbet Syrup (page 144) instead of alcohol
3 peaches, preferably white-fleshed, peeled and lightly rubbed with lemon juice
½ quantity Vanilla Ice Cream (page 137)

THE LEMON FILLING: Combine all the ingredients for the filling in a small saucepan and bring to the boil over low heat, whisking continuously. As soon as the mixture starts to bubble, transfer it to a bowl and leave to cool at room temperature. When it is cold, cover with clingfilm and refrigerate.

THE RAVIOLI DOUGH: Put the first four ingredients in a bowl and work to a smooth dough with your fingertips. Cover with clingfilm and refrigerate for 30 minutes.

THE ORANGE AND PASSION FRUIT SAUCE: Put the orange juice and sugar in a small saucepan and reduce by one-third over low heat. Transfer to a bowl, leave to cool, then halve the passion fruit and scoop out the seeds with a teaspoon into the orange sauce. Keep at room temperature.

FILLING THE RAVIOLI: Divide the dough into two pieces, one 45% of the dough, the other 55%.

On a lightly floured surface, roll the smaller piece of dough into a 2 mm/½ in thick 28 × 19 cm/11 × 7½ in rectangle, using a pasta machine or rolling pin. Fill the piping bag with the lemon filling and pipe eighteen small balls onto the sheet of dough in staggered rows, six along the longer side, and three along the shorter side (1). Brush the dough around the balls with eggwash.

Roll out the remaining dough into a thin 30 × 21 cm/ 12 × 8½ in rectangle and lay this over the first sheet of dough. Using your fingertips, very delicately press down around the balls of filling.

Using the non-cutting edge of the 3 cm/1¼ in pastry cutter, press lightly around the balls of filling. Cut out the eighteen ravioli with the larger, fluted cutter (2) and lay them on a very lightly floured sheet of greaseproof paper.

THE BANANAS: Peel and cut each into eighteen diagonal slices, then arrange them in threes on a baking sheet. Sprinkle with demerara sugar and caramelize the little heaps of banana with a blowtorch (3).

SPECIAL EQUIPMENT:
Plain 3 cm/1¼ in pastry cutter
Fluted 5 cm/2 in pastry cutter
Piping bag with a plain 5 mm/¼ in nozzle
Blowtorch
Pasta maker or a rolling pin

Serves 6
Preparation time: 1 hour 20 minutes
Cooking time: 7 minutes

NOTE:
During the winter, substitute very ripe pears for the peaches.

THE SABAYON: Prepare this not more than half an hour in advance. Keep the sabayon in a bain-marie for the shortest possible time until ready to use.

COOKING THE RAVIOLI: Bring 1 litre/1¾ pints water to the boil with 30 g/1 oz caster sugar, drop in the ravioli and mint leaves and cook over low heat for 7 minutes. Meanwhile, heat the serving plates.

PRESENTATION: Halve the peaches. Slice each half very thinly and arrange one sliced half in a rosette in the centre of each heated plate, leaving a gap in the middle for the ice cream.

Place three ravioli at the edge of each plate, then three heaps of caramelized bananas. Spoon a little orange and passion fruit sauce over the ravioli. Coat the sliced peaches with sabayon (4) and glaze to a hazelnut colour with the blowtorch (5). Top the peaches with a scoop of ice cream and serve immediately.

BAKED APPLE IN A GOLDEN CAGE WITH CRUNCHY APPLE PEARLS

Pomme en cage dans sa croûte dorée et ses perles croquantes

A RUSTIC DESSERT, FULL OF AUTUMNAL FLAVOURS. YOU CAN OMIT THE GOLDEN CAGES, BUT THEY DO ADD AN ARTISTIC DIMENSION TO A SIMPLE AND INEXPENSIVE DISH, AND ARE NOT AT ALL DIFFICULT TO MAKE.

INGREDIENTS:

150 g/5 oz trimmings of Jean Millet's or Quick Puff Pastry (pages 24 and 25), or Flan Pastry (page 22)

Flour for dusting

Eggwash (1 egg yolk mixed with 1 soup spoon milk and a pinch of salt)

6 apples (preferably Coxes), each about 150 g/5 oz

50 g/2 oz butter

100 g/4 oz dried apricots, finely diced

60 g/2 oz runny honey

80 g/3 oz toasted flaked almonds

250 g/9 oz caster sugar

250 ml/9 fl oz Apricot Coulis (see Fruit Coulis, page 51)

SERVES 4

Preparation time: 50 minutes

Cooking time: 30 minutes

THE GOLDEN CAGES: On a lightly floured surface, roll out the pastry trimmings into a square about 2 mm/¹⁄₁₂ in thick. Roll the lattice rolling pin over the pastry in one direction only (1). Using a chef's knife, cut the pastry square into 4 smaller squares. Drape one square over a hemispherical mould, teasing the pastry lightly with your fingertips to give a latticed effect (2). Cut off the excess pastry around the base of the mould with the pastry cutter. Prepare three more pastry cages in this way and refrigerate for 20 minutes.

Meanwhile, preheat the oven to 180°C/350°F/gas 4.

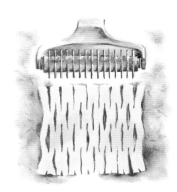

1

BAKING THE CAGES: Brush the pastry cages with eggwash, taking care not to let it drip onto the moulds. Bake in the preheated oven for 7–8 minutes, then leave to cool at room temperature. When the cages are almost cold, lift them carefully off the moulds.

2

THE BAKED APPLES: Reduce the oven temperature to 150°C/300°F/gas 2.

Wash four apples in cold water, wipe dry and, using the tip of a knife, make an incision all round the middle to ensure even cooking. Remove the cores with an apple corer, then arrange the apples in a roasting pan greased with all the butter.

In a bowl, mix the diced apricots, honey and 40 g/1½ oz flaked almonds. Divide this filling between the cavities in the apples and pile up the excess in a dome on top of the fruit. Bake for 30 minutes, basting the apples every 10 minutes with the cooking juices and butter from the roasting pan. Keep the cooked apples warm in the pan.

THE CRUNCHY APPLE PEARLS: Peel the remaining two apples with a vegetable peeler. Use the melon baller to scoop out twenty-four balls of apple. In a small, heavy-

SPECIAL EQUIPMENT:

4 hemispherical moulds, 9 cm/3½ in diam., 4.5 cm/1¾ in deep, lightly greased on the outside and chilled

Lattice rolling pin

10 cm/4 in plain pastry cutter

7 mm/³⁄₈ in melon baller

based saucepan, cook the sugar without water, stirring continuously. As soon as it turns to a very pale caramel, take the pan off the heat.

Spread the remaining flaked almonds on a baking tray. Quickly dip the apple balls one at a time in the caramel, then lay them on the almonds. With your fingertips, bring up the almonds slightly around the apple balls, taking care not to touch the barely set caramel coating (see photo, opposite). Keep at room temperature.

PRESENTATION: Place a baked apple in the centre of each serving plate and moisten with the cooking juices from the pan. Pour the cold apricot coulis around the edge, and make a border of six crunchy apple pearls. Carefully place the pastry cages over the apples and serve at once.

COULIBIAC OF WINTER FRUITS
Coulibiac aux fruits d'hiver

ALTHOUGH THIS DESSERT MAY NOT LOOK AS SPECTACULAR AS SOME, IT HAS
A WONDERFUL FLAVOUR, AND THE SCENT OF THE FRUITS WHICH PERVADES
THE ROOM AS YOU CUT IT OPEN AT THE TABLE IS A KNOCKOUT.

INGREDIENTS: ❋
250 g/9 oz rhubarb
190 g/7 oz caster sugar
2 bananas
80 g/3 oz butter
Juice of 1 lemon
2 apples (preferably Coxes),
    about 200 g/7 oz each
A pinch of ground cinnamon
400 g/14 oz Brioche dough
    (page 19)
Flour for dusting
4 pancakes, 18 cm/7 in
    diam., made with
    ⅓ quantity Pancake batter
    (page 27)
100 g/4 oz moist dried
    apricots, coarsely diced
100 g/4 oz apricot jam,
    mixed with the pulp of 2
    passion fruit
Eggwash (1 egg yolk mixed
    with 1 soup spoon milk
    and a pinch of salt)

Serves 6
Preparation time: 40
    minutes
Cooking time: 35 minutes

THE RHUBARB: Peel the stalks and cut into 6 cm/2⅜ in lengths. Rinse
in cold water and place in a saucepan with 110 g/4 oz sugar and
100 ml/4 fl oz water. Bring to the boil and turn off the heat as soon
as the liquid bubbles. Leave the rhubarb to cool in the poaching syrup
and drain when cold.

THE BANANAS: Peel, then, starting from one end, run your thumb downwards to divide them lengthways into their three segments. In a frying pan,
brown the bananas over high heat for a few seconds with 40 g/ 1½ oz each
of butter and sugar, but do not cook them. Place on a plate.

THE APPLES: Peel and core, and use the apple corer to cut as many tubes
as possible from the apple flesh. In the frying pan, brown the tubes
over high heat for 1 minute with 40 g/1½ oz each butter and sugar.
Sprinkle with cinnamon and lemon juice and place on a plate.

ASSEMBLING THE COULIBIAC:
On a lightly floured sur-
face, carefully roll out
the brioche dough into a
30 × 20 cm/12 × 8 in rec-
tangle. Cover this with
the cold pancakes (1).
Down the middle, lay a
20 cm/8 in line of half
of the bananas, rhubarb,
apples and diced apricots
(2). Use a spoon to spread
half the apricot jam and
passion fruit mixture
over the fruits, then lay
on the remaining fruits and spread over the rest of the jam.
Fold the pancakes over the fruits and brush the four edges of
the brioche dough with eggwash (3).

Fold one of the longer sides of the dough over the
pancake-wrapped fruits. Brush the top of the dough with
eggwash, then bring the other side up over the first side (4).
With a rolling pin, lightly flatten the two ends of the dough
(5), trim off a little of the excess, brush with eggwash and
fold up the ends. Turn the coulibiac over onto a baking sheet
and refrigerate for 20 minutes.

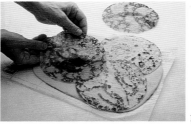

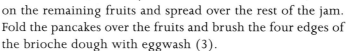

SPECIAL EQUIPMENT:
Apple corer

NOTE:
To gild the lily, serve a
kirsch-scented Sabayon (page
53) with the coulibiac, but
this is not really necessary.

Meanwhile, preheat the oven to 180°C/350°F/gas 4.

BAKING THE COULIBIAC: Brush the coulibiac with eggwash. With the tip of a sharp knife, score a pattern of sunray lines over the surface (6). Use the tip of the knife to cut two little chimneys in the top of the coulibiac. Bake in the preheated oven for 35 minutes.

6

PRESENTATION: Serve the piping hot coulibiac whole at the table and slice with a very sharp knife.

WALNUT PITHIVIERS WITH PISTACHIO COULIS
Pithiviers aux noix, coulis à la pistache

I ADORE THIS DIVINE AUTUMN OR WINTER DESSERT. FRESH WALNUTS ARE
IN SEASON FROM OCTOBER TO NOVEMBER, GIVING TWO MONTHS PLEASURE.

INGREDIENTS: ❋
750 g/1½ lbs Jean Millet's
    Puff Pastry (page 24)
A pinch of flour
24 walnuts, preferably fresh,
    skinned and quartered
180 g/6 oz Frangipane
    (page 43)
Eggwash (1 egg yolk mixed
    with 1 soup spoon milk
    and a pinch of salt)
20 g/¾ oz icing sugar
250 g/9 oz caster sugar
Oil, for greasing
120 g/4½ oz pistachios,
    skinned
300 ml/11 fl oz Crème
    Anglaise (page 40)

Serves 6
Preparation time: 35
    minutes
Cooking time: about 15
    minutes

ASSEMBLING THE PITHIVIERS: 20 minutes before baking the pithiviers, preheat the oven to 220°C/425°F/gas 7.

On a lightly floured surface, roll out 40% of the pastry into a 30 × 20 cm/12 × 8 in rectangle. Cut the rectangle in half lengthways, then into three widthways to make six small, regular squares. Place on a dampened baking sheet. Reserve twenty-four of the best walnut quarters for caramelizing, and mix the remainder into the frangipane cream. Heap this mixture in the middle of each pastry square and brush the edges of the pastry around the mixture with a little eggwash.

Roll out the remaining pastry into a 45 × 30 cm/18 × 12 in rectangle and cut into six regular squares. Invert these onto the top of the filled squares and press the edges with your fingertips to seal them thoroughly.

CUTTING OUT AND DECORATING THE PITHIVIERS: Press the non-cutting edge of the pastry cutter onto one of the Pithiviers (1). Using a small, very sharp knife, cut the pastry outside the cutter into twelve to fifteen little 'ears', making three of them slightly more pronounced (2). Lift off the pastry cutter and repeat the operation with the other five Pithiviers.

Brush the top of the Pithiviers with eggwash. With the tip of a knife, trace criss-cross lines on the little 'ears'. Use the knife tip to score curved rays like the arcs of a circle from the centre to the outer edges of the Pithiviers (3).

BAKING THE PITHIVIERS: Bake in the hot oven for 14 minutes, reducing the oven temperature to 190°C/375°F/gas 5 after 10 minutes. Remove the Pithiviers from the oven and increase the temperature to 240°/475°F/gas 9. Dust the tops of the Pithiviers with a veil of icing sugar and return them to the hot oven for a minute or two, until they have an attractive glaze, like a varnish. Remove from the oven and transfer them with a palette knife to a wire rack.

SPECIAL EQUIPMENT:
8 cm/3¼ in diam. pastry
    cutter

NOTES:
All the elements of this dessert can be prepared the day before. Bake the Pithiviers just before the meal and keep near a heat source, taking care that they do not dry out, until ready to serve.

The uncooked Pithiviers can be frozen for at least a week. Glaze and decorate them after defrosting.

CARAMELIZING THE WALNUTS: Put the caster sugar in a small, heavy-based saucepan, and dissolve over low heat, stirring continuously with a wooden spatula. As soon as the sugar has dissolved, take the pan off the heat and use a fork to dip the reserved walnuts one at a time into the sugar. Place on a lightly-oiled baking sheet.

THE PISTACHIO COULIS: Put 80 g/3 oz of the pistachios in a food processor with the crème anglaise and process for 3 minutes, then pass through a fine strainer and put into a sauceboat. Use a chef's knife to chop the remaining pistachios.

PRESENTATION: Place the warm Pithiviers on individual serving plates. Pour a ribbon of pistachio coulis around them, scatter on little heaps of chopped pistachios and arrange four caramelized walnut quarters on each plate. Serve at once.

CHAPTER SEVEN

LARGE DESSERTS AND GATEAUX

These convivial, imposing desserts are often served on special occasions, such as a feast day, a family reunion or a gathering of friends. They are presented in all their glory and served at the table.

They are made on a base of light biscuit, meringue, sponge or puff pastry and filled with a variety of delectable fruit mousses. They should always be served chilled, either just as they are or with a fruit coulis.

Since these gâteaux can be successfully frozen for several days, you might like to make two at a time. Then if unexpected guests arrive, with a wave of your magic wand, you can conjure up an astonishing home-made dessert from the freezer. They also make the most wonderful gifts to take to friends.

Glazing the Cardinal Gâteau

CARDINAL GATEAU
Entremets Cardinal

SILKY-SMOOTH, RICH, FRUITY AND GLORIOUS, THIS DESSERT IS A GREAT
FAVOURITE OF MY CLIENTS AT THE WATERSIDE INN — AND OF MINE TOO. IT
MAY EVEN SERVE TEN PEOPLE IF YOUR GUESTS ARE NOT TOO GREEDY!

INGREDIENTS:

RASPBERRY PARFAIT

200 g/7 oz bitter couverture
or best quality cooking
chocolate, chopped
100 g/4 oz caster sugar
1 whole egg
2 egg yolks
2 gelatine leaves, separately
soaked in cold water and
well drained
250 ml/9 fl oz raspberry
purée, sieved
300 ml/11 fl oz whipping
cream, whipped to a
ribbon consistency

1 × 20 cm/8 in round
chocolate Genoise Sponge
(page 33), cut into a disc
3–5 mm/⅛-¼ in thick
650 g/1½ lbs raspberries
(reserve 200 g/7 oz of
the best for decoration)

GLAZE

50 ml/2 fl oz grenadine
syrup
50 ml/2 fl oz raspberry
jam, sieved

Serves 8–10
Preparation time: 45
minutes, plus 2–6 hours
chilling

THE RASPBERRY PARFAIT: Put the chocolate in a bowl and stand it in a
bain-marie set over medium heat to melt. Put 2 tablespoons of water
and the sugar in a small saucepan and bring to the boil over low heat,
skimming the surface and brushing down the inside of the pan from
time to time with a pastry brush dipped in cold water. When the
syrup has boiled for a couple of minutes, put in the sugar
thermometer. When the temperature reaches 116°C/240°F, place the
whole egg and the yolks in the bowl of the electric mixer and begin
to whisk at low speed. As soon as the syrup reaches 121°C/250°C,
take the pan off the heat. Wait for a minute, until the syrup stops
bubbling, then pour it onto the eggs in a thin stream, mixing all the
time. Add 1 gelatine
leaf and leave the mixer
running on low speed
for 5 minutes. Still at
low speed, whisk in the
melted chocolate, mix
for a minute or two
until you have a
homogeneous mixture,
then stop the motor.

With a wire whisk,
delicately fold 200 ml/
7 fl oz of the raspberry
purée into the whipped
cream. Using a spatula,
fold the raspberry-
flavoured cream into the egg and chocolate mixture. Do not
overwork this raspberry parfait, which must be used immediately.

ASSEMBLING THE GATEAU: Lay the chocolate sponge on the cake board.
Place the ring around the sponge, then half-fill it with raspberry
parfait. On top, arrange 450 g/1 lb of the raspberries in a single layer,
packing them tightly together without crushing them, then fill the
ring with the remaining parfait. Smooth the surface with a palette
knife. Transfer the gâteau to the freezer for 2–3 hours, or refrigerate
for 5–6 hours.

THE GLAZE: Combine the grenadine, jam and the remaining raspberry
purée in a small saucepan and boil for 2 or 3 minutes. Take the pan
off the heat and add the remaining gelatine leaf, then gently pass this

SPECIAL EQUIPMENT:

1 dessert ring, 22 cm/8½ in
diam., 4 cm/1½ in deep
Rigid cake board, 22 cm/
8½ in diam.
Sugar thermometer
Blowtorch (optional)

NOTES:

The unglazed gâteau can be
frozen for a week; glaze it
just before serving, or a few
hours in advance.
    I do not moisten the
chocolate sponge with syrup
in this dessert, as the
raspberry parfait is so
creamy that the sponge
would be saturated.
Like all parfaits, this should
be served ice cold.

jelly through a muslin-lined sieve and keep at room temperature. Just as the glaze becomes almost cold, it will begin to thicken without solidifying. This is the moment to use it to glaze the gâteau. Leave the ring on during this process.

If the gâteau is in the freezer, take it out and leave at room temperature for about 20 minutes. If it is in the fridge, you can glaze it immediately. Pour half the glaze over the top of the gâteau, smooth with a palette knife, then return the gâteau to the fridge for 5 minutes. As soon as the glaze has set, pour on the remainder and keep the dessert in the fridge until ready to serve.

PRESENTATION: To remove the dessert ring, run a blowtorch briefly around the edge of the ring, or slide a knife blade dipped in hot water between the edge of the gâteau and the ring. Lift off the ring by rotating it upwards, or place the dessert on a tin and slide the ring downwards (see page 17). Place the gâteau on a pretty round serving plate. Arrange the reserved raspberries in attractive semi-circles around the top to delineate the individual portions, and serve at once.

CHOCOLATE MINT SNAILS
Le colimaçon chocolat menthe

THIS EASY AND QUICK TO MAKE DESSERT IS A PERFECT TEATIME TREAT FOR CHILDREN OR ADULTS. FOR ADDED EFFECT, TOP WITH CHOCOLATE CURLS (PAGE 154) AND SERVE WITH A COFFEE-FLAVOURED CREME ANGLAISE (PAGE 40).

INGREDIENTS: ✳
¾ quantity chocolate Genoise Sponge mixture (page 33)
1 quantity Mint Mousse (page 48)
Icing sugar for dusting

Makes 3 gâteaux, each serving 4
Preparation time: 20 minutes
Cooking time: 8 minutes

THE CHOCOLATE SPONGE: Preheat the oven to 200°C/400°F/gas 6.

Make the chocolate genoise sponge mixture following the method on page 33. Spread the mixture evenly onto the lined baking sheet, smoothing it with a palette knife. Bake the sponge in the preheated oven for 8 minutes.

Slide the Silpat or paper onto a cooling rack and leave the sponge until cold. Lay a tea towel, then another rack over the cold sponge and invert it. Peel off the Silpat or paper and use a serrated knife to trim off about 5 mm/¼ in from the edges of the sponge.

Spread the half-set mint mousse over the sponge, leaving an empty 2 cm/¾ in border all round. Refrigerate for 30 minutes, then roll up the shorter side of sponge like a Swiss roll, using the tea towel to help you. Refrigerate for at least 2 hours before serving.

PRESENTATION: Using a serrated knife, cut the roll into three equal pieces. Stand the pieces upright on a plate like snail shells and dust with icing sugar. Serve well chilled and slice the 'snails' at the table.

SPECIAL EQUIPMENT:
60 × 40 cm/24 × 16 in baking sheet lined with Silpat or silicone paper

NOTE:
The 'snails' can be frozen for a week, so if you prefer, serve only one or two and freeze the rest. Defrost in the fridge for 3 hours before serving.

BLACK AND WHITE SAINT-HONORÉ
Saint-Honoré noir et blanc

SINCE MY YOUTH, I HAVE ALWAYS REGARDED A SAINT-HONORÉ AS THE ULTIMATE GASTRONOMIC AND
VISUALLY APPEALING DESSERT. IN THIS BLACK AND WHITE VERSION, THE COMBINATION OF THE VANILLA AND
CHOCOLATE CHANTILLY CREAMS IS SUBLIME AND A TESTAMENT TO THE COOK'S DEXTERITY.

INGREDIENTS: ❊
200 g/7 oz trimmings of
　Jean Millet's or Quick
　Puff Pastry (pages 24
　and 25)
Flour for dusting
1 quantity Choux Paste
　(page 26)
200 g/7 oz caster sugar
Eggwash (1 egg yolk mixed
　with 1 soup spoon milk
　and a pinch of salt)
VANILLA CHANTILLY CREAM
600 ml/1 pint well-chilled
　double cream
60 g/2 oz icing sugar
1 split vanilla pod

CHOCOLATE CHANTILLY
CREAM
250 ml/9 fl oz well-chilled
　whipping cream
150 g/5 oz bitter couverture
　or best quality cooking
　chocolate, heated to
　50°C/122°F

Serves 8
Preparation time: 50
　minutes, plus 1 hour
　chilling
Cooking time: 35 minutes

THE PASTRY BASE: On a lightly floured surface, roll out the pastry into
a neat circle 2 mm/1/12 in thick. Roll this over the rolling pin, then
unroll it onto a baking sheet dampened with cold water. Lay the ring
on the pastry and, using the tip of a knife, cut round it to make a
24 cm/9½ in pastry circle. Prick with a fork and refrigerate for
20 minutes.

PIPING OUT THE CHOUX PASTE: Preheat the oven to 200°C/400°F/gas 6.
　Fill the piping bag fitted with the 12 mm/½ in nozzle with choux
paste. Starting from the centre of the pastry base and working
outwards, pipe out a spiral, holding the nozzle fractionally above the
base. Stop piping 3 cm/1¼ in from the edge of the pastry to leave a
clear border. Brush this border with eggwash, then pipe on a raised
circle of choux paste, holding the nozzle well above the pastry. Brush
the choux circle with eggwash and bake the base in the preheated
oven for 35 minutes.
　Using the piping bag fitted with the 5 mm/¼ in nozzle, pipe
seventeen small 2 cm/¾ in choux puffs onto the lightly-greased
baking tray. Brush with eggwash and press the puffs lightly with the
back of a fork. Bake in the oven with the pastry base for 20 minutes.
Make a small hole in the bottom of the choux puffs with the tip of a
small knife, place them and the pastry base on a cooling rack and
leave at room temperature until cold.

MAKING THE CARAMEL: Put 50 ml/2 fl oz water in a small, heavy-based
saucepan and add the 200 g/7 oz sugar. Bring to the boil over low
heat, skim the surface, then wash down the inside of the pan with a
pastry brush dipped in cold water. Stop cooking as soon as the sugar
becomes a pale amber caramel. Pierce one side of the choux puffs
with the tip of a small knife, and dip the tops one at a time into the
caramel (1). Place the puffs on a baking sheet.

THE VANILLA AND CHOCOLATE CHANTILLY CREAMS: Put the double
cream and icing sugar in a bowl and scrape in the inside of
the vanilla pod. Whip to a ribbon consistency.
　In another bowl, whip the whipping cream to a ribbon
consistency, then whisk in the melted chocolate, without
beating over-vigorously.

ASSEMBLING THE SAINT-HONORÉ: Using the piping bag with the
5 mm/¼ in nozzle, fill the choux puffs with the vanilla

SPECIAL EQUIPMENT:
2 baking sheets, 1 lightly
　greased
1 dessert ring, 24 cm/
　9½ in diam.
Piping bag with a plain
　12 mm/½ in nozzle
Piping bag with a plain
　5 mm/¼ in nozzle
2 piping bags, each fitted
　with a Saint-Honoré
　nozzle

Chantilly cream. Stick them onto the choux pastry crown, attaching them on one by one with a little caramel (2). Fill the Saint-Honoré base with a 1.5 cm/⅝ in deep layer of vanilla Chantilly cream.

Fill one of the piping bags fitted with a Saint-Honoré nozzle with vanilla Chantilly and the other with chocolate Chantilly. Pipe in staggered bands of chocolate Chantilly, interlacing them evenly with bands of vanilla Chantilly (3 and 4). Refrigerate the Saint-Honoré for 1 hour before serving.

PRESENTATION: Place the Saint-Honoré on a round serving plate and slice it with a very sharp knife.

FLOATING ISLAND WITH DATES
Ile flottante aux dattes

I DREAMT UP THIS DESSERT DURING MY TIME IN NORTH AFRICA. THE DELICIOUS DATES WHICH
GROW ALL OVER THE REGION WERE THE INSPIRATION FOR THIS VARIATION ON THE CLASSIC
FLOATING ISLAND WITH ALMONDS OR PRALINES. IT IS A WONDERFUL AUTUMN OR WINTER DISH.

INGREDIENTS:

180 g/6 oz caster sugar

6 dates, stoned and halved
lengthways

6 dates, finely diced

A tiny pinch of ground star
anise

¼ quantity Crème Anglaise
flavoured with vanilla
(page 40)

MERINGUE

4 egg whites

85 g/3 oz caster sugar

Serves 4

Preparation time: 20
minutes

Cooking time: 20 minutes

CARAMELIZING THE BASIN OR MOULD: In a small, heavy-based saucepan set over low heat, dissolve the sugar without water, stirring continuously with a wooden spatula. When it turns an attractive caramel colour, pour two-thirds into the basin or mould. Protect your hands with a tea towel and roll the mould around to coat the inside thoroughly with caramel. Quickly arrange the halved dates side by side to within about 1.5 cm/⅝ in of the top of the mould, placing the uncut surface against the caramel.

Invert the mould onto a wire rack placed squarely on the work surface so that the caramel sets more or less uniformly on the sides of the mould.

PREPARING THE MERINGUE: Preheat the oven to 140°C/275°F/gas 1.

Using a bowl and whisk or an electric mixer, beat the egg whites until half-risen. Add the sugar and continue to beat until very stiff and well-risen. Add the diced dates and star anise and whisk for just a few seconds more.

Pour the meringue into the mould and gently smooth the surface.

COOKING THE FLOATING ISLAND: Place on a baking sheet and cook in the warm oven for 20 minutes. Insert a fine metal skewer into the centre of the floating island to check whether it is cooked; the skewer should come out shiny and clean. Cook for a few minutes more if necessary. Leave the cooked floating island to cool at room temperature in the basin or mould for 30 seconds before unmoulding.

PRESENTATION: Using a tea towel to hold the mould, unmould the hot but not scalding floating island by inverting it a few centimetres above a round, shallow serving plate. If the caramel has thickened, making it difficult to unmould, heat the base of the basin or mould for a few seconds over a gas flame. Pour the chilled crème anglaise all round the floating island, then refrigerate for 15–20 minutes.

Meanwhile, reheat the remaining caramel in a warm oven or microwave until slightly liquid. Spoon an even coating over the top of the dessert.

The floating island can be served as soon as the caramel has set, about 15 minutes after coating. Let your guests help themselves with a spoon to the dessert and the accompanying crème anglaise.

SPECIAL EQUIPMENT:

Round heatproof basin, or a
stainless steel
hemispherical mould,
16 cm/6½ in diam. at
the opening, 8 cm/3¼ in
deep

NOTES:

After its final coating of
caramel, the dessert can if
necessary be kept in the
fridge for an hour before
serving without affecting the
crunchiness of the caramel.

Take great care when
making caramel-based
desserts. Hot caramel diffuses
its heat through the mould,
so take every precaution not
to burn yourself.

BANANA AND CARAMEL MOUSSE GATEAU

Entremets mousse bananes et caramel

THE COMBINATION OF THE TWO MOUSSES AND DELICATE SPONGE WITH THE
LIGHTLY CARAMELIZED BANANAS MAKES THE TIME SPENT IN PREPARING THIS
DESSERT WELL WORTH WHILE.

INGREDIENTS: ❊
140 g/4½ oz chocolate
    Cigarette Paste (page 28)
1 quantity Joconde Sponge
    mixture (page 31)
8 bananas, about 200 g/
    7 oz each
60 g/2 oz butter
100 g/4 oz caster sugar
⅔ quantity (600 g/1 lb
    6 oz) Caramel Mousse
    (page 46)
1 quantity Banana Mousse
    (page 48)
100 ml/4 fl oz Apple Jelly
    (page 59)

Makes 2 gâteaux, each
    serving 8
Preparation time: 40
    minutes, plus about 1½
    hours freezing

THE PATTERNED SPONGE: Preheat the oven to 250°C/500°F/gas 10.

Using a palette knife, spread the cigarette paste all over the sheet of Silpat or silicone paper as thinly and evenly as possible. With the tip of your index finger, mark out small banana-shaped arcs 2 cm/¾ in long all over the surface of the paste, spacing them 2 cm/¾ in apart. Place in the freezer for about 10 minutes to harden the paste.

Spread the joconde sponge mixture over the cigarette paste, smooth with a palette knife, then bake in the very hot oven for 2–3 minutes until just firm but still moist. Leave the cooked sponge to cool slightly for 10 minutes, then invert it onto a cooling rack and remove the Silpat or silicone paper. Keep at room temperature.

CARAMELIZING THE BANANAS: Peel the bananas and cut them diagonally into 1 cm/½ in thick rounds. In a non-stick frying pan, sauté half the bananas over high heat for 2 minutes with half the butter and half the sugar, then transfer to a plate. Sauté the remaining bananas in the same way.

Reserve the sixteen best lightly-caramelized banana rounds for decorating the top of the dessert. Place the two flan rings on a baking sheet lined with clingfilm and arrange the rest of the bananas inside. Place in the freezer for 30 minutes.

ASSEMBLING THE GATEAUX: Cut three 4 cm/1½ in wide strips from the length of the sponge and two 20 cm/8 in discs from the rest. Place the two dessert rings on the cake bases and line the rings with the bands of rodoïde or acetate. Press on the bands of sponge, patterned-side against the acetate, cutting and splicing to line the inside of the rings completely.

Place the sponge discs in the bottom of the rings. Divide the caramel mousse between the rings. Unmould the frozen sliced bananas and place them on the mousse, without pressing them down. Put the half-assembled gâteaux in the freezer for 30 minutes.

Finish by filling the rings with banana mousse. Smooth the surface with a palette knife and freeze again for 30 minutes.

PRESENTATION: At least 4 hours before serving, place the gâteaux in the fridge for 2 hours, then glaze with apple jelly. Remove the dessert rings and bands of rodoïde or acetate. Arrange the reserved banana rounds in an arc on one side of each gâteau. Place the desserts on serving plates and keep in the fridge until ready to serve. They should be served well-chilled.

SPECIAL EQUIPMENT:
60 × 40 cm baking sheet
    lined with Silpat or
    silicone paper
2 dessert rings, 22 cm/
    8½ in diam., 5 cm/2 in
    deep
2 bands of rodoïde or
    acetate, 72 × 5 cm/
    28 × 2 in
2 rigid cardboard cake bases,
    24 cm/9½ in diam.
2 flan rings, 16 cm/6½ in
    diam., 1.5 cm/⅝ in deep

NOTES:
It is impossible to make this dessert successfully if you reduce the quantities, hence the necessity to make two gâteaux. One can be frozen for another occasion. They freeze well, unglazed, for up to a week; glaze them a few hours before serving.

YELLOW PEACH SOUVERAIN
Souverain aux pêches jaunes

THIS ATTRACTIVE DESSERT IS EASY TO MAKE. IF POSSIBLE, USE FRESHLY POACHED PEACHES IN SEASON, BUT TINNED PEACHES ARE OF EXCELLENT QUALITY AND SIMPLIFY THE PREPARATION. IF YOU WISH, SERVE THE SOUVERAIN WITH A STRAWBERRY COULIS (PAGE 51)

INGREDIENTS: ❀
220 g/8 oz yellow peaches in syrup (drained weight)
1 Genoise Sponge (page 33), 22 cm/8½ in diam., 5 cm/2 in thick
550 g/1 lb 3 oz Mousseline Cream (page 42)
200 ml/7 fl oz Sorbet Syrup (page 144), mixed with 50 ml/2 fl oz kirsch (optional)
1 quantity Italian Meringue (page 37), freshly made with 6 egg whites, and cooled
60 g/2 oz flaked almonds, toasted

Serves 8
Preparation time: 25 minutes

PREPARATION: Reserve one attractive peach half to decorate the dessert, finely dice the rest and mix them into the mousseline cream.

Slice the genoise sponge horizontally into three 1.5 cm/⅝ in thick discs (1) and brush with the kirsch-flavoured sorbet syrup (2).

ASSEMBLING THE SOUVERAIN: Lay one sponge disc on the cake base and spread over half the mousseline cream with a palette knife. Top with a second sponge disc and spread with the remaining mousseline cream (3). Finish with the third disc and press lightly with your fingertips.

Using a palette knife, coat the top and sides of the dessert with a 5 mm/¼ in thick layer of meringue (4). Take a handful of flaked almonds in your right hand and, holding the dessert with your left hand, press the almonds all round the sides (5).

Fill the piping bag fitted with a Saint-Honoré nozzle with Italian meringue and, starting from the centre of the dessert, swirl on curved arcs of meringue all over the surface to make a daisy effect (6). Brown the edges lightly with a blowtorch, or place briefly under a salamander. Place the peach half in the centre of the dessert and refrigerate for at least an hour.

PRESENTATION: Place the souverain on a round serving plate and slice it at the table.

SPECIAL EQUIPMENT:
22 cm/8½ in round cardboard cake base
Piping bag with a Saint-Honoré nozzle
Blowtorch or salamander

APPLE CHARLOTTE WITH APPLE CRISPS
Charlotte aux pommes et ses chips

THIS DESSERT NEEDS NO ACCOMPANYING SAUCE OR COULIS. THE CRUNCHY APPLE CRISPS MAKE A MARVELLOUS CONTRAST WITH THE SMOOTH, CREAMY BAVAROIS.

INGREDIENTS: ❋

3 apples (preferably Coxes),
  total weight about 500 g/
  1 lb 2 oz

80 g/3 oz caster sugar
1 quantity Apple Bavarois
  (page 44)
30 × 20 cm/12 × 8 in
  sheet of Hazelnut
  Dacquoise (page 31)
1 tablespoon Decorating
  Chocolate (page 186)
  (optional)

APPLE JELLY
All the apple trimmings,
  including the cores and pips
125 g/4½ oz caster sugar
½ lemon, chopped
1 split vanilla pod
3 gelatine leaves, soaked in
  cold water and well
  drained
250 ml/9 fl oz water

Makes 2 charlottes, each
  serving 8
Preparation time: 1 hour 15
  minutes

THE APPLE CRISPS AND SLICES FOR DECORATION: Preheat the oven to 180°C/350°F/gas 4.

Wash but do not peel the apples, wipe them dry and halve them. Cut four wafer-thin slices from the middle of the two best halves, lay them on a lightly greased baking sheet, sprinkle with about 1 teaspoon sugar and cook in the oven for 6 minutes. Turn over the apple slices and cook for another 4 minutes. Place on a plate and leave to cool at room temperature.

Lay the six apple halves flat side-down. Cut out a tube from each (see left) and cut the tubes into wafer-thin slices (see right), discarding the core end. Arrange these on the second baking sheet and sprinkle with the remaining sugar. Cook in the oven for 10−15 minutes, until pale golden. Leave to cool on the baking sheet. When the crisps are cold, lift them off with a palette knife and keep in an extremely dry place so that they remain crunchy.

THE APPLE JELLY: Make the jelly using the listed ingredients, following the method on page 59, then leave the jelly to cool.

ASSEMBLING THE CHARLOTTE: Place the cake tin or cardboard mould on the Silpat or silicone paper. Slide this onto a baking sheet and arrange two apple slices at each end of the rectangle. Make the bavarois following the method on page 44 and pour it into the mould as soon as it begins to set. Trim the edges of the hazelnut dacquoise to fit the mould, then lay it over the mousse, press lightly with your fingertips and place the charlotte in the freezer for at least 1 hour or in the fridge for at least 3 hours.

PRESENTATION: Invert the mould containing the charlotte onto the work surface. Remove the Silpat or paper, then slide a small knife blade between the bavarois and mould and lift off the mould. Cut the charlotte in half widthways to make two desserts. Glaze the two charlottes with half-set apple jelly. If you like, pipe on the words 'Apples' or 'Pommes' with the decorating chocolate. Lightly press the apple crisps all round the edges of the charlottes, place one or both on a serving plate and serve well-chilled.

NOTE:
Once you have removed the mould and divided the charlotte, you can return one half to the freezer before glazing with apple jelly. It will keep well for up to a week.

SPECIAL EQUIPMENT:
Rectangular cake tin,
  30 × 20 × 4 cm/
  12 × 8 × 1½ in, or a
  cardboard mould of the
  same dimensions covered
  in clingfilm
4 cm/1½ in pastry cutter
2 non-stick baking sheets,
  1 lightly greased
Silpat or silicone paper

JEWELLED FRUIT GATEAU
Diamant de fruits, mousse au citron vert

AS IT IS DIFFICULT TO MAKE A SATISFACTORY CITRUS MOUSSE IN SMALL
QUANTITIES, YOU WILL NEED TO PREPARE TWO OF THESE WONDERFULLY
REFRESHING GATEAUX — A GOOD EXCUSE FOR A LITTLE GREEDY INDULGENCE!

INGREDIENTS: ❅
100 g/4 oz redcurrants
150 g/5 oz strawberries
150 g/5 oz kiwi fruit
1 plain Genoise Sponge (page 33), 20 cm/8 in diam., 5 cm/2 in thick
150 ml/5 fl oz Sorbet Syrup (page 144)
25 ml/1 fl oz kirsch
1 quantity Lime Mousse (page 47)
2 soup spoons Decorating Chocolate (page 186)
100 ml/4 fl oz Apple Jelly (page 59)

Makes 2 gâteaux, each serving 8
Preparation time: 35 minutes, plus 2 hours freezing or 6 hours chilling

SPECIAL EQUIPMENT:
2 cardboard cake bases, 24 cm/10 in diam.
2 dessert rings, 22 cm/8½ in diam., 5 cm/2 in deep
Blowtorch (optional)

PREPARING THE FRUIT: Use a fork to strip the redcurrants from their stalks without damaging the fruit, and place in a bowl. Hull the strawberries, cut them into 5 mm/¼ in dice and place in another bowl. Peel the kiwi fruit and cut 8 attractive slices from the middle, then halve these; dice the rest of the kiwi like the strawberries. Place in a bowl, cover with clingfilm and refrigerate all the fruit.

THE GENOISE SPONGE: Mix the sorbet syrup with the kirsch. Use a serrated knife to cut two 5 mm/¼ in thick rounds from the sponge. Brush these with the kirsch-flavoured syrup.

ASSEMBLING THE GATEAUX: Cover the cardboard cake bases with clingfilm. Place a dessert ring over each base and arrange 8 kiwi semi-circles against the clingfilm to make a border inside the rings. Scatter one-third of the diced strawberries and kiwi and half the redcurrants into the rings (1), then cover the fruit with a layer of lime mousse (2).

Mix the remaining fruit into the rest of the lime mousse and fill up the rings to within 5 mm/¼ in of the top. Lay a circle of sponge over each gâteau, syrup-side down (3). Press lightly with your fingertips, then cover the gâteaux with clingfilm and place in the freezer for at least two hours, or in the fridge for at least 6 hours.

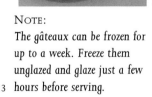

NOTE:
The gâteaux can be frozen for up to a week. Freeze them unglazed and glaze just a few hours before serving.

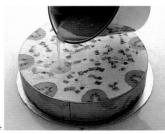

GLAZING THE GATEAUX: Remove the clingfilm, invert the gâteaux onto the work surface, sponge-side down and remove the cake bases. Glaze with the almost set apple jelly (4) and spread with a palette knife (5). Fill a greaseproof paper cone with the decorating chocolate and pipe on a modern geometric design (6). Return the gâteaux to the fridge until ready to serve.

PRESENTATION: Briefly run a blowtorch round the outside of the rings, or slide the tip of a knife dipped in hot water between the inside of the rings and the desserts. Lift off the rings, rotating them slightly, or place the gâteaux on a tin and slide the rings downwards (see page 17). Serve immediately, or freeze.

LIQUORICE GATEAU WITH A PEAR FAN

Délice à la réglisse, éventail de poires

THIS UNUSUAL LIQUORICE-SCENTED DESSERT IS VERY SIMPLE TO PREPARE.
THE COMBINATION OF THE TWO FLAVOURS IS EXCEPTIONALLY GOOD.

INGREDIENTS: ❊

1 quantity *Spiced Cake*
 mixture (*page 29*)
2 pears, about 200 g/7 oz
 each, peeled, halved and
 poached in syrup
1 quantity *Liquorice*
 Bavarois (*page 44*)
1 pear, about 120 g/4 oz,
 peeled, but with a small
 collar of skin left on near
 the stalk, poached whole
 in syrup
60 ml/2 fl oz *Apple Jelly*
 (*page 59*)

Serves 8
Preparation time: 30
 minutes, plus 1 hour
 freezing

THE SPICED CAKE BASE: Bake the spiced cake in the greased dessert ring, following the method on page 29. Bake for only 40 minutes, then leave on a cooling rack at room temperature.

ASSEMBLING THE GATEAU: Place the second dessert ring on the cardboard cake base and line the inside with the band of rodoïde. With a small sharp knife, cut three of the pear halves into 5 mm/¼ in thick slices. Delicately dab them dry, then arrange them in a rosette all over the cake base and up against the band of rodoïde.

Pour one-third of the liquorice bavarois over the pears in the ring and place in the freezer for 10 minutes.

Finely dice the fourth pear half and mix it into the remaining bavarois, then pour this mixture into the dessert ring. With a serrated knife, slice the spiced cake into a disc of an even thickness of about 1 cm/½ in. Lay the cake disc over the bavarois in the ring, pressing down lightly with your fingertips. Freeze for at least 1 hour.

PRESENTATION: At least 2 hours before serving the dessert, invert it,

Press the sliced pear lightly to make it into a fan

remove the cardboard cake base and place it under the gâteau on a serving plate. Refrigerate for 1 hour, then glaze with the apple jelly. Remove the dessert ring and band of rodoïde.

Pat dry the whole poached pear and use a small sharp knife to cut out the core from the bottom of the fruit without spoiling the shape. With the same knife, slice down and all round the pear from the bottom of the collar at 5 mm/¼ in intervals, press lightly to fan it out, then arrange it on the centre of the dessert. Brush lightly with apple jelly and refrigerate until ready to serve. Serve the gâteau very cold.

SPECIAL EQUIPMENT:

2 dessert rings, 22 cm/8½ in
 diam., 5 cm/2 in deep,
 1 lightly greased
1 band of rodoïde or acetate,
 75 × 5 cm/ 30 × 2 in
1 rigid cardboard cake base,
 24 cm/9½ in diam.,
 covered in clingfilm
Silpat or silicone paper

NOTES:

The gâteau keeps well in the freezer for up to a week. Glaze it and decorate with the pear fan several hours before serving.

If you prefer, a Chocolate Sponge base (page 34) makes an excellent substitute for the spiced cake. Bake a sheet and cut out two rounds to make a double thickness to form the base of the gâteau.

MILLE-FEUILLE OF GINGER MOUSSE WITH CRUNCHY QUINCES

Mille-feuille, mousse gingembre et croquants de coings

COOKED QUINCES ARE DELICIOUS, ESPECIALLY WHEN THEY ARE STILL SLIGHTLY CRUNCHY.
THE GRENADINE ENHANCES THE FLAVOUR OF THIS LOVELY FRUIT.

INGREDIENTS: ❋
400 g/14 oz Quick Puff
    Pastry (page 25)
Flour for dusting
500 ml/18 fl oz Sorbet
    Syrup (page 144)
2 quinces, total weight about
    400 g/14 oz
Juice of 1 lemon
125 ml/4½ fl oz grenadine
½ quantity freshly-made
    Ginger Mousse (page 49)
30 g/1 oz icing sugar

Serves 8
Preparation time: 45
    minutes, plus 45 minutes
    chilling

PREPARING THE PASTRY: On a lightly floured work surface, roll out the pastry into a 60 × 40 cm/24 × 16 in rectangle, 2 mm/¹⁄₁₂ in thick. Roll the pastry around the rolling pin, then unroll it onto a baking sheet lined with silicone paper. Refrigerate for at least 30 minutes.

POACHING THE QUINCES: Put the syrup in a saucepan and bring to the boil. Peel the quinces and rub them with lemon juice. Poach in the syrup for 15 minutes if they are very ripe, or for 30 minutes if they are hard and slightly unripe. Add the grenadine a few minutes before the cooking time is up, then leave the quinces to cool in the poaching syrup at room temperature. Refrigerate them once they are completely cold.
  Preheat the oven to 180°C/350°F/gas 4.

BAKING THE PASTRY: Prick the pastry with a fork, cover it with a sheet of silicone paper and lay the second baking sheet on top. This will prevent the pastry from rising too unevenly during cooking.
  Bake in the preheated oven for 8 minutes until the pastry is pale golden. Remove the top baking sheet and silicone paper, slide the pastry sheet onto a cooling rack and leave at room temperature.

SPECIAL EQUIPMENT:
1 dessert ring, 18 cm/7 in
    diam., 4 cm/1½ in deep
    (optional)
1 band of rodoïde or acetate,
    57 × 4 cm/22 × 1½ in
2 baking sheets, 60 × 40 cm/
    24 × 16 in
1 cardboard cake base,
    18 cm/7 in diam.
Metal skewer, for decorating
    the mille-feuille

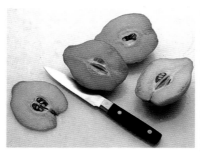

CUTTING THE QUINCES: Cut one quince into ten even segments. Halve the second quince lengthways and cut off one 3 mm/⅛ in slice (see photo, left). Finely dice the rest of the fruit and put half in a sauceboat with some of the poaching syrup. Put the segments and slice of quince in a bowl and keep in the fridge.

NOTE:
This crisp and creamy dessert freezes very well inside the rodoïde band. Defrost it slowly for 3 hours in the fridge before the final stages of presentation.

ASSEMBLING THE MILLE-FEUILLE: Prepare the ginger mousse, following the method on page 49. As soon as it begins to set, add the remaining diced quinces and start assembling the mille-feuille. Remove the paper from underneath the pastry, then place the dessert ring on the pastry and cut round it with a small, sharp knife to make four circles.

Lay one pastry circle on the cake base. Encircle it with the band of rodoïde or acetate and secure the band with sticky tape. Pour one-third of the ginger mousse over the pastry base and smooth with a soup spoon. Lay a second pastry circle on top and repeat the operation twice more, finishing with the fourth pastry circle. Leave to set in the fridge for at least 2 hours, or in the freezer for 45 minutes.

PRESENTATION: Heat the metal skewer along two-thirds of its length over a gas flame.

Remove the band of rodoïde or acetate from around the mille-feuille and sprinkle the top generously with icing sugar. When the skewer is red-hot, lay it across the surface of the mille-feuille at 2 cm/¾ in intervals to mark out caramelized but not burnt lines. Reheat the skewer as often as necessary and mark out another set of lines to make a regular diamond pattern.

Place the mille-feuille on a serving plate, arrange the quince slice in the centre and the segments around the base. Serve the mille-feuille chilled but not frozen, and serve the diced quinces in syrup separately in the sauceboat.

CHAPTER EIGHT

TARTS AND TARTLETS

Whichever type of pastry you use as a tart base, it should always be very thin, well-cooked and crisp. Ideally, tarts should be filled with very ripe fresh fruits, sun-ripened and bursting with sugar. They are delicious served warm or cold, but should never be chilled. They are appetizing even when you are not hungry, and children adore them.

Tarts are simple and inexpensive to make. Whether they be rustic or elegant, with their glowing colours they are always alluring and mouth-wateringly good. Delicately spread between the pastry and the fruit are wonderful soft pillows of cream, which make these tarts into the undisputed champions of desserts.

Almost all uncooked tarts can be frozen for several days. Bake them just an hour or two before serving and be patient enough to let them cool a little before sinking in your teeth . . . .

Adding rhubarb to the cream-filled tartlet

RHUBARB TARTLETS
Tartelettes à la rhubarbe

IF YOU PREFER, MAKE ONE LARGE TART INSTEAD OF THE SMALL
TARTLETS

INGREDIENTS: ❋
600 g/1¼ lbs tender young
  rhubarb
200 ml/7 fl oz sweet white
  wine, preferably Sauternes
2 tablespoons water
150 g/5 oz caster sugar
1½ tablespoons grenadine
  syrup
Flour for dusting
250 g/9 oz Sweet Short
  Pastry (page 20)
200 ml/7 fl oz whipping
  cream, whipped to a
  ribbon consistency with
  25 g/1 oz caster sugar
100 g/4 oz Pastry Cream
  (page 39)

Serves 8
Preparation time: 30
  minutes
Cooking time: 7 minutes

PREPARING THE RHUBARB: Scrape the stalks, removing any fibrous threads. Cut the rhubarb into 5–6 cm/2–2⅜ in chunks. Choose the two most tender chunks and cut them into julienne.

Put the wine, water, sugar and grenadine into a shallow pan and bring to the boil. Drop in the rhubarb julienne for 30 seconds, then lift them out with a slotted spoon and place in a bowl with a couple of spoons of the cooking syrup.

With the syrup still boiling in the pan, add the rhubarb chunks, then lower the heat and poach gently for about 30 minutes. Leave the rhubarb to cool in the syrup and, when it is cold, drain in a sieve for 30 minutes. Do not discard the syrup, which can be used to make a sorbet or champagne cocktail.

Meanwhile, preheat the oven to 180°C/350°F/gas 4.

THE TARTLET CASES: On a lightly floured work surface, roll out the pastry to a thickness of 3 mm/⅛ in. Cut out eight circles with the pastry cutter and use these to line the tartlet tins. Crimp the edges of the pastry with your fingertips to make a border slightly higher than the top of the tins. Refrigerate the pastry cases for 10 minutes.

BAKING THE TARTLET CASES: Prick the bases with a fork and bake in the preheated oven for 7 minutes. Leave in the tins to cool slightly, then carefully unmould the pastry cases on to a wire rack.

FILLING THE TARTLETS AND PRESENTATION: Use a whisk to mix the whipped cream with the pastry cream, and divide the mixture between the tartlet cases. Spoon in the poached rhubarb and scatter the barely-cooked rhubarb julienne over the top. Serve the tartlets on individual plates at room temperature.

SPECIAL EQUIPMENT:
8 non-stick or lightly
  buttered tartlet tins,
  10 cm/4 in diam.,
  2 cm/¾ in deep
10 cm/4 in plain pastry
  cutter

NOTES:
All the components of this dessert can be prepared in advance; the tartlets will take only 8 minutes to fill at the last moment, or at most 1 hour before serving. If you fill them any earlier, the pastry will become soggy. Do not refrigerate these tartlets, or the rhubarb will lose its flavour.

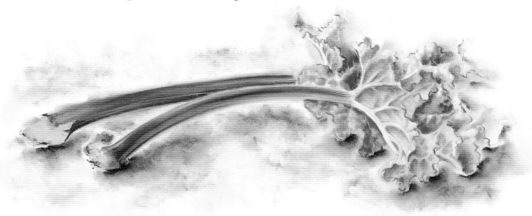

FRUIT TARTLETS WITH GLAZED FIVE SPICE SABAYON
Grandes tartelettes aux fruits, gratinées aux cinq épices

THE WARMTH OF THE SABAYON AND THE HEAT OF THE GRILL DEVELOP THE
SCENT OF THE FRUITS IN A SPECTACULAR WAY, AND THE FIVE SPICES ADD A
MUSKY FLAVOUR TO THE SABAYON — A TRULY HEADY COMBINATION.

INGREDIENTS:

420 g/14 oz Shortcrust
(page 20), or Quick Puff
Pastry trimmings (page
25)

Flour for dusting

720 g/1½ lbs assorted
fruits (eg: bananas,
bilberries, raspberries,
redcurrants, blackberries),
according to your taste
and the season

1 quantity Sabayon (page
53)

½ teaspoon five spice powder

18 wild strawberries for
decoration (optional)

6 small mint sprigs

Serves 6

Preparation time: 20
minutes

Cooking time: 11 minutes

PREPARING THE PASTRY CASES: On a lightly floured surface, roll out the
pastry to a thickness of 2 mm/⅟₁₂ in. Cut out six circles with the pastry
cutter and line the tartlet tins, lightly pinching up the edges of the
pastry to make a border slightly higher than the tins. Refrigerate for
10 minutes.

Meanwhile, preheat the oven to 180°C/350°F/gas 4.

BAKING THE PASTRY CASES: Prick the bottom of the pastry cases with a
fork. Line with a circle of greaseproof paper and fill with baking or
dried beans. Bake in the preheated oven for 10 minutes. Remove the
beans and paper and return the pastry cases to the oven for 1 minute
to ensure that the insides are well cooked. Take them out of the oven
and unmould onto a cooling rack.

THE FRUITS: Peel, wash and hull as necessary. Cut into pieces or
rounds, depending on the size, and keep at room temperature.

THE SABAYON: Follow the recipe on page 53, flavouring the sabayon
with sweet white wine, kirsch or pear liqueur, according to your
taste. When the sabayon has
puffed up, sprinkle on the
five spice powder and keep at
room temperature while you
assemble the tartlets.

Preheat a salamander or
the grill to very hot.

PRESENTATION: Arrange the
fruits in the tartlet cases, coat
generously with two-thirds
of the sabayon and glaze
lightly under the hot grill or
salamander for a few
seconds. Immediately place
the tartlets on warmed plates
and pour the remaining
sabayon in a ribbon around
them. Arrange three wild
strawberries and a small
sprig of mint on each tartlet
and serve at once.

SPECIAL EQUIPMENT:

6 tartlet tins, 12 cm/5 in
diam., 2 cm/¾ in deep

16 cm/6 in plain pastry
cutter

CHOCOLATE AND RASPBERRY TART

Tarte au chocolat et aux framboises

THIS IS ONE OF MY CLIENTS' FAVOURITE DESSERTS. IN WINTER, THE
RASPBERRIES CAN BE REPLACED BY FINELY SLICED POACHED PEARS.

INGREDIENTS: ❈
250 g/9 oz Sweet Short
    Pastry (page 20)
Flour for dusting
250 g/9 oz raspberries
250 ml/9 fl oz whipping
    cream

GANACHE
200 g/7 oz plain couverture
    or best quality cooking
    chocolate, finely chopped
25 g/1 oz liquid glucose
50 g/2 oz butter, diced

A few Chocolate Curls
    (page 154) (optional)
A pinch of icing sugar

Serves 8
Preparation time: 20
    minutes
Cooking time: 10
    minutes

PREPARING THE PASTRY BASE: On a lightly floured surface, roll out the
pastry into a circle about 2 mm/¹⁄₁₂ in thick. Roll the pastry around
the rolling pin, then unroll it over the flan ring so as not to spoil the
shape. Line the ring with the pastry and pinch up the edges with your
fingertips to make an even border standing above the top of the ring.
Slide the tart base onto a baking sheet and leave in the fridge to rest
for at least 20 minutes.

BAKING THE PASTRY BASE: Preheat the oven to 180°C/350°F/gas 4.

Prick the pastry base with a fork. It is not necessary to line it with
paper or fill it with baking beans. Bake for 10 minutes.

Meanwhile, reserve a dozen of the best raspberries for decoration
and halve the rest. Slide the cooked pastry base onto a cooling rack,
carefully remove the ring and leave at room temperature. When the
base is cold, cover the bottom with the halved raspberries.

THE CHOCOLATE GANACHE FILLING: Put the cream in a saucepan and
bring to the boil. Take the pan off the heat and add the chocolate and
glucose, stirring with a whisk to make a smooth cream. Now whisk
in the butter, a small piece at a time.

SPECIAL EQUIPMENT:
A dessert ring, 24 cm/9½ in
    diam., 2 cm/¾ in deep

NOTES:
You can use a Shortbread
pastry (page 21) instead of
sweet short pastry, but it is
much more fragile and
delicate to work with.

Instead of one large tart,
you might prefer to make
small tartlets.

FINISHING THE TART: As soon as the ganache is ready, pour it into the tart base and leave to cool at room temperature. Once cold, refrigerate for an hour or two before serving.

PRESENTATION: Dust the chocolate curls with icing sugar and arrange them on the tart. Decorate the tart with the reserved raspberries and serve on a china or silver plate.

CURD CHEESE TART
Tarte au fromage

I ADORE THIS 'GRANNY FOOD' TART. IN SUMMER, I MAKE IT WITH PUFF PASTRY TRIMMINGS, BUT IN WINTER I PREFER THE EXTRA SWEETNESS OF SWEET SHORT PASTRY.

INGREDIENTS:
350 g / 12 oz Sweet Short Pastry (page 20)
Flour for dusting
150 g / 5 oz soft curd cheese (whatever fat content you prefer)
50 g / 2 oz caster sugar
150 ml / 5 fl oz milk
3 eggs, separated
Juice of 1 lemon
Zest of 1 lemon, thinly slivered and blanched
20 g / ¾ oz flour, plus extra for dusting
30 g / 1 oz cornflour
20 g / ¾ oz icing sugar

SERVES 8
Preparation time: 25 minutes
Cooking time: 35 minutes

THE PASTRY CASE: On a lightly floured surface, roll out the pastry into a circle about 2 mm / ¹⁄₁₂ in thick. Use it to line the dessert ring, and place on a baking sheet. Refrigerate for 20 minutes.
Meanwhile, preheat the oven to 180°C/350°F/gas 4.

THE CHEESE FILLING: In a bowl, whisk together the curd cheese, sugar, milk, egg yolks, lemon juice and zest, flour and cornflour. Beat the egg whites stiffly and delicately fold them into the mixture with a spatula. Fill the pastry case with the mixture and bake the tart in the preheated oven for 20 minutes. Reduce the oven temperature to 150°C/300°F/gas 2 and bake for a further 15 minutes.
Take the tart out of the oven and immediately place it on a cooling rack. Carefully lift off the flan ring and leave the tart to cool at room temperature until barely cold.

PRESENTATION: Lightly dust the top of the tart with icing sugar and place it on a fine china plate. Serve it just cold, but never chilled.

SPECIAL EQUIPMENT:
A dessert ring, 22 cm/8½ in diam., 2 cm/¾ in deep, lightly greased

NOTES:
Never refrigerate this tart, or it will lose all its flavour.
I sometimes substitute a few drops of orange flower essence for the lemon zest.

RICE TART SCENTED WITH LAPSANG SOUCHONG AND LYCHEES

Tarte au riz au parfum de lapsang souchong et fruits de litchies

THIS TART IS PARTICULARLY DELICIOUS IN WINTER. I SOMETIMES SPRINKLE ON A VEIL OF CASTER SUGAR AND LIGHTLY CARAMELIZE THE TART WITH A BLOWTORCH TO REINFORCE THE SCENT OF THE TEA. OBVIOUSLY IT DOES NOT THEN NEED GLAZING WITH LYCHEE SYRUP. THIS CREAMY DESSERT NEEDS NO ACCOMPANYING SAUCE OR COULIS.

INGREDIENTS:
350 g/12 oz Sweet Short
    Pastry (page 20)
Flour for dusting
Eggwash (1 egg yolk mixed
    with 1 soup spoon milk
    and a pinch of salt)
750 ml/26 fl oz milk
75 g/3 oz pudding rice
75 g/3 oz caster sugar
10 g/⅓ oz Lapsang
    Souchong tea, wrapped in
    a piece of muslin
180 g/6 oz lychees in syrup
    (drained weight; reserve
    the syrup)
100 ml/4 fl oz whipping
    cream, whipped to a
    ribbon consistency

Serves 8
Preparation time: 30
    minutes
Cooking time: 30 minutes

THE PASTRY CASE: On a lightly floured surface, roll out the pastry into a circle 3 mm/⅛ in thick. Use it to line the flan ring and place on a baking sheet. Refrigerate for 20 minutes.

Meanwhile, preheat the oven to 200°C/400°F/gas 6.

BLIND BAKING THE PASTRY CASE: Prick the bottom of the pastry in several places with a fork. Line the base with greaseproof paper, fill with baking or dried beans and bake in the preheated oven for 20 minutes.

Remove the beans and paper and delicately brush the inside and bottom of the pastry case with a little eggwash. Return it to the oven for another 5 minutes. Place the tart on a cooling rack, remove the ring and leave at room temperature.

COOKING THE RICE: Heat the milk in a small saucepan. As soon as it comes to the boil, scatter in the rice like rain and cook gently for 15 minutes, stirring occasionally with a spatula. Add the sugar and muslin-wrapped tea and cook gently for another 15 minutes, stirring from time to time. Take the pan off the heat, remove the tea and leave the rice to cool slightly in the pan for 10–15 minutes.

FILLING THE TART: Reserve one-third of the best lychees for decoration and halve them. Coarsely dice the remainder and stir them into the rice with a spatula, then delicately fold in the whipped cream. Gently pour the mixture into the pastry case. Arrange the halved lychees tastefully on top and leave the tart to cool at room temperature for at least an hour.

When the tart is cold, boil the lychee syrup to reduce it slightly and leave to cool for a few minutes. With a pastry brush, use a little to glaze the top of the tart very lightly.

PRESENTATION: Place the tart on a serving plate and serve it cold but not chilled.

SPECIAL EQUIPMENT:
A dessert ring, 22 cm/
    8½ in diam., 2 cm/¾ in
    deep, lightly greased

NOTE:
If fresh lychees are available, use about twenty. Just peel and stone them; they will not need poaching in syrup, although you should glaze them with syrup from a tin of lychees.

Pine Nut and Praline Tart

Tarte aux pignons et pralines

Serve this delicious tart by itself or with a Honey Sauce (page 55) in summer, and a warm or cold Chocolate Sauce (page 55) in winter.

Ingredients:

300 g/11 oz Flan Pastry (page 22)

Flour for dusting

120 g/4 oz softened butter

200 g/7 oz tant pour tant (equal quantities of ground almonds and icing sugar, sifted together)

3 eggs

175 g/6 oz mixed glacé fruits, at least 2 varieties (eg: angelica, oranges, cherries), finely diced

60 g/2 oz sultanas, macerated in 60 ml/ 2 fl oz Armagnac for 6 hours

120 g/4 oz pine nuts

16 pralines

Icing sugar for dusting (optional)

Serves 8

Preparation time: 25 minutes

Cooking time: 30 minutes

PREPARING THE PASTRY CASE: On a lightly floured surface, roll out the pastry into a circle 2 mm/½ in thick. Roll it around the rolling pin, then unroll it over the ring, so as not to spoil the shape. Line the ring with the pastry and pinch up the edges between your forefinger and thumb to make a smooth, even border raised slightly above the rim of the ring. Slide the pastry case onto a baking sheet and leave it to rest in the fridge for at least 20 minutes.

THE FILLING: In a bowl, work the softened butter with a spatula until smooth, then stir in the tant pour tant and then the eggs, one at a time. When the mixture is well blended, add the glacé fruits and the macerated sultanas.

Preheat the oven to 200°C/400°F/gas 6.

BAKING THE TART: Prick the base with a fork, pour in the filling and spread it evenly with a palette knife. Cover the surface with the pine nuts, then space the pralines evenly around the edge. Press the pine nuts lightly with your fingertips to push them down on the filling, and bake the tart in the hot oven for 10 minutes. Lower the oven temperature to 170°C/325°F/gas 3 and bake for a further 20 minutes.

Take the tart out of the oven and leave until almost completely cold before removing the dessert ring.

PRESENTATION: Place the tart on a plate and dust lightly with icing sugar if you like. It is best served barely warm; on no account refrigerate it.

Special equipment:

A dessert ring, 24 cm/9½ in diam., 2 cm/¾ in deep

APRICOT DARTOIS
Dartois aux abricots

TINNED APRICOTS ARE ALWAYS OF EXCELLENT QUALITY, WHICH IS WHY I USE
THEM FOR THIS DESSERT.

INGREDIENTS: ❋

450 g / 1 lb Jean Millet's or
Quick Puff Pastry (pages
24 and 25)

Flour for dusting

150 g / 5 oz Frangipane
(page 43)

Eggwash (1 egg yolk mixed
with 1 soup spoon milk
and a pinch of salt

250 g / 9 oz (drained
weight) tinned apricot
halves in syrup

Icing sugar for dusting

300 ml / 11 fl oz Red Fruit
Coulis (see Fruit Coulis,
page 51)

SERVES 6

Preparation time: 20
minutes

Cooking time: 25 minutes

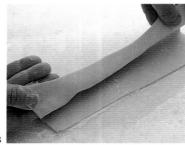

PREPARING THE DARTOIS BASE: On a lightly floured surface, roll 200 g/ 7 oz of the pastry into a 27 × 12 cm/11 × 5 in rectangle. Roll this around the rolling pin, then unroll it onto a baking sheet lightly dampened with cold water. Prick the pastry with a fork.

Using a spoon, spread the frangipane along the length of the pastry, leaving a clear 2 cm/ ¾ in border on either side (1). Brush these pastry borders with eggwash. Pat dry the apricots and arrange them on the frangipane (2).

Roll out the remaining pastry into a 27 × 13 cm/11 × 5½ in rectangle. Fold the pastry in half lengthways without applying pressure (3). Make incisions down the length of the pastry about every 4 mm/⅙ in with the heel of a chef's knife, leaving a 2 cm/¾ in strip intact on the two outside edges (4). Unfold the pastry into its original shape. Drape it over the rolling pin and unroll it onto the apricot-filled rectangle (5). Lightly press the edges together with your fingertips and refrigerate the dartois for 30 minutes.

BAKING THE DARTOIS: Preheat the oven to 200°C/400°F/gas 6.

Using a chef's knife, trim off about 3 mm/⅛ in pastry along the length of the rectangle. Delicately and sparingly brush the top of the pastry with eggwash. Liberally brush the sides with more eggwash. With the tip of a small, sharp knife, make light, diagonal incisions in the borders, then along the edges (6).

NOTES:

The dartois can be prepared the day before and kept in the fridge. Bake and glaze it shortly before serving. It is best served just warm.

128

6

Bake in the preheated oven for 25 minutes. Increase the temperature to 220°C/425°F/gas 7, dust the dartois with icing sugar and return it to the oven for 1–2 minutes, or place it under a hot salamander for a few seconds, until beautifully glazed.

PRESENTATION: Serve the dartois on a long plate and cut it with a very sharp knife. Serve the red fruit coulis separately.

LATTICED MIRABELLE TARTLETS
Tartelettes fines aux mirabelles en cage

ALTHOUGH THESE SIMPLE, LIGHT TARTLETS ARE BEST MADE WITH FRESH
MIRABELLES IN AUTUMN, THEY ARE ALSO EXCELLENT MADE WITH BOTTLED
MIRABELLES IN WINTER.

INGREDIENTS: ❋
450 g/1 lb trimmings of
Jean Millet's or Quick
Puff Pastry (pages 24
and 25)
Flour for dusting
100 g/4 oz Pastry Cream
(page 39)
84 stoned mirabelles,
poached in syrup or
bottled, or 18 fresh
Victoria plums, stoned,
each cut into 6 and
poached in syrup for 30
seconds
Eggwash (1 egg yolk mixed
with 1 soup spoon milk
and a pinch of salt)

Serves 6
Preparation time: 35
minutes
Cooking time: 18 minutes

PREPARING THE PASTRY BASES: On a lightly floured surface, roll out two-thirds of the pastry to a thickness of 2 mm/1⁄12 in. Using the pastry cutter, cut out six rounds and turn them over onto a baking sheet lightly dampened with cold water. Refrigerate for 20 minutes.

THE LATTICE STRIPS: On the lightly floured surface, roll out the remaining pastry into a rectangle about 16 × 8 cm/6½ × 3¼ in and 3 mm/⅛ in thick. Place on a baking sheet and refrigerate for 30 minutes.

ASSEMBLING THE TARTLETS: Preheat the oven to 190°/375°F/gas 5.

Prick the pastry bases with a fork and divide the pastry cream between them, spreading it evenly with a spoon. Arrange fourteen well-drained mirabelles or three segmented plums on the pastry cream. Brush the pastry rectangle with eggwash, cut it lengthways into 3 mm/⅛ in strips, then halve these widthways. Arrange five strips slantwise on each tartlet, then another five to form a lattice. Trim the lattice if necessary. Refrigerate for 10 minutes.

BAKING THE TARTLETS: Bake the tartlets in the preheated oven for 18 minutes, until golden brown. Use a palette knife to transfer them delicately to a cooling rack and keep at room temperature.

PRESENTATION: Place the tartlets on plates and serve them plain, while still slightly warm.

SPECIAL EQUIPMENT:
12 cm/5 in plain pastry
cutter

NOTE:
The tartlets can be prepared
right up to the final stage a
day in advance and kept in
the fridge. Bake just before
serving, or during the meal.

PRINCESS TART WITH BILBERRIES
Tarte princesse aux myrtilles

SERVE THIS DELICIOUS TART AT ROOM TEMPERATURE TO ENHANCE THE
SUBTLE FLAVOURS OF BILBERRIES, ORANGE AND CHIBOUST CREAM WITH A
THICK, RICH DOUBLE COATING OF CARAMEL.

INGREDIENTS:
250 g/9 oz Flan Pastry
    (page 22)
Flour for dusting
Eggwash (1 egg yolk mixed
    with 1 soup spoon milk
    and a pinch of salt)
450 ml/16 fl oz double
    cream
4 eggs
125 g/4½ oz caster sugar,
    plus 100 g/4 oz for
    caramelizing the tart
Finely grated zest of
    ½ orange
200 g/7 oz bilberries
½ quantity freshly-made
    Chiboust Cream (page
    39)

Serves 8
Preparation time: 35
    minutes
Cooking time: 25 minutes

THE PASTRY CASE: Preheat the oven to 220°C/425°F/gas 7.
On a lightly floured surface, roll out the pastry into a circle 2 mm/½ in thick. Place the dessert ring on a baking sheet and line it with the pastry. Pinch up the edges to make an attractive, evenly crimped border. Refrigerate for about 20 minutes.

BLIND BAKING THE PASTRY CASE: Prick the bottom of the pastry case with a fork, line with a circle of greaseproof paper and fill with baking or dried beans. Bake in the hot oven for 15 minutes.
Remove the beans and paper. Brush all over the inside of the tart with eggwash and return it to the oven for a further 5 minutes. Leave it in the ring at room temperature.
Reduce the oven temperature to 200°C/400°F/gas 6.

THE FILLING: In a bowl, lightly mix the double cream, eggs, 125 g/4½ oz sugar and the finely grated orange zest.

BAKING THE TART: Reserve the twenty-six best bilberries, spread the remainder over the base of the tart and pour on the cream filling. Immediately bake in the heated oven for 25 minutes. Take the tart out of the oven and neaten the border with a sharp knife, then carefully lift off the flan ring. Place the tart on a wire rack and leave to cool at room temperature.

THE CHIBOUST CREAM AND GLAZE: Roll the band of rodoïde or acetate around the tart and secure it with two pieces of sticky tape. Spread the freshly-made Chiboust cream over the tart up to the top of the band, and smooth the surface with a palette knife. Place in the freezer for 30 minutes or in the fridge for at least 1 hour. Fill the piping bag with the remaining Chiboust cream.
After freezing or refrigerating the tart, carefully remove the sticky tape and the rodoïde band by sliding a knife blade between it and the Chiboust cream. Heat the salamander or grill to as hot as possible.
Sprinkle 50 g/2 oz sugar over the Chiboust cream on top of the

SPECIAL EQUIPMENT:
A dessert ring, 24 cm/9½ in
    diam., 2 cm/¾ in deep,
    lightly greased
Piping bag with a plain
    1 cm/½ in nozzle
80 × 4 cm/32 × 1½ in
    band of rodoïde or acetate
Salamander or grill
Blowtorch (optional)

NOTES:
The uncaramelized tart
freezes well for up to a week.
Place in the fridge for at
least 3 hours to bring it
slowly to the correct
temperature before
caramelizing the top. Why
not make two tarts and freeze
one to enjoy a few days after
the first?

tart and caramelize it lightly by passing the salamader 1 mm/¼₄ in above the surface of the cream, or by placing the tart under the very hot grill.

Repeat the operation to make a second coating of caramel, using all but 20 g/¾ oz of the sugar. Leave the tart to cool at room temperature for a few minutes, then pipe the remaining Chiboust cream into twenty-six rosettes all around the edge. Sprinkle these with the remaining sugar and caramelize them with a blowtorch or leave them plain. Top each rosette with an attractive bilberry.

PRESENTATION: Place the tart on a round serving plate and slice it with a very sharp knife as soon as it has been caramelized, or certainly within an hour.

FIG AND FRESH ALMOND TARTLETS

Tartelettes aux figues et amandes fraîches

THESE SUMMER TARTLETS ARE SIMPLE TO MAKE; THEY LOOK RAVISHING AND
HAVE A DELICATE FLAVOUR. THEY ARE PERFECT IN JUNE AND JULY WHEN
FIGS ARE IN FULL SEASON AND FRESH ALMONDS APPEAR IN THE MARKETS.

INGREDIENTS:

250 g/9 oz Shortcrust
  (page 20)
Flour for dusting
600 g/1¼ lbs Pastry Cream
  (page 39)
100 ml/4 fl oz whipping
  cream, whipped to a
  ribbon consistency
7 very ripe figs, about
  65 g/2½ oz each
48 fresh almonds, shelled
  and skinned, for decoration
50 g/2 oz flaked almonds,
  toasted

ALMOND COULIS

70 fresh almonds, shelled
  and skinned
300 ml/11 fl oz whipping
  cream
Juice of 1 lemon
2 tablespoons milk
  (optional)

Serves 6
Preparation time: 55
  minutes
Cooking time: 10 minutes

PREPARING THE PASTRY CASES: On a lightly floured surface, roll out the shortcrust to a thickness of 2 mm/⅟₁₂ in. Cut out six rounds with a plain 13 cm/5 in pastry cutter and use them to line the tartlet tins. Refrigerate for 20 minutes.

Meanwhile, preheat the oven to 180°C/350°F/gas 4.

BAKING THE PASTRY CASES: Prick the pastry bases with a fork. Line them with a circle of greaseproof paper and fill with baking beans. Bake blind for 10 minutes, then remove the beans and paper and unmould the cases onto a cooling rack.

THE ALMOND COULIS: Coarsely chop the 70 almonds with a heavy chef's knife and place in a food processor with the cream. Process for 1 minute to make a slightly grainy coulis. Transfer to a bowl, stir in the lemon juice and refrigerate. If the coulis is too thick, thin it with the milk.

FILLING THE TARTLETS: Using a whisk, mix the pastry cream with the lightly whipped cream. Divide the mixture between the pastry cases, making a little mound in the centre. Cut six of the figs into eight segments and arrange these on the tartlets, leaving the stem end protruding slightly over the edge of the pastry cases.

Cut the remaining fig into 6 rounds and place one in the centre of each tartlet. Split 24 almonds lengthways and place 8 halves between the fig segments on each plate. Halve the remaining almonds horizontally and arrange them on the fig round like daisy petals.

PRESENTATION: Place the tartlets on individual plates; they look wonderful on claret-coloured and slightly opaque plates. Pour the almond coulis around the tartlets, decorate with toasted flaked almonds and serve immediately.

SPECIAL EQUIPMENT:
Plain 13 cm/5 in pastry
  cutter
6 tartlet tins, 10 cm/4 in
  diam., 2 cm/¾ in deep

NOTE:
If you cannot find fresh, milky almonds in their green shells, use skinned dried almonds soaked in cold milk for several hours. These cannot, however, compare with the velvety smoothness of fresh almonds.

CHOCOLATE BOATS

Barquettes chocolat

THESE LITTLE BOATS ARE SIMPLE TO PREPARE AND MAKE AN EXCELLENT
LUNCHTIME DESSERT. SERVE THEM ALONE OR WITH A COFFEE-FLAVOURED
CRÈME ANGLAISE (PAGE 40).

INGREDIENTS: ❄
160 g/5 oz Shortbread
    Pastry (page 21) or Sweet
    Short Pastry (page 20)
Flour for dusting
120 g/4 oz Frangipane
    (page 43)
200 g/7 oz Chocolate
    Chantilly Cream
    (page 42)
15 g/½ oz unsweetened
    cocoa powder

Serves 6
Preparation time: 25
    minutes
Cooking time: 15 minutes

LINING THE MOULDS: Arrange the barquette moulds in a row. On a lightly floured surface, roll out the pastry into a rectangle 40 cm/ 16 in long, 12 cm/5 in wide, 2 mm/1/12 in thick. Roll the pastry around the rolling pin, then unroll it over the line of moulds. Use your lightly floured thumb to push the pastry delicately into each mould. Roll the rolling pin across the top of the moulds to cut the pastry. Using a piece of floured pastry trimming, press down the pastry to ensure that it takes on the shape of the mould. Refrigerate for 20 minutes.

Meanwhile, preheat the oven to 180°C/350°F/gas 4.

BAKING THE PASTRY BOATS: Prick the base of the pastry cases with a fork, then use a palette knife to fill them with frangipane and smooth the surface. Bake in the preheated oven for 15 minutes. Remove the pastry boats from the oven, unmould immediately and arrange on a cooling rack. Leave to cool completely.

SPECIAL EQUIPMENT:
6 barquette moulds, 9 cm/
    3½ in long, 5 cm/2 in
    wide, 1.5 cm/⅝ in deep

NOTES:
The pastry boats can be frozen for up to a week. Remove from the freezer 2 hours before serving and place in the fridge. Dust with cocoa at the last moment.

Sweet short pastry is easier to work than shortbread pastry, but has a less delicate and fine flavour.

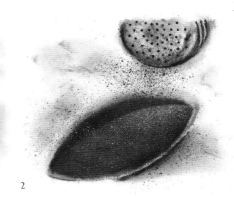

FILLING THE PASTRY BOATS: Use palette knife to heap the chocolate Chantilly into 2.5 cm/1 in high mounds on the pastry cases and spread it along their length to resemble little boats (1). Keep in the fridge.

PRESENTATION: Generously dust the Chantilly with cocoa (2). Arrange the boats on individual plates and serve very cold.

CHAPTER NINE

ICE CREAMS AND SORBETS

Ices originated in China before the 16th century. Their popularity spread all over the world and continues to grow. Nowadays, a wide range of reasonably-priced ice cream makers is available for domestic use, enabling you to make an ice cream or sorbet in less than half an hour, so it is perfectly feasible to whip up a home-made ice even after a day's work. It is simplicity itself to make sorbets from fruit or vegetables, sweetened, plain or flavoured with aromatics. Concocting a sorbet is rather like creating a cocktail. Being low in calories, sugar and cholesterol, sorbets make the perfect 'diet' dessert.

Custard-based ice creams are best churned just before serving. Since the recipes in this chapter are intended for domestic consumption only, my ice creams contain no stabilizers or preservatives, which makes them all the more delicious. However, the custard mixture can be pasteurized if you wish by poaching it at 79.4°C/175°F for 15 seconds.

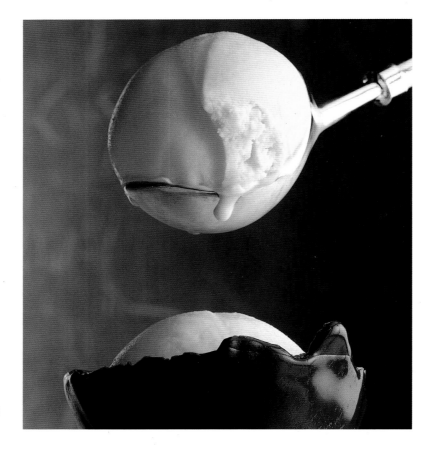

Ice cream in chocolate shells (see recipe page 143)

VANILLA ICE CREAM
Glace vanilla

INGREDIENTS:
CREME ANGLAISE:
6 egg yolks
125 g/4 oz caster sugar
500 ml/18 fl oz milk
1 vanilla pod, split

100 ml/4 fl oz double
cream

Makes about 700 ml/
1¼ pints
Preparation time: 15
minutes

THE CREME ANGLAISE: Make a Crème Anglaise with the listed ingredients, following the method on page 40. Strain through a conical strainer and leave to cool, stirring occasionally.

CHURNING THE ICE CREAM: Churn in an ice cream maker until slightly thickened, then add the double cream and churn for another 10–15 minutes.

PISTACHIO ICE CREAM
Glace pistache

I ADORE THE COMBINATION OF PISTACHIO AND VANILLA ICE CREAM AND OFTEN SERVE THEM IN TANDEM. THIS ICE CREAM ALSO FEATURES IN MY TRIO OF ICE CREAMS IN CHOCOLATE SHELLS (PAGE 143).

INGREDIENTS:
½ quantity Crème Anglaise
(page 40), made without
vanilla
60 g/2 oz pistachio paste,
or 80 g/3 oz pistachios,
skinned and finely crushed
in a small mortar
75 ml/3 fl oz double cream

Serves 6
Preparation time: 20
minutes, plus about 15

THE CREME ANGLAISE: Follow the method on page 40, omitting the vanilla. As soon as the crème anglaise is ready, pour it onto the pistachio paste or crushed pistachios, whisking continuously. Leave to cool completely, stirring from time to time.

CHURNING THE ICE CREAM: Pass the crème anglaise through a conical strainer and churn in an ice cream maker. As soon as it begins to thicken slightly, add the double cream and continue to churn for about 10–15 minutes, depending on your machine.

PRESENTATION: Serve the ice cream in shallow dishes. If you like, garnish with a few skinned and caramelized pistachios (see Pistachio Crème Brûlée, page 67).

MEADOWSWEET ICE CREAM
Glace reine des prés

MEADOWSWEET FLOWERS HAVE A SUBTLE, AROMATIC PERFUME AND WERE ONCE USED
FOR FLAVOURING BEER, MEAD AND WINE. I HAVE USED THEM TO MAKE ICE CREAM
SINCE I WAS CHEF TO MADEMOISELLE CECILE DE ROTHSCHILD IN THE 1960S.

INGREDIENTS:
½ quantity *Crème Anglaise*
  (page 40), made without
  vanilla
10 g/⅓ oz dried
  meadowsweet flowers
75 ml/3 fl oz double cream

Serves 6
Preparation time: 15
  minutes, plus about 15
  minutes churning

THE CREME ANGLAISE: Follow the method on page 40, omitting the
vanilla. As soon as the crème anglaise is ready, add the meadowsweet
flowers and leave to infuse for 20 minutes, then pass the crème
anglaise through a conical strainer. Leave to cool completely, stirring
from time to time.

CHURNING THE ICE CREAM: Churn the crème anglaise in an ice cream
maker. When it begins to thicken slightly, add the double cream and
continue to churn for about 10–15 minutes more, depending on
your machine.

PRESENTATION: Serve this ice cream plain in shallow dishes.

NOTE:
Meadowsweet is sold in
almost every pharmacy in
France and is available in
Britain from herbalists. It
has anti-rheumatic and
diuretic properties and is
often drunk as an infusion,
using 20–30 g/⅔–1 oz per
litre/1¾ pints of boiling
water.

CARAWAY ICE CREAM
Glace carvi

I ENJOY THIS CARAWAY-FLAVOURED ICE CREAM ON ITS OWN OR AS AN
ACCOMPANIMENT TO CHOCOLATE DESSERTS, SUCH AS BITTER CHOCOLATE
AND CARAMELIZED WALNUT DELIGHT (PAGE 162).

INGREDIENTS:
½ quantity *Crème Anglaise*
  (page 40), made without
  vanilla
50 g/2 oz caraway seeds
75 ml/3 fl oz double cream

Serves 6 (makes about
  850 ml/1½ pints)
Preparation time: 20
  minutes, plus about 15
  minutes churning

THE CREME ANGLAISE: Follow the method on page 40, omitting the
vanilla. As soon as it is ready, add the caraway seeds and leave to infuse
for 5 minutes. Pass the crème anglaise through a conical strainer and
leave to cool, stirring from time to time.

CHURNING THE ICE CREAM: Pour the cooled crème anglaise into an ice
cream maker and churn until slightly thickened. Add the cream and
churn for another 10–20 minutes, until firm.

ALMOND ICE CREAM WITH A BORDER OF FIGS
Glace au lait d'amandes et cordon de figues

THE COLOUR AND FLAVOUR OF A RASPBERRY COULIS SERVED SEPARATELY IN A SAUCEBOAT WILL COMPLEMENT THIS
DELICIOUS ICE CREAM, ALTHOUGH IF THE FIGS ARE REALLY RIPE AND OOZING JUICE, IT WILL NOT BE NECESSARY.

INGREDIENTS:
½ quantity Crème Anglaise
  (page 40)
100 g/4 oz ground almonds
100 ml/4 fl oz double
  cream
3 fresh figs, peeled
2 tablespoons best quality
  chocolate liqueur
  (optional)
12 almonds, peeled, soaked
  in milk and split

SERVES 6
Preparation time: 20
  minutes, plus about 15
  minutes churning

THE CREME ANGLAISE: Follow the method on page 40. As soon as the
crème anglaise is ready, take the pan off the heat and add the ground
almonds. Place in a bowl and leave until completely cold, whisking
from time to time.

CHURNING THE ICE CREAM: Pass the crème anglaise through a conical
strainer and churn in an ice cream maker. As soon as the mixture
thickens slightly, add the double cream and churn for another 10–15
minutes, depending on your machine.

PRESENTATION: Cut each fig into eight segments and, if you wish,
moisten them with chocolate liqueur. Fill six shallow bowls with
almond ice cream. Arrange the fig segments in a border around the
edge, place four almond halves on the ice cream and serve.

FROMAGE FRAIS SORBET WITH WHITE PEPPER
Sorbet au fromage blanc poivré

THIS UNUSUAL SORBET IS EXCELLENT SERVED WITH BERRY FRUITS, SUCH AS WILD STRAWBERRIES
AND RASPBERRIES. COMPLEMENT THE FLAVOUR WITH SOME HAZELNUT TUILES (PAGE 172).

INGREDIENTS:
350 ml/12 fl oz Sorbet
  Syrup (page 144)
400 g/14 oz fromage frais
  or white curd cheese
  (whatever fat content you
  prefer)
50 ml/2 fl oz lemon juice,
  strained
2 g/¹⁄₁₅ oz white
  peppercorns, finely crushed

Serves 6
Preparation time: 10
  minutes, plus about 15
  minutes churning

PREPARATION: Lightly mix the cold sorbet syrup into the fromage frais,
then add the lemon juice and crushed peppercorns. Transfer the
mixture to an ice cream maker and churn for about 15 minutes,
depending on your machine. Serve immediately, or keep in the
freezer until ready to serve.

PRESENTATION: Scoop the sorbet into a glass bowl or individual dishes,
using an ice cream scoop dipped into iced water to make each ball.

NOTE:
Churn the sorbet soon after
adding the pepper to the
mixture, or the flavour will
be too strong.

Igloo with Vanilla Ice Cream and Mirabelles

Igloo glace vanille aux mirabelles

CHILDREN ADORE THIS INTRIGUING AND ORIGINAL DESSERT, WITH ITS WONDERFUL FLAVOUR COMBINATION OF MERINGUE, ICE CREAM AND MIRABELLES. IT CAN BE SIMPLIFIED BY MAKING ONE LARGE IGLOO, USING A SALAD OR MIXING BOWL AS A MOULD. THE PREPARATION WILL BE LESS FIDDLY; MAKE A MUCH LARGER CHIMNEY TO FLAMBÉ THE IGLOO, AND CUT INTO PORTIONS AT THE TABLE.

INGREDIENTS:

1.25 litres / 2¼ pints Vanilla Ice Cream (page 137)

1 quantity freshly made Meringue Topping made with Egg Whites (page 35)

300 g / 11 oz (drained weight) tinned or freshly poached mirabelles in syrup, chilled

200 ml / 7 fl oz syrup from the mirabelles

1 vanilla pod, cut into very fine slivers (optional)

8 tablespoons mirabelle eau-de-vie

8 small bands of rice paper, 10 × 2 cm / 4 × ¾ in, rolled up to form chimneys

Serves 8

Preparation time: 1 hour 15 minutes, plus freezing

LINING THE MOULDS: Chill a baking sheet and eight serving plates. Line the 8 moulds with the vanilla ice cream, spreading it with a soup spoon. Make a hemispherical cavity about 3 cm / 1¼ in diameter, 2 cm / ¾ in deep in the centre of each, then place in the freezer for at least 1 hour.

After this, cut a 1 cm / ½ in hole in the bottom of the ice cream in each mould and lift out the ice cream in the cutter; the resulting hole will be the chimney. Immediately return the moulds to the freezer.

ASSEMBLING THE IGLOOS: Prepare the meringue topping and fill the piping bag and a paper icing cone with the mixture.

Reserve about twenty of the best mirabelles for decoration. Fill the cavities in the igloos with the remaining well-chilled and well-drained mirabelles. Run a blowtorch lightly over the outside of the moulds and unmould the igloos onto the chilled baking sheet. Place the rice paper chimneys in the holes in the igloos.

Pipe the meringue topping over the igloos and smooth the surface with a palette knife, taking care not to block the chimneys. Replace in the freezer for 30 minutes to ensure that the ice cream does not melt. The igloos are now ready to serve. Just pipe on the outline of ice blocks, using the meringue in the paper cone.

PRESENTATION: Transfer the igloos onto well-chilled serving plates, with the aid of a triangular palette knife. Use the remaining meringue in the piping bag to form an entrance porch to each igloo, and

decorate these in the same way as the igloos. Brown lightly with the blowtorch.

Arrange 5 mirabelle halves on one side of each plate around the igloo, with the vanilla slivers and mirabelle syrup. At the table or sideboard, lightly warm the mirabelle eau-de-vie, pour into the chimneys and ignite. Serve immediately.

SPECIAL EQUIPMENT:

8 hemispherical moulds, 9 cm / 3½ in diam., 4.5 cm / 1¾ in deep, chilled in the freezer

Plain 1 cm / ½ in pastry cutter

Piping bag with a plain 5 mm / ¼ in nozzle

Blowtorch

NOTE:

It is essential to work fast when coating the igloos with the meringue, so that the ice cream does not melt. The kitchen should not be too warm.

TRIO OF ICE CREAMS IN CHOCOLATE SHELLS

Tierce de glaces dans leur coque de couverture

AN ICED DESSERT FOR A GRAND OCCASION. THREE FLAVOURS OF ICE CREAM IN
DELICIOUS BITTER CHOCOLATE SHELLS, TIPPED WITH A TOUCH OF GOLD AND SERVED
WITH STRAWBERRY JUICE. A FITTING GRAND FINALE TO AN ELEGANT MEAL.

INGREDIENTS: ✳

400 g/14 oz bitter
couverture, tempered (page
154), or best quality
cooking chocolate, melted
and kept liquid

2 sheets of gold leaf
(optional)

½ quantity Pistachio Ice
Cream (page 137)

½ quantity Caraway Ice
Cream (page 138)

½ quantity Almond Ice
Cream (page 139)

12 pistachios, skinned

A pinch of caraway seeds

4 almonds, skinned, soaked
in milk for 1 hour, then
split

200 ml/7 fl oz Strawberry
Juice (page 51)

2 limes, all peel and pith
removed, cut into segments

Serves 4

Preparation time: 35
minutes

THE CHOCOLATE SHELLS: One at a time, dip the bottom two-thirds of the
moulds into the liquid chocolate. Let the excess run off for a few
seconds before inverting the moulds onto a wire rack. Leave the
chocolate to harden in a cool place (but not in the fridge).

As soon as the chocolate has hardened, repeat the operation to
make a second coating (see above). Refrigerate the shells for 1 hour.
Once the chocolate has set, detach the clingfilm from inside the
moulds, then carefully lift the shells off the moulds. Very delicately
peel off the clingfilm from inside the shells.

Arrange the shells on a wire rack and, if you wish, dab a touch of
gold leaf here and there on the borders of the shells.

PRESENTATION: Place three chocolate shells on each plate and fill each
one generously with a portion of different ice cream. Sprinkle a few
caraway seeds over the caraway ice cream, place three pistachios on
the pistachio ice cream and two almond halves on the almond ice
cream.

Pour the strawberry juice onto the plates and scatter on the lime
segments. Serve immediately.

SPECIAL EQUIPMENT:

12 round stainless steel or
china moulds, approx.
5 cm/2 in diam. at the
base, 8 cm/3¼ in diam.
at the top, 5 cm/2 in
high; the whole exterior
surface wrapped in
clingfilm to give a smooth
surface

NOTES:

Each chocolate shell weighs
about 20 g/⅔ oz, so you
will have up to 150 g/5 oz
melted couverture left over.
However, you must start
with the full 400 g/14 oz
for dipping the moulds.

Cooking chocolate will
not give the same glossy
sheen as couverture.

SORBET SYRUP
Sirop à sorbet

THIS SYRUP IS USED FOR MAKING ALL TYPES OF SORBET.

INGREDIENTS:
750 g/1 lb 10 oz sugar
650 ml/22 fl oz water
90 g/3 oz liquid glucose

Makes about 1.4 litres/
2½ pints
Preparation time: 5 minutes

In a saucepan, bring all the ingredients to the boil, stirring occasionally with a spatula. Boil for about 3 minutes, skimming any impurities from the surface if necessary. If you have a saccharometer, the reading should be 30° Beaumé or 1.2624 density. Strain the syrup through a conical strainer and use when completely cold.

SPECIAL EQUIPMENT:
Beaumé scale saccharometer
(optional)

NOTE:
The syrup will keep for 2
weeks in the fridge in an
airtight container or covered
with clingfilm

BANANA SORBET
Sorbet à la banane

YOU NEED VERY RIPE BANANAS FOR THIS SORBET, BUT IF THEY HAVE ANY
BLACK PATCHES, CUT THESE AWAY WITH A SHARP KNIFE.

INGREDIENTS:
500 g/1 lb 2 oz ripe
bananas (peeled weight)
Juice of 2 lemons
250 ml/9 fl oz milk
200 ml/7 fl oz Sorbet
Syrup (page 144)
Flavourings (optional):
½ vanilla pod, split,
or 50 ml/2 fl oz rum, or
a good pinch of ground
cinnamon

Serves 8 (makes about
1 kg/2¼ lbs)
Preparation time: 25
minutes, plus about 20
minutes churning

THE SORBET MIXTURE: Cut the bananas into rounds and mix immediately with the lemon juice to prevent the fruit from oxidizing and turning black. In a saucepan, bring the milk to the boil and immediately add the bananas and sorbet syrup. Simmer at 95°C/203°F for about 5 minutes. At this stage, you can add your chosen flavouring, then turn off the heat.

Remove the vanilla pod and purée the mixture in a blender for 2 minutes, until it is homogeneous and smooth, then pass it through a conical strainer. Leave to cool completely at room temperature, stirring with a spatula from time to time.

CHURNING THE MIXTURE: The sorbet mixture should be churned as soon as the bananas have cooled, as they will cause it to oxidize and turn brown. Churn the cold mixture in an ice cream maker for about 20 minutes, depending on your machine. The sorbet should have a firm consistency.

PRESENTATION: Serve this sorbet plain in shallow dishes, or garnished with half a banana lightly brushed with Chocolate Sauce (page 55).

SPECIAL EQUIPMENT:
Cooking thermometer

NOTE:
I give the peeled weight of
the bananas as the skins vary
in thickness depending on the
variety of the fruit.

PINEAPPLE SORBET IN A PINEAPPLE SHELL

L'Ananas en sorbet dans sa coque

INGREDIENTS: ✽
1 very ripe pineapple, about
    1.4 kg/3 lbs
250 ml/9 fl oz Sorbet
    Syrup (page 144)
Juice of 1 lemon
6–8 crystallized violets

THE RIBBON (OPTIONAL)
1 tablespoon melted butter
70 g/2½ oz Tulip Paste
    (page 28)
A pinch of cocoa powder

Serves 6

*Preparation time: 45
    minutes, plus 25 minutes
    for the ribbon*

PREPARING THE PINEAPPLE: Divide the pineapple lengthways into 60% and 40%, making sure that the larger piece, which will be used as the shell, stands stably on the work surface. Keep the leaves attached.

Using a knife with a fine blade, cut round the flesh 1 cm/½ in inside the skin to release the flesh, then use a spoon to detach the rounded bottom part, enabling you to remove the pineapple flesh in one piece. Prepare the other piece of pineapple in the same way.

Reserve the larger shell in the fridge and discard the smaller shell. Cut the pieces of pineapple flesh into 5 mm/¼ in semi-circular slices. Cut the best of these into 12 triangular pieces. Heat the sorbet syrup, poach the pineapple triangles for 20 minutes, then leave to cool in the poaching syrup at room temperature. When they are cold, drain them, reserving the syrup for the sorbet.

THE SORBET: Put all the raw pineapple pieces and pulp into a food processor with half the sorbet syrup. Process for 2 minutes to make a thick coulis, then pass through a fine strainer into a bowl and add the rest of the syrup and the lemon juice. Churn in an ice cream maker for about 20 minutes, until firm. Transfer the sorbet to a container and place in the freezer while you make the ribbon.

THE RIBBON: Preheat the oven to 180°C/350°F/gas 4.

Lay a strip of parcel tape on a baking sheet, then lay the other two parallel to it, spacing the strips 4 cm/1½ in apart. Brush the gaps between the tape very lightly with melted butter. Chill the baking sheet in the fridge for a few minutes, then spread some plain tulip paste as thinly as possible over the two buttered gaps.

Colour the remaining paste with the cocoa, place in a decorating cone and pipe slightly diagonal lines onto the bands of plain paste. Remove the parcel tape and bake the ribbons in the preheated oven for about 4 minutes, until pale golden brown. Take the ribbons out of the oven and, using scissors, immediately cut one of the bands into three equal lengths and fold them into a bow. Cut the second band slightly on the slant into two equal lengths, then slightly crumple them to resemble the two free ends of a ribbon. Keep at room temperature.

PRESENTATION: Spoon half the sorbet into the pineapple shell, then fill it with balls of sorbet, using two different-sized scoops. Top with two small balls in the centre. Arrange the candied pineapple triangles among the balls (you can caramelize them with a blowtorch if you wish). Decorate the balls of sorbet with crystallized violets. Place the pineapple on a large serving plate and arrange the pastry ribbon and bows over the pineapple leaves. Serve immediately.

SPECIAL EQUIPMENT:
*3 strips of parcel tape,
    30 × 5 cm/12 × 2 in
    (for the ribbon)*
*Paper decorating cone (for
    the ribbon)*
Blowtorch (optional)

NOTES:
*The ribbon is an extra
refinement which can be
omitted, although it looks so
attractive that I think it is
worth the effort.*

*All the preparation for
this dessert can be done the
day before; just churn the
sorbet before, or better still,
during the meal to give a
deliciously soft texture.*

*Fill the pineapple shell at
the last moment; it only
takes 5 minutes. For a
marvellous buffet dish, stand
the pineapple shell in a
shallow dish on a bed of
crushed ice.*

Apple Sorbet
Sorbet aux pommes

INGREDIENTS:
300 g/11 oz apples,
    preferably Granny Smiths
300 ml/11 fl oz water
80 g/3 oz caster sugar
40 g/1½ oz liquid glucose
Juice of ½ lemon
½ vanilla pod, split

Serves 6
Preparation time: 10
    minutes, plus about 15
    minutes churning

COOKING THE APPLES: Wash in cold water and cut each apple into 6 or 8 segments. Place in a saucepan with all the other ingredients. Cover and cook over low heat until the apples are almost puréed. Remove the vanilla pod, then liquidize everything else in a blender for 2 minutes to make a very liquid purée. Pass this through a fine conical strainer and leave to cool at room temperature.

CHURNING THE SORBET: As soon as the apple purée is completely cold, churn it in an ice cream maker for 15–20 minutes, depending on your machine. The sorbet should still be quite soft and velvety, so do not churn it for too long.

PRESENTATION: Serve the sorbet as it is, or scoop out the flesh from small raw apples and fill the cavities with apple sorbet.

NOTES:
I do not remove the apple peel or cores, since they contain so much flavour. To enhance this further, you could add 50 ml/2 fl oz Calvados at the end of churning.

Adjust the quantity of sugar to suit the sweetness or tartness of the apples.

Iced Melon Surprise
Melon glacé en surprise

INGREDIENTS:
4 very ripe melons,
    500–600 g/1 lb 2 oz–
    1¼ lbs each
100 ml/4 fl oz Sorbet
    Syrup (page 144)
Juice of ½ lemon
1 quantity Spun Sugar
    (page 182)
24 wild strawberries
Crushed ice (optional)

Serves 4
Preparation time: 25
    minutes, plus about 15
    minutes churning

THE MELONS: Using a knife with a very thin, long blade, divide each melon with six zigzag cuts, starting about two-thirds from the bottom and cutting diagonally into the centre (see photo opposite). Discard the melon seeds. Use a 1 cm/½ in melon baller to scoop out six small balls of flesh from inside each lid, and refrigerate.

Scoop out the rest of the melon flesh with a soup spoon and place in a food processor with the sorbet syrup and lemon juice. Purée for about 2 minutes, to make a kind of thick coulis, then pass it through a sieve and keep in the fridge until ready to churn into a sorbet.

THE SPUN SUGAR: Follow the recipe on page 182, but do not spin the sugar into angel's hair more than 30 minutes before serving the dessert, or the humidity may cause the strands to soften and lose their ethereal quality.

THE SORBET: Pour the melon coulis into an ice cream maker and churn for 10–15 minutes until semi-firm.

PRESENTATION: Put the melon shells into shallow dishes or a bowl two-thirds filled with crushed ice. Using an ice cream scoop, generously fill the shells with balls of sorbet. Arrange a melon ball and a strawberry between each zigzag. Lay a veil of spun sugar on top of each melon and serve immediately.

NOTES:
My favourite melons are Cavaillon or Charentais, which have by far the best flavour. However, other good quality varieties are available throughout the year.

It is difficult to spin sugar successfully in small quantities, so you will need to use 250 g/9 oz sugar for this recipe.

Iced Melon Surprise

Chocolate Sorbet
Sorbet au chocolat

I often accompany my desserts with a chocolate sorbet, especially in winter. Of course it is also delicious served on its own accompanied by some petits fours served on a separate plate.

INGREDIENTS:
400 ml/14 fl oz water
100 ml/4 fl oz milk
150 g/5 oz caster sugar
40 g/1½ oz liquid glucose
30 g/1 oz unsweetened
   cocoa powder
100 g/4 oz bitter couverture
   or best quality cooking
   chocolate, chopped

Serves 8
Preparation time: 15
   minutes, plus about 15
   minutes churning

PREPARATION: Combine the water, milk, sugar, glucose and cocoa in a saucepan and bring to the boil, stirring continuously with a whisk. Simmer over a gentle heat for 2 minutes. Take the pan off the heat, add the chopped chocolate and stir with the whisk for 2 minutes, then pass through a conical strainer into a bowl. Leave to cool at room temperature, then refrigerate.

20 minutes before serving, pour the mixture into an ice cream maker and churn for about 15 minutes, until the sorbet has set. Serve at once, or keep in the freezer.

PRESENTATION: Scoop the sorbet into balls, dipping the scoop into iced water before making each ball. Serve in a large glass compote dish or individual glasses

Grapefruit Granita with Crisp Wafer Biscuits
Granité de pamplemousse dans sa coque et ses dentelles croustillantes

This refreshing dessert with a difference sparkles like diamonds.

INGREDIENTS:
3 very ripe grapefruit,
   preferably pink
50 ml/2 fl oz Sorbet Syrup
   (page 144)
150 g/5 oz caster sugar
4 tablespoons Pastry Cream
   (page 39)
Crushed ice for serving

Serves 6
Preparation time: 20
   minutes, plus freezing

EMPTYING THE GRAPEFRUIT SHELLS: Using the tip of a small sharp knife, make an incision all round the grapefruit without spoiling the segments. Slide a soup spoon into the incision between the skin and segments and ease away the flesh without damaging the skin. Refrigerate the shells. Separate the segments and keep the six best for the garnish.

THE GRAPEFRUIT GRANITA: Purée the rest of the segments with the sorbet syrup in a blender for 1 minute, then pass through a conical strainer. Pour the resulting juice into a shallow stainless steel dish and place in the freezer. Stir the juice with a fork every 30 minutes until it has frozen into large crystals; depending on the temperature of your freezer, this may take 1½ hours (at −25°C/−13°F) or up to 3 hours (at −10°C/14°F).

THE CARAMELIZED GRAPEFRUIT SEGMENTS: In a small heavy-based saucepan, gently cook the sugar without water to a very pale caramel, stirring continuously with a spatula. Turn off the heat and, using a

SPECIAL EQUIPMENT:
Wafer-thin 6 cm/2⅜ in
   diam. template
Non-stick baking sheet, or a
   sheet of Silpat

NOTE:
This dessert can equally well
be made with oranges

fork, dip the grapefruit segments into the sugar, one at a time. Place on a very lightly oiled baking sheet and keep at room temperature.

Grapefruit Granita with Crisp Wafer Biscuits

THE CRISP WAFERS: Preheat the oven to 180°C/350°F/gas 4.

Place the template on a non-stick baking sheet or Silpat, put in a little pastry cream and spread it with a palette knife. Move the template along and repeat the operation until you have used all the pastry cream to make at least twelve wafers (more than a dozen will allow for breakages). Bake for 3 minutes, until pale golden. Lift them off the baking sheet with a palette knife while still hot, and crumple them slightly with your fingertips. Place the crisp wafers on a wire rack.

PRESENTATION: Place a little crushed ice in the bottom of six stemmed glass bowls. Fill the grapefruit shells with the granita and arrange them on the ice. Half-bury a caramelized grapefruit segment in the granita. Place a couple of wafers at the base of each glass, or serve them separately. Serve immediately.

CHAPTER TEN

CHOCOLATE

From prehistoric times, the cacao tree, from which cocoa beans come, has grown wild in Central America. The Mayas were the first people to cultivate the trees, and later the Aztecs used cocoa beans not only to make chocolate-based drinks, but also as currency: one slave cost three beans. Christopher Columbus was the first European to discover the bean, which subsequently became popular in the French court in 1615 through the Spanish Infanta.

Cacao trees are grown in thirty-five tropical countries, but 80% of the world's production comes from six countries, four of them in West Africa — the Ivory Coast, Ghana, Cameroon and Nigeria, which accounts for 52% of this yield. In less than a century, the yield of cacao trees has increased from 115,000 metric tonnes to more than two million.

Tempering chocolate with a palette knife (see page 154)

The three varieties of cacao tree are Criollo, Forastero (which represents 70% of the world's production) and Trinitario. Criollo, which produces only 10% of the crop, is the best and most sought-after cocoa. All the trees are very fragile. They need a warm humid climate, but are sensitive to wind, sunshine, disease and pests, so they are often grown alongside other fruit trees, particularly banana palms, whose broad leaves offer perfect shady protection to this valuable crop.

The process from tree to table is complicated, involving many precise steps, each requiring expertise and constant attention. From a simple bean with very few additions comes a superbly complex, rich, tantalizing taste.

The cocoa pod reaches maturity after five to six months. Each cacao tree produces two annual harvests. In Africa, the main crop is between September and December, with a second small gathering in May and June. The harvest is cracked open within a week of picking and any rotten pods are discarded.

The seeds, which are covered in a sweet white pulp, are fermented under banana leaves for five to seven days, and are stirred regularly to circulate the air. This fermentation is very important to develop the flavour. During the process, the seeds turn from light purple to rich brown.

The next stage is the critical drying process, which enhances the flavour and reduces the humidity to prevent mould. Nowadays, a few factories use industrial blowers to blow warm air onto the seeds, but most are still traditionally sun-dried. After three to seven days drying, the seeds take on their new name of 'cocoa beans' and are then shipped from their country of origin to the factory, to be transformed into chocolate.

The beans are cleaned, dusted and waste is removed. To separate the nibs from the shell and germ, the beans are warmed and winnowed. Only the nibs are then roasted or ground, depending on the desired end product. The roasted beans are coarsely ground, then further refined into a mass known as cocoa paste or liquor. This is used as an ingredient in chocolate-making, or is pressed again to separate the liquid (cocoa butter) from the dry particles (cake). The cocoa butter is deodorized and has the colour removed, while the cake is ground and sifted into cocoa powder. The cocoa paste is mixed with sugar (and powdered milk for milk chocolate), then ground again to a refined, silky texture.

Now follow two long stages called 'conching', which remove any remaining humidity and sourness and fully develop the flavour. Conching can take up to five days. The first process, 'dry conching', aerates the cocoa paste, sugar, milk and flavouring to make the particles even smoother. The second is 'liquid conching', when cocoa butter is added. The resulting liquid chocolate is then sent to the manufacturers, or moulded into blocks for confectioners.

COUVERTURE: Couverture is the finest chocolate used for commercially- and hand-made chocolates and pâtisserie. French legislation determines the following ingredients for couverture:

Dark chocolate is 31% cocoa butter and 16% pure cocoa. Milk chocolate is at least 31% total fats, and contains a maximum of 55% sugar. White chocolate is at least 20% cocoa butter and maximum of 50% sugar. The finest, richest, densely flavoured couverture can have a 76% cocoa solids content; anything above this percentage will taste too bitter.

Couverture can be melted and remoulded after tempering (see page 154). It is used for dipping, decoration and piping. This prized product of pâtissiers can be as important as their skill. The craft of the master is balanced by the quality of the couverture. The taste of the chocolate is reflected in the price you pay. The fruit aroma of the beans cannot deceive the palate with a poor quality product.

Chocolate-based desserts are among my favourites. Generally, they require more care and time than other desserts, but they feature on everyone's hit parade. I like them crunchy, creamy, shiny, featherlight, melting in the mouth – need I say more?

Clockwise from top left: Decorating Chocolate run-outs: Chocolate Teardrop: Modelling Chocolate rose, leaf and stem: Honeycomb Chocolate Discs: Chocolate Curls: Chocolate Fans: Dark and White Modelling Chocolate roses and leaves

TEMPERED COUVERTURE

This process applies to all couverture, and gives it a wonderful sheen; however, when a recipe calls only for melted couverture, it is not necessary to temper it. Cooking chocolate never needs to be tempered, since it cannot achieve the same high gloss as couverture.

Chop the couverture with a heavy knife and melt in a hot cupboard or electric chocolate warmer at the following temperatures:

50°–55°C/122°–131°F for fondant, bittersweet and bitter couverture; 50°C/122°F for milk chocolate, 45°C/113°F for white chocolate. It is essential to use a chocolate thermometer for this process.

Pour about 80% of the melted couverture onto a marble work surface and work it with a triangular scraper or large palette knife, continuously bringing it up over itself until it cools to 26°–27°C/78.8°–80.6°F. Use the triangle or knife to scrape up the chocolate from the work surface and mix it with the untempered couverture. Mix the mass with a spatula until it is all the same temperature (28°–29°C/82.4°–84.2°F for white chocolate, and 30°–32°C/86°–89.6°F for plain or bitter chocolate). If it is a few degrees too hot, pour about one-third back onto the work surface and repeat the operation until it reaches the correct temperature.

The couverture is now ready to use for dipping, coating sweets, moulding etc. Keep it at the correct temperature in a chocolate warmer. Ideally, all chocolate work should be done at a room temperature of 18°–22°C/64.4°–71.6°F, and a humidity level of not more than 50–60%.

CHOCOLATE CURLS AND FANS
Copeaux et éventails chocolat

INGREDIENTS:
100 g/4 oz plain couverture, melted to 35°C/95°F
20 g/¾ oz white couverture, melted to 35°C/95°F

Makes a 30 × 20 cm/ 12 × 8 in sheet
Preparation time: 10 minutes

CHOCOLATE CURLS: Invert the heated baking sheet onto the work surface. Using the white chocolate in the piping cone, draw fine, even lines spacing them close together or further apart, as you prefer. Pour the melted dark couverture evenly over the lines and smooth evenly with a palette knife. Refrigerate for 15 minutes.

Place the baking sheet on the work surface and push the scraper between the chocolate and the baking sheet with short, rapid movements to roll the chocolate into curls (see photo opposite).

CHOCOLATE FANS: Invert the heated baking sheet onto the work surface. Pour on the melted dark couverture and spread it evenly with a palette knife. Using the white chocolate in the piping cone, draw fine even lines all over the surface of the dark chocolate. Refrigerate for 15 minutes.

Place the baking sheet on the work surface. Holding one side of the chocolate with your index finger, push the scraper between the chocolate and the baking sheet with a short, rapid movement to pleat the chocolate into fans (see photo above).

SPECIAL EQUIPMENT:
30 × 20 cm/12 × 8 in baking sheet, preheated to 55°C/131°F
Metal scraper
Paper piping cone

NOTES:
If the chocolate has become too hard after 15 minutes in the fridge, leave it to soften at room temperature for a few minutes before shaping the curls or fans. They will keep well in a cool place for 5 days.

HONEYCOMB CHOCOLATE DISCS
Alvéoles chocolat

THESE CHOCOLATE DISCS RESEMBLE THE CELLS OF A HONEYCOMB AND GIVE A LIGHT, ALMOST AIRY DECORATIVE EFFECT. TEMPERING THE CHOCOLATE MAKES THEM WONDERFULLY SHINY. USE SMALL DISCS TO DECORATE INDIVIDUAL DESSERTS, OR A LARGE DISC FOR A GÂTEAU.

INGREDIENTS:
50 g/2 oz plain couverture, tempered (see page 154)
50g/2 oz white couverture, tempered (see page 154)

Makes twelve 7 cm/2¾ in diam. discs
Preparation time: 10 minutes

Using a pastry brush, spread the plain couverture all over the bumpy side of the bubble wrap (1), then refrigerate for 15 minutes. After this time, use a palette knife to spread the white couverture over the plain couverture (2) and refrigerate for at least another 15 minutes.

Carefully peel the clingfilm-covered bubble wrap off the chocolate honeycomb. Very lightly warm the pastry cutter over a gas flame and cut out twelve chocolate discs. These can be used immediately.

SPECIAL EQUIPMENT:
30 × 25 cm/12 × 10 in sheet of plastic bubble wrap, covered with clingfilm
7 cm/2¾ in pastry cutter

NOTES:
The discs can be made with only one type of chocolate, but you will not achieve the pretty speckled or marbled effect obtained with dark and white chocolate.

The honeycomb discs will keep well for 5 days.

1

2

MODELLING CHOCOLATE
Chocolat plastique

YOU CAN MAKE BEAUTIFUL CHOCOLATE FLOWERS BY TINTING WHITE MODELLING
CHOCOLATE WITH FOOD COLOURINGS, SUCH AS PINK, YELLOW AND ORANGE.

INGREDIENTS:

DARK CHOCOLATE
250 g/9 oz dark couverture,
    melted to 45°C/113°F
100 g/4 oz liquid glucose
    and 60 ml/ 2 fl oz Sorbet
    Syrup (page 144), boiled
    together and cooled to
    35°C/95°F

WHITE CHOCOLATE:
250 g/9 oz white
    couverture, melted to
    45°C/113°F
25 g/1 oz cocoa butter,
    melted and mixed into the
    couverture (for stockist,
    see page 190)
150 g/5 oz liquid glucose
    and 25 ml/1 fl oz Sorbet
    Syrup, boiled together and
    cooled to 35°C/95°F

Makes about 420 g/14 oz
(9–12 roses)
Preparation time: 10
    minutes

MAKING THE MODELLING CHOCOLATE: (This method applies for both dark and white chocolate.) Add the glucose and syrup mixture to the melted chocolate and mix well with a spatula. Pour the mixture onto a marble or formica work surface and continue to mix with the spatula until the chocolate is completely cold and crystallized. Wrap it in clingfilm or a sheet of polythene until ready to use.

TO MAKE CHOCOLATE OR MARZIPAN ROSES: Dust the work surface very lightly with icing sugar. Roll out 35–40 g/1¼–1½ oz chocolate or marzipan to a thickness of 2 mm/ ½2 in, then cut out nine 4 cm/ 1½ in discs with a plain pastry cutter (1). Roll the trimmings into a small ball.

Roll this ball on the work surface with your hand into an

oval or 'bud'. Press one end of the bud against the work surface so that it stands upright (2).

Use the modelling tool to thin down one-half of the edge of each of the nine discs (3). These will be the petals.

Wrap the first petal around the bud, placing the thinned edge at the top, without completely enveloping the bud (4). Use your thumb to curve up the thicker edges of the other petals.

Now, always keeping the thinner edge at the top, build up the other petals over the bud wrapped in its first petal, overlapping them (5). Do not squeeze too hard; just press lightly with your fingertips to attach the base of the petals to the bottom of the bud to resemble an open rose in full bloom.

NOTES:
You will need about 35 g/ 1¼ oz folding chocolate to make a rose. If you wish, tint white folding chocolate with food colourings to obtain pinks, yellows, oranges etc.

Marzipan roses can be modelled in exactly the same way as chocolate flowers. Both will keep well in a dry place at room temperature for several days.

5   6

Press the base of the flower with your fingertips to make it open out even more. With a knife, cut 5 mm/¼ in off the base of the rose to make it stable (6).

WHITE CHOCOLATE LAYER CAKE
Délice ivoirine

A SCOOP OF CHOCOLATE SORBET (PAGE 148) GOES WELL WITH THIS DESSERT, WHICH IS ALSO DELICIOUS BY ITSELF. IT LOOKS PLAIN AND UNADORNED, BUT IS RICH AND CREAMY.

INGREDIENTS: ❊
½ quantity chocolate Genoise Sponge mixture (page 33)
120 ml/4 fl oz Sorbet Syrup (page 144), mixed with 50 ml/2 fl oz Cognac (optional)
1 quantity White Chocolate Mousse (see White Chocolate Dome, page 165)
200 g/7 oz Chocolate Glaze (page 186)

Serves 22
Preparation time: 35 minutes

THE CHOCOLATE SPONGE: Preheat the oven to 200°C/400°F/gas 6.

Spread the sponge mixture over half the baking sheet (ie: 40 × 30 cm/ 16 × 12 in). Bake in the preheated oven for 8 minutes. Slide the Silpat or paper onto a cooling rack and leave the sponge until cold. Cover the cold sponge with a tea towel, then a cooling rack, and invert it.

Peel off the Silpat or paper. Cut the sponge into two 35 × 11 cm/ 14 × 4½ in bands (the size of the cardboard frames), trimming off the outside edges. Moisten with sorbet syrup, place in the bottom of the frames and put them on a baking sheet. Using a palette knife, fill the frames with white chocolate mousse and level the surface as smoothly as possible. Place in the freezer for at least 30 minutes.

PRESENTATION: Shortly before serving, take the desserts out of the freezer and immediately use a palette knife to glaze the tops with warmish (but not too hot) chocolate glaze. Only run the palette knife once over the surface so that the icing sets immediately. Dip a knife blade into hot water and slide it between the inside of the frames and the mousse, then remove the frames. Cut each band into eleven rectangles and place on individual plates. Serve the dessert very cold, almost frozen.

SPECIAL EQUIPMENT:
2 frames made from rigid cardboard covered with foil, 35 cm/12½ in long, 14 cm/4½ in wide, 2.5 cm/1 in deep
60 × 40 cm/24 × 16 in baking sheet lined with Silpat or silicone paper

NOTE:
Because of its composition, it is impossible to make a smaller quantity of this dessert successfully, but you can keep one frozen for a week. Glaze it only just before serving.

CHOCOLATE TEARDROPS WITH WHITE CHOCOLATE MOUSSE AND GRIOTTINES

Larmes de chocolat, mousse ivoirine et griottines

I CLASS THIS DELECTABLY ELEGANT, RESTRAINED DESSERT AS ONE OF MY 'CHOCOLATIER'S FOLLIES'.

INGREDIENTS: ❋
250 g/9 oz bitter
  couverture, tempered (see
  page 154)
1 quantity *White Chocolate*
  Mousse (see White
  Chocolate Dome, page
  165)
72 griottines (small cherries
  in eau-de-vie syrup)
250 ml/9 fl oz eau-de-vie
  syrup from the griottines,
  reduced by one-third over
  low heat
40 g/1½ oz *Tulip Paste*
  (page 28), flavoured wih
  a pinch of cocoa powder
½ quantity *Chocolate Sorbet*
  (page 148)
6 sprigs of mint

Serves 6
Preparation time: 1 hour

THE TEARDROP SHAPES: Using a rocking motion, gently dip one side only of each strip of rodoïde or acetate into the surface of 200 g/7 oz of the tempered couverture (1), or lay the strips on the work table and coat the surface with the thinnest possible layer of couverture.

As soon as the couverture begins to set, stand the first strip upright with the chocolate on the inside, pinch the two ends together in a loop and secure them with a paperclip to make a teardrop shape (2). Place the teardrops on a baking sheet lined with greaseproof paper and refrigerate for 30 minutes.

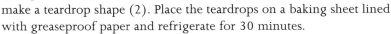

FILLING THE TEARDROPS: Using the piping bag fitted with the plain nozzle, fill the teardrops one-third full with the white chocolate mousse. Arrange 8 griottines in each teardrop, then fill up with mousse and smooth the surface with a palette knife. Refrigerate until ready to serve.

THE CHOCOLATE TULIP PASTE: Preheat the oven to 180°C/350°F/gas 4.

Using the template, spread the paste into six rounds on a non-stick baking sheet. Cook in the preheated oven for 3–4 minutes. Lift off the rounds one at a time with a palette knife and place them in six of the moulds, using the seventh mould to press them into basket shapes to hold the chocolate sorbet.

THE CHOCOLATE FILIGREE: Fill a paper piping cone with some of the remaining melted couverture and pipe very fine filigree patterns no bigger than 4 cm/1½ in diameter onto the sheet of rodoïde or acetate. Place in the fridge.

PRESENTATION: Remove the paperclips and plastic strips from the teardrops and put one on each plate. Using the piping cone, pipe a line of chocolate along the length of each drop and fill it with the cold reduced eau-de-vie syrup. Arrange three griottines on each plate and one on each teardrop, and place a sprig of mint beside it. Fill the pastry baskets with a small scoop of chocolate sorbet and place one on each plate. Delicately peel off the chocolate filigree patterns and stand them aslant on the chocolate sorbet. Serve the dessert extremely cold, almost frozen.

SPECIAL EQUIPMENT:
6 strips of rodoïde or acetate,
  26 × 4.5 cm/10 × 1¾ in
1 sheet of rodoïde or acetate,
  30 × 20 cm/12 × 8 in
Piping bag with a plain
  1 cm/½ in nozzle
6 cm/2⅜ in diam. template
7 moulds, approx. 7.5 cm/
  3 in diam. at the top,
  4 cm/1½ in diam. at the
  base, 2.5 cm/1 in deep
6 paperclips
Paper piping cone

NOTE:
All the elements of this
dessert can be prepared a day
in advance. Arrange all the
different goodies on the plates
just before serving.

CHOCOLATE CAPPUCCINO MOUSSES
Mousse au chocolat, glace café

THIS EASY DESSERT CAN BE MADE A DAY OR TWO IN ADVANCE. IF YOU LIKE, YOU CAN ADD A DASH
OF TIA MARIA TO THE COFFEE CREAM, BUT I PREFER IT PLAIN. THE CONTRAST BETWEEN THE
UNSWEETENED COFFEE CREAM AND THE HALF-SET RICH, SUGARY CHOCOLATE MOUSSE IS UNIQUE.

INGREDIENTS: ❋
250 g/9 oz plain couverture
    or best quality cooking
    chocolate
6 egg whites
125 g/4½ oz caster sugar
4 egg yolks
150 ml/5 fl oz whipping
    cream
1 tablespoon instant coffee
    powder
1 tablespoon unsweetened
    cocoa powder

Serves 4
Preparation time: 20
    minutes

PREPARATION: Chop the chocolate with a chef's knife, place in a bowl and stand it in a bain-marie set over medium heat. Remove from the heat as soon as the chocolate has melted. Beat the egg whites until half-risen, then, still whisking, add the sugar, a little at a time and beat to a very firm snow. Stir the yolks, then 50 ml/2 fl oz of the cream into the melted chocolate and immediately fold in the beaten egg whites delicately with a spatula. As soon as the mixture becomes homogeneous, divide it between the shallow bowls or cups and place in the fridge.

PRESENTATION: Just before serving, dissolve the instant coffee in a scant 2 tablespoons of water. With a fork or whisk, whip the remaining cream into a light, runny foam, then add the coffee. Top the chocolate mousses with the foam, sprinkle with a little cocoa and serve immediately.

SPECIAL EQUIPMENT:
4 shallow serving bowls or
    wide-mouthed, shallow
    cups, 12 cm/4½ in
    diam., 5 cm/2 in deep

CHOCOLATE MILLE-FEUILLE DIAMONDS
Diamants de mille-feuille chocolat

THE CRUNCHY TEXTURE OF THE COUVERTURE MAKES A WONDERFUL
CONTRAST WITH THE LUSCIOUS, CREAMY FILLING

INGREDIENTS: ❋
30 g/1 oz white couverture,
    just melted and tepid
220 g/8 oz plain couverture,
    tempered (see page 154)
125 g/4 oz Coffeee
    Chantilly (page 42)
125 g/4 oz Chocolate
    Chantilly (page 42)
200 ml/7 fl oz Caramel
    Sauce (page 55)

Serves 6
Preparation time: 40
    minutes

THE COUVERTURE DIAMONDS: Lay one sheet of rodoïde on a baking sheet. Fill the paper cone with the tepid white couverture and pipe on a network of vertical, horizontal and diagonal lines. As soon as they have hardened, spread the tempered plain couverture over them. Lay the second sheet of rodoïde on top and very lightly roll a rolling pin over the surface to eliminate all the air bubbles and even up the surface. Leave in a cool place (but on no account in the fridge) until the couverture is set.

Lift off the top sheet of rodoïde. Very slightly warm a thin knife blade over a gas flame and cut three 7 cm/2¾ in wide bands along the length of the couverture. Cut each band slightly on the diagonal into six 3.5 cm/1⅜ in rectangles, lightly warming the knife blade.

Fill one piping bag with coffee Chantilly and one with chocolate Chantilly. Onto twelve of the rectangles, pipe alternating 1 cm/½ in balls of coffee and chocolate cream.

SPECIAL EQUIPMENT:
2 sheets of rodoïde or acetate,
    23 cm/9 in long,
    21 cm/8½ in wide
Paper piping cone
2 piping bags with plain
    1 cm/½ in nozzles

Top six of the cream-filled rectangles with six more cream-filled rectangles, then finish with an unfilled rectangle, placing it with the pattern upwards. Leave the mille-feuille diamonds in the fridge for at least 30 minutes before serving.

NOTE:

This dessert can be prepared several hours in advance: stack the plates on rings and keep them in the fridge. Spoon the caramel sauce onto the plates at the last moment.

PRESENTATION: Place the diamonds on individual serving plates and spoon some caramel sauce beside them. Serve cold.

CHOCOLATE TRUFFLE TRIANGLES
Palets-triangles

THESE ARE THE RICHEST, MOST INDULGENT CHOCOLATES IMAGINABLE.

INGREDIENTS:

GANACHE

55 ml/2 fl oz double cream

170 g/6 oz best quality plain chocolate or dark couverture, melted

80 g/3 oz butter, softened and whipped

15 ml/1 tablespoon aged Armagnac (at least 10 years old)

250 g/9 oz bitter couverture, tempered (page 154), for dipping

Makes 12 triangles, about 35 g/1¼ oz each

Preparation time: 40 minutes

THE GANACHE: In a small saucepan, boil the cream for 1 minute, then cool at room temperature to 35°–40°C/95°–104°F. At this stage, pour the cream onto the melted chocolate and whisk to make a completely homogeneous mixture. Keep in a cool place.

When the ganache has cooled to 20°C/68°F, whisk in small pieces of butter, one at a time. Finally add the Armagnac and whisk until the ganache is smooth and very shiny.

SHAPING THE GANACHE: Pour it into the tray or inside the rulers and smooth the surface with a palette knife. Chill in the fridge for 3 hours.

DIPPING THE TRIANGLES: Invert the tray onto a board and peel off the clingfilm or slightly warm a knife blade over a gas flame, slide it between the inside of the rulers and the ganache and remove the rulers. Slice the ganache rectangle in half along its length to make two bands. Cut each band into three 5.5 cm/2¼ in squares, making six squares in all. Slightly warm the knife blade again and cut each square diagonally to make twelve 5.5 × 5.5 × 8 cm/2¼ × 2¼ × 3¼ in triangles. Using the dipping fork, dip the triangles one at a time into the tempered couverture. Let the excess drip off before placing the triangles on the lined baking sheet. Cover them immediately with the rodoïde triangles (this will make them beautifully shiny) and press lightly with a broad palette knife. Keep in a cool place away from any humidity, which would ruin the shine on the chocolate coating.

PRESENTATION: Remove the rodoïde triangles only just before serving the chocolates so that they remain very glossy. Serve them piled into a pyramid on a round plate.

SPECIAL EQUIPMENT:

A two-pronged fork for dipping

A tray covered with clingfilm, 16.5 cm/6½ in long, 11 cm/4½ in wide, 1.2 cm/½ in deep, or 4 metal confectioner's rulers placed on a baking sheet covered with clingfilm

Chocolate thermometer

Twelve 6.5 × 6.5 × 9 cm/ 2½ × 2½ × 3½ in triangles of rodoïde or acetate

Baking sheet lined with silicone or greaseproof paper

NOTE:

The chocolate-dipped triangles will keep well in a cool place for 5 days.

BITTER CHOCOLATE AND CARAMELIZED WALNUT DELIGHT WITH CARAWAY ICE CREAM

Délice au chocolat amer et cerneaux de noix, glace carvi

YOU CAN TRULY BE PROUD OF THIS MARVELLOUS DESSERT. THE SUBLIME COMBINATION OF CHOCOLATE MOUSSE, WALNUTS AND ICE CREAM AMPLY JUSTIFIES THE TIME SPENT ON ITS PREPARATION.

INGREDIENTS: ❋

CHOCOLATE MOUSSE
4 teaspoons water
100 g/4 oz caster sugar
1 egg, plus 2 extra yolks
275 ml/½ pint whipping
    cream, whipped to a
    ribbon consistency
175 g/6 oz bitter couverture
    or best quality cooking
    chocolate, warmed to
    37°C/98.6°F

CARAMELIZED NUT
    CRUNCHES
75 g/3 oz walnut halves, plus
    75 g/3 oz caster sugar
20 walnut halves, plus
    250 g/9 oz caster sugar

60 g/2 oz Tulip Paste
    (page 28)
30 × 20 cm/12 × 8 in
    sheet baked Joconde Sponge
    (page 31)
150 g/5 oz Chocolate Glaze
    (page 186)
½ quantity Caraway Ice
    Cream (page 138)
500 ml/18 fl oz Honey
    Sauce (page 55)
Zests of 2 limes, cut into
    thin slivers and blanched
    twice
Oil for greasing

Serves 10
Preparation time: 1½ hours,
    plus 2 hours freezing

THE CARAMELIZED NUT CRUNCHES: Put the 75 g/3 oz sugar without any water into a small, heavy-based saucepan, and dissolve over low heat, stirring with a spatula to obtain a pale, nutty caramel. Add the 75 g/3 oz walnuts and mix well. Pour onto a lightly-oiled baking tray and leave at room temperature. When the nuts have cooled, crush them coarsely with a rolling pin to make small nut crunches.

THE TULIP PASTE BASKETS: Preheat the oven to 180°C/350°F/gas 4.

Using the template, spread ten small circles of tulip paste on a non-stick baking sheet, flattening them with a palette knife. Bake for 3–4 minutes, then immediately lift off the circles one at a time with a palette knife and place them in ten of the moulds, pressing down lightly with the eleventh mould to shape little shallow baskets for the ice cream.

THE JOCONDE SPONGE: Using the pastry cutter, cut out ten circles from the baked sponge. Place these in the dessert rings, arrange on a baking sheet and leave at room temperature.

THE CHOCOLATE MOUSSE: Put the water in a saucepan, add the sugar and bring to the boil over low heat. Wash down the inside of the pan with a pastry brush dipped in cold water, and cook the sugar until the temperature reaches 115°C/240°F. Now work the egg and yolks in a bowl, either by hand or with an electric mixer. As soon as the sugar reaches 121°C/250°F, turn off the heat, leave the syrup to rest for 1 minute, then pour it gently onto the eggs, whisking continuously until completely cold. Add the melted chocolate, then stir in the nut crunches with a spatula. Finally, fold in the whipped cream. Fill the dessert rings with this chocolate mousse, smooth the surface with a palette knife and freeze for at least 2 hours.

THE CARAMELIZED WALNUTS AND CARAMEL DECORATION: In a small, heavy-based saucepan, heat the 250 g/9 oz sugar without water over low heat, stirring continuously, until pale caramel. Immediately turn off the heat. Dip the 20 walnut kernels in the caramel, one at a time, and use a fork to transfer them to a lightly oiled baking tray. If the caramel becomes too thick while you are dipping the walnuts, reheat it over very low heat. Keep the caramelized walnuts in a dry place.

Dip the prongs of a fork in the caramel (reheated if necessary) and swirl the sugar into whatever shape you like – spirals, criss-crosses

SPECIAL EQUIPMENT:
10 dessert rings, 6.5 cm/
    2½ in diam., 3 cm/1¼ in
    deep
11 moulds approx. 7.5 cm/
    3 in diam. at the top,
    4 cm/1½ in diam. at the
    base, 2.5 cm/1 in deep
6 cm/2⅜ in diam. wafer-
    thin template
6.5 cm/2½ in pastry cutter
Sugar thermometer
Non-stick baking sheet, or a
    sheet of Silpat
Blowtorch (optional)

NOTES:
All the separate elements of
this dessert can be prepared
several hours before the meal.

The mousses freeze well
for a week, so make them a
few days in advance.

etc. – as it runs off onto a non-stick baking sheet or a sheet of Silpat. Repeat to make about ten caramel decorations. Keep in a dry place.

GLAZING THE MOUSSES: Pour a little chocolate glaze onto one un-moulded mousse and smooth the surface with a palette knife. Glaze all the mousses in this way.

PRESENTATION: Gently heat the outside of the rings with a blowtorch, or run a knife blade dipped in hot water between the rings and the mousses. Remove the rings by rotating them gently upwards.

Place a mousse on each plate, then a basket filled with a 4 cm / 1 ½ in scoop of caraway ice cream. Arrange a caramel decoration aslant on the ice cream and place one walnut half on the mousse and another on the ice cream. Spoon a little honey sauce and some lime zest between the mousses and baskets of ice cream, and serve at once.

WHITE CHOCOLATE DOMES WITH RASPBERRY PARFAIT AND DARK CHOCOLATE CURLS

Dômes aux deux chocolats et ses framboises

I PARTICULARLY LOVE THIS DESSERT FOR ITS SMOOTH SHAPE AND THE VISUAL AND GASTRONOMIC CONTRAST BETWEEN THE PURITY OF THE WHITE MOUSSE AND THE RICHNESS OF THE DARK PARFAIT. ALTHOUGH IT DOES TAKE TIME, IT IS QUITE SIMPLE TO PREPARE, AND THE PLEASURE IT GIVES YOUR GUESTS WILL BE TINGED WITH ENVY AND ADMIRATION OF YOUR SKILL.

INGREDIENTS:

Italian Meringue (page 37), made with 100 g/ 4 oz egg whites and 75 g/ 3 oz caster sugar

1 quantity Raspberry Parfait (see Cardinal Gâteau, page 103)

WHITE CHOCOLATE MOUSSE

200 g/7 oz white couverture or best quality cooking chocolate, chopped

50 g/2 oz butter, melted

450 ml/16 fl oz whipping cream, whipped to a ribbon consistency

350 g/12 oz raspberries

30 × 20 cm/12 × 8 in sheet of baked Joconde Sponge (page 31), cut into ten 8 cm/3¼ in circles

80 Chocolate Fans or Curls (page 154)

10 mint sprigs

200 g/7 oz thick Raspberry Coulis (see Fruit Coulis, page 51)

Serves 10

Preparation time: 30 minutes

THE ITALIAN MERINGUE: Follow the recipe on page 37. Do not make the meringue in advance; it should be freshly made and just cold.

THE RASPBERRY PARFAIT: Make this after you have prepared the meringue, following the recipe on page 103. Do not prepare it more than 30 minutes in advance.

THE WHITE CHOCOLATE MOUSSE: Put the white couverture in a small bowl and stand it in a bain-marie. Heat over medium heat to 40°C/104°F, stirring occasionally.

Whisk the melted butter into the warm couverture without overworking it. Still using a whisk, fold in one-third of the cold whipped cream, then the meringue. Finally fold in the rest of the cream very delicately until the mousse is perfectly blended.

ASSEMBLING THE DOMES: Using the piping bag, pipe about 50 g/2 oz mousse into the bottom of the moulds. Using a palette knife, spread the mousse up the insides of the moulds to cover them completely, then place in the freezer to harden for 10–15 minutes.

THE RASPBERRIES: Reserve about thirty of the best for decoration. Arrange six raspberries in the bottom of each mould on top of the hardened mousse. Fill up the moulds with the raspberry parfait and smooth the surface with a palette knife. Top each one with a joconde sponge circle, pressing it delicately and lightly with your fingertips onto the parfait. Cover the moulds with clingfilm and keep in the freezer until ready to serve.

PRESENTATION: Heat the outside of the moulds for 2 or 3 seconds with a blowtorch, or by dipping them briefly into boiling water. Invert the moulds onto serving plates and unmould the domes. Arrange the chocolate fans or curls around the base. Place three raspberries and a mint sprig on top of each dome. Pour a little raspberry coulis around the domes on one side of the plates and serve very cold, but not frozen.

SPECIAL EQUIPMENT:

Chocolate thermometer

10 hemispherical moulds, 9 cm/3½ in diam., 4.5 cm/1¾ in high

Piping bag with a plain 1 cm/½ in nozzle

Blowtorch (optional)

NOTE:

This dessert can be frozen for at least a week, so you could serve the domes at more than one meal.

CHAPTER ELEVEN

PETITS FOURS

Petits fours come in many forms, but of course they are always small. Their colours range from glowing to brilliant to understated, depending on the type. They are particularly delicious when freshly made, since they hate humidity, heat and especially the cold. Sadly, not many people really appreciate them, and still fewer have mastered the art of preparing them.

But what delight, what luxury to nibble one or two petits fours with your coffee! It is a mistake to offer too much choice; my advice is to serve only two or three well-made varieties.

In this chapter, you will find a large selection of petits fours. Some are more appropriate to certain seasons than others. For example, you would serve Blackcurrant Jellies in summer and Chocolate Tuiles in winter. My own personal favourites to serve with coffee are the *petits fours secs* or chocolate petits fours, such as Hazelnut Tuiles, Little Lemon Cakes and Chocolate Quenelles.

Petits fours also go very well with ice creams and sorbets and certainly justify the time spent in preparing them.

Dipping a pineapple segment into syrup

CANDIED PINEAPPLE SEGMENTS
Fruits déguisés à l'ananas

A PETIT FOUR TO SHOW OFF YOUR SKILLS, WHICH IS WELL WORTH THE
EFFORT INVOLVED IN THE PREPARATION.

INGREDIENTS:
1 pineapple, about 1.5 kg/
    3¼ lbs
120 g/4 oz marzipan, made
    with 33% almonds
Icing sugar for dusting

SYRUP
400 g/14 oz caster sugar
250 ml/9 fl oz water
COOKED SUGAR
250 g/9 oz caster sugar
50 g/2 oz liquid glucose
100 ml/4 fl oz water

Makes 20
Preparation time: 1 hour 10
    minutes

SPECIAL EQUIPMENT:
Small copper sugar pan, or a
    heavy-based saucepan
Two-pronged fork for dipping
Plain 1.5 cm/⅝ in pastry
    cutter
Sugar thermometer
1 lightly-oiled baking sheet

PREPARING THE PINEAPPLE: Using a very sharp knife, cut off the two ends of the pineapple and remove all the skin from the fruit. Cut eight attractive slices, about 5 mm/¼ in thick, from the peeled pineapple. Remove the fibrous core with the pastry cutter.

POACHING THE PINEAPPLE RINGS: Dissolve the caster sugar in the water to make a syrup and bring to the boil. Drop in the pineapple rings and poach gently at 90°C/194°F for 1 hour. Turn off the heat and leave the pineapple to cool slightly in the syrup. When the rings are barely warm, arrange them delicately on a draining rack and leave until completely cold.

Dust the work surface with icing sugar. Roll out the marzipan to the same diameter as the pineapple and 3 mm/⅛ in thick. Pile four pineapple rings on the marzipan. Trim off any excess marzipan from around the edge and the centre with a small, sharp knife, following the contours of the pineapple. Turn over the four rings and top with the remaining rings so that the marzipan is sandwiched between the two. Cut each 'sandwich' into five regular segments and place on a wire rack.

COOKING THE SUGAR: Combine the water, sugar and glucose in the sugar pan and bring to the boil over low heat. Skim the surface and wash down the inside of the pan with a pastry brush dipped in cold water. Put in the thermometer and cook to 151°C/303.8°F. Turn off the heat and leave the sugar to bubble down for 2 minutes.

Insert the dipping fork into the centre of the pineapple segments and dip them in the cooked sugar, one by one (see photo, opposite). As soon as they are coated with sugar, take them out and leave them to drain for 2 or 3 seconds. Place on a lightly-oiled baking sheet and leave until cold.

PRESENTATION: Ideally, the pineapple segments should be served on a silver platter, to set off the beautiful sheen of the sugar coating.

BLACKCURRANT JELLIES
Pâté de fruits

THESE PETITS FOURS ARE AMONGST THE SIMPLEST TO MAKE, YET ONE OF THE TASTIEST. IT IS A RARE PERSON WHO EATS FEWER THAN FOUR OR FIVE IN ONE GO! YOU COULD USE STRAWBERRIES OR APRICOTS INSTEAD OF BLACKCURRANTS; THEY ARE PARTICULARLY DELICIOUS WHEN THE FRUITS ARE IN HIGH SEASON.

INGREDIENTS:
200 g/7 oz fresh or frozen blackcurrant pulp (drained weight)
180 g/6 oz caster sugar
15 g/½ oz pectin mixed with 20 g/¾ oz caster sugar
50 g/2 oz granulated sugar

Makes 35
Preparation time: 15 minutes

THE JELLY MIXTURE: In a heavy-based saucepan, heat the blackcurrant pulp to 50°C/122°F. Add the 180 g/6 oz caster sugar and bring to the boil. Skim the surface, add the pectin and sugar mixture and cook to 103°C/217.4°F. Take the pan off the heat and leave the fruit to bubble down for 10 seconds.

Pour the mixture into the tray or rulers and leave to cool at room temperature for at least 2 hours.

PRESENTATION: Remove the jelly from the tray or rulers and cut into thirty-five 2 cm/¾ in cubes. Roll them delicately in the granulated sugar and arrange on a plate, alone or with other petits fours.

SPECIAL EQUIPMENT:
Sugar thermometer
A tray, 14 cm/6 in long, 10 cm/4 in wide, 1.5 cm/⅝ in deep, lined with cling film, or 4 metal confectioner's rulers, placed on a baking sheet covered with clingfilm

NOTES:
Fruit jellies will keep for a week in a cool but not humid place.

If you want to make a larger quantity, cook the mixture to 105°C/221°F instead of 103°C/217.4°F

CANDIED GRAPEFRUIT PEEL
Aiguillettes de pamplemousse confites

ONLY THE GRAPEFRUIT PEEL IS USED FOR THIS RECIPE, SO SERVE THE CHILLED SEGMENTS WITH A COUPLE OF SPOONS OF THE POACHING SYRUP FOR A REFRESHING DESSERT.

INGREDIENTS:
1 grapefruit, about 360 g/ 12 oz, washed
400 g/14 oz caster sugar
300 ml/10 fl oz water
50 g/2 oz granulated sugar

THE GRAPEFRUIT: Using a very sharp knife with a flexible blade, cut off a 5 mm/¼ in sliver from the top and bottom of the fruit. Starting from the top of the grapefruit and following its contour, cut off about five strips of peel, 6 cm/2⅜ in long and 5 cm/2 in wide, removing all the pith and membrane from the fruit. Cut each strip into five long, thin batons.

NOTES:
These delicious petits fours keep well at room temperature for 3 days, but will lose some of their soft texture after a day or two.

168

Makes 25
Preparation time: 25
  minutes
Cooking time: 1½ hours

POACHING THE BATONS: Place in a saucepan, cover with cold water and bring to the boil. Refresh, drain and repeat the process four times.

Put the sugar and water in a saucepan and gently bring to the boil. Immediately drop in the five-times-blanched grapefruit batons. Poach gently without boiling at about 90°C/194°F for about 1½ hours.

Leave the batons to cool slightly in the poaching syrup. Place on a wire rack while still just warm and drain until completely cold, then roll them in the granulated sugar.

PRESENTATION: Place the batons in paper petits fours cases and serve with coffee, by themselves or with other petits fours.

SPECIAL EQUIPMENT:
Sugar thermometer

MINI-TARTLETS WITH BERRY FRUITS
Mini-tartelettes aux fruits rouges

I CAN NEVER HAVE ENOUGH OF THESE PETITS FOURS. DECORATE THEM WITH BLACKCURRANTS, GRAPES, WILD STRAWBERRIES OR WHAT YOU WILL.

INGREDIENTS: ❈
Flour for dusting
120 g/4 oz Sweet Short
  Pastry (page 20)
1 soup spoon strawberry or
  raspberry jam
170 g/6 oz Frangipane
  (page 43)
100 ml/4 fl oz whipping
  cream, whipped with
  10 g/⅓ oz icing sugar
20 attractive raspberries,
  small strawberrries, small
  clusters of redcurrants or
  bilberries
20 small mint leaves

Makes 20
Preparation time: 20
  minutes
Cooking time: 8 minutes

MAKING THE TARTLETS: Preheat the oven to 180°C/350°F/gas 4.

On a lightly floured work surface, roll out the pastry to a thickness of 2 mm/1⁄12 in. Cut out twenty rounds and line the tins with them. Using a paper cone, pipe a little jam into the bottom of the pastry cases. Fill with frangipane and bake in the preheated oven for 8 minutes. Unmould the tartlets onto a cooling rack.

PRESENTATION: Just before serving, pipe a rosette of whipped cream onto each tartlet. Decorate with the fruit of your choice and a mint leaf. Arrange the tartlets on a china plate, or better still, on a silver platter with other petits fours.

SPECIAL EQUIPMENT:
20 tartlet tins, 4.5 cm/
  1¾ in at the top, 2.5 cm/
  1 in diam. at the base,
  1 cm/½ in deep
Paper piping cone
Piping bag with a fluted
  1 cm/½ in nozzle
5 cm/2 in fluted pastry
  cutter

NOTE:
The pastry cases must be freshly baked, so it is essential to serve the tartlets the day they are made.

PROVENCAL CARAMEL CUPS

Coques au caramel provençales

MY FRIEND DANIEL GIRAUD FROM VALENCE GAVE ME THE RECIPE FOR THESE
PROVENCAL PETITS FOURS, WITH THEIR CRISP CHOCOLATE SHELLS AND DIVINELY SOFT
CARAMEL CENTRES. THEY ARE A GREAT FAVOURITE AT THE WATERSIDE INN.

INGREDIENTS:

200 g/7 oz milk chocolate
   couverture, tempered (page
   154)
70 g/2½ oz caster sugar
20 g/⅔ oz butter
25 ml/1 fl oz whipping cream

THE CHOCOLATE CUPS: Dip the outside of the paper cases one by one
into the tempered couverture and place on a baking sheet lined with
clingfilm. Leave to harden in a cool place, but not the fridge. Repeat
the operation to give a second coating of chocolate. When this has
hardened, delicately peel off the paper cases one by one. The
chocolate cups will weigh about 5 g/⅙ oz each. Keep them in a cool
place away from any humidity.

SPECIAL EQUIPMENT:

Small heavy-based saucepan
20 rigid paper sweet cases,
   4 cm/1½ in at the
   opening, 2.5 cm/1 in at
   the base, 1.5 cm/⅝ in
   deep

60 g/2 oz fondant

20 g/⅔ oz highly perfumed runny honey

25 g/1 oz toasted flaked almonds

Makes 20

Preparation time: 40 minutes

THE CARAMEL FILLING: Put the sugar in the pan and dissolve it over low heat without water, stirring continuously with a spatula. As soon as it turns to a pale golden caramel, turn off the heat. Stir in the butter, then the cream and finally the fondant and honey. Stir until the mixture is smooth and homogeneous, then add the almonds and fold them in delicately so as not to break them too much. Leave the mixture to go completely cold in a cool place. Fill the chocolate cups with the cold filling and keep in the fridge until ready to serve.

PRESENTATION: Arrange the caramel cups on a small plate or tray and serve with coffee. They will be much appreciated.

Left to right: Provençal Caramel Cups, Piped Almond Petits Fours, Chocolate Tuiles, Little Lemon Cakes, Candied Pineapple Segments, Chocolate Quenelles, Mini-Tartlets with Berry Fruits, Hazelnut Tuiles, Macaroons, Blackcurrant Jellies with Candied Grapefruit Peel

CHOCOLATE QUENELLES
Quenelles au chocolat

DO NOT HESITATE TO PROVIDE THREE OR FOUR OF THESE WONDERFUL
CHOCOLATE TREATS PER PERSON.

INGREDIENTS:

1 quantity Ganache (see
  Chocolate Truffle
  Triangles, page 161),
  made with whisky instead
  of Armagnac
150 g/5 oz bitter couverture,
  melted
100 g/4 oz unsweetened
  cocoa powder, sifted

Makes about 32
Preparation time: 20
  minutes

THE GANACHE: Prepare it following the recipe on page 161. As soon as
it is ready, form it into small quenelles, using two teaspoons, and
place them on a sheet of greaseproof or silicone paper. Refrigerate for
at least 2 hours.

FINISHING THE QUENELLES: Using a fork, dip them quickly one at a time
into the melted couverture, then roll them in the cocoa and place on
a wire rack. Keep in a cool place until ready to serve.

PRESENTATION: It is best to serve the quenelles in little paper cases so
that your guests are not showered with cocoa as they pick them up.
Serve them alone or with other petits fours.

NOTE:
The quenelles will keep in a
cool place for 5 days.

HAZELNUT TUILES
Tuiles noisette

THESE TUILES ARE DELICIOUS SERVED WITH ICE CREAM OR ON THEIR
OWN WITH COFFEE.

INGREDIENTS:
70 g/2½ oz egg whites
90 g/3½ oz caster sugar
15 g/½ oz flour
100 g/4 oz very finely
  ground hazelnuts
4 teaspoons hazelnut oil

Makes about 50
Preparation time: 15
  minutes
Cooking time: 10 minutes

THE PASTE: In a small bowl, beat the egg whites 5 or 6 times with a
fork until slightly frothy. Add the sugar, mix it in with a spatula, then
mix in the flour and ground hazelnuts and finally the hazelnut oil.
Cover with clingfilm and leave at room temperature for 1 hour.
  Meanwhile, preheat the oven to 220°C/425°F/gas 7.

SHAPING AND BAKING THE TUILES: Work the mixture with a spatula for a

SPECIAL EQUIPMENT:
1 wafer-thin template,
  7 cm/2¾ in diam.
2 lightly greased, well-
  chilled baking sheets
1 gutter-shaped tuile mould,
  or a rolling pin

NOTE:
The tuiles will keep well for
a week in an airtight
container in a dry
atmosphere, so you can treat
yourself to some home-made
petits fours with your
morning coffee.

few seconds. Lay the template on one chilled baking sheet, put in a little tuile mixture and level it out to the sides with a palette knife. Move the template a little way along and use all the mixture to make about twenty-five tuiles in this way.

Place the tuiles in the hot oven and lower the temperature to 200°C/400°F/gas 6. Bake for about 5 minutes, until very pale golden. Take the tuiles out of the oven and immediately, using a palette knife, lift them one at a time onto the tuile mould or rolling pin. Leave to cool. Shape and bake a second batch in the same way.

PRESENTATION: Arrange the tuiles on a plate and dust with a light veil of icing sugar or serve them plain.

CHOCOLATE TUILES
Tuiles au chocolat

THESE TUILES SHOULD BE STORED IN A COOL, DRY PLACE . . . BUT THEY MAY NOT REMAIN THERE FOR LONG. ONCE YOU HAVE TASTED ONE, THE SHEER PLEASURE WILL TEMPT YOU TO EAT AT LEAST ANOTHER FOUR, SO I SUGGEST YOU PROVIDE THIRTY TUILES FOR SIX PEOPLE!

INGREDIENTS:
250 g/9 oz plain or white couverture or best quality cooking chocolate, chopped
75 g/3 oz nibbed almonds, toasted and cooled

Makes 30
Preparation time: 15 minutes

PREPARING THE TUILES: Temper the couverture (following the method on page 154) and stir in the toasted almonds. Place the template on one of the strips of rodoïde and fill with about 1 tablespoon of the chocolate and almond mixture. Move the template a little distance away and spread in the mixture again, repeating the process to make a maximum of five tuiles per strip.

As soon as you have prepared the first strip, slide it onto the tuile mould or rolling pin to curve the rodoïde and thus the tuiles, and leave to cool. Lift the tuiles off the rodoïde only after the chocolate has set and just before serving, so that they keep their brilliant shine.

SPECIAL EQUIPMENT:
Cardboard template, 6 cm/ 2⅜ in diam.
6 strips of rodoïde or flexible acetate, about 10 cm/ 4 in wide
Gutter-shaped tuile mould or rolling pin

NOTE:
Before spreading plain couverture in the template, you could smear the rodoïde strips with a little melted white couverture, using the tip of your index finger to give an attractive marbled effect of white on brilliant brown. This will make the tuiles even prettier.

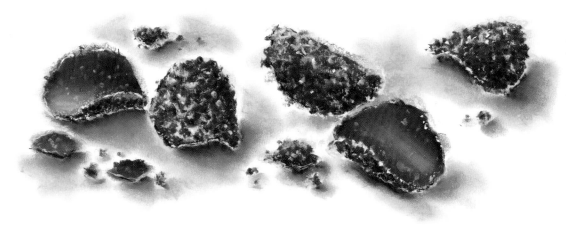

SOFT MACAROONS
Macarons tendres ou 'Progrès'

INGREDIENTS:

200 g/7 oz tant pour
    tant (equal quantities of
    icing sugar and ground
    almonds, sifted together)
15 g/½ oz flour, sifted
37.5 g/1½ oz cornflour
45 ml/1½ fl oz tepid milk
175 ml/6 fl oz egg whites
150 g/5 oz caster sugar
60 g/2 oz flaked almonds
15 g/½ oz icing sugar

Makes about 35
Preparation time: 25
    minutes
Cooking time: 12 minutes

PREPARATION: Preheat the oven (preferably a convection fan oven) to 160°–170°C/325°F/gas 3.

Combine the tant pour tant, flour, cornflour and milk in a bowl and carefully blend with a spatula.

Beat the egg whites until half-risen, then whisk in the sugar, a little at a time, until the whites are very firm and almost like meringue. Delicately and gradually fold the egg whites into the tant pour tant mixture with a slotted spoon. As soon as it becomes homogeneous, stop working the mixture, and put it into a piping bag with a plain nozzle. It must be used immediately.

PIPING AND COOKING THE MACAROONS: Line the baking sheets with your chosen paper or Silpat and pipe on seventy 4 cm/1½ in balls of the macaroon mixture, spacing them 4 cm/1½ in apart. Sprinkle the macaroons with a few flaked almonds, then dust with a light veil of icing sugar. Bake in the preheated oven for 12 minutes.

Remove the macaroons from the oven and slide the paper or Silpat onto cooling racks. When the macaroons are cold, assemble them in pairs, pressing them very lightly together.

PRESENTATION: Arrange the macaroons on a plate lined with a doily and serve them alone or with other petits fours.

SPECIAL EQUIPMENT:

Piping bag with a plain
    7 cm/2¾ in nozzle
Four 30 × 20 cm/12 × 8 in,
    or two 60 × 40 cm/
    24 × 16 in baking sheets,
    lined with greaseproof or
    silicone paper or Silpat

NOTES:

Make large macaroons by
piping them into 6 cm/
2⅜ in balls. Sandwich these
with a praliné-flavoured
Buttercream (page 41).

Macaroons freeze well for
3 or 4 days, but they are at
their delectable best served on
the day they are made, when
they are divinely melting,
and almost creamy

PISTACHIO MACAROONS
Macarons à la pistache

INGREDIENTS:

350 g/12 oz icing sugar
300 g/11 oz ground
    almonds
350 g/11 oz egg whites
250 g/9 oz icing sugar
85 g/3 oz pistachio paste
2 drops of green food
    colouring

Makes 90
Preparation time: 35
    minutes
Cooking time: 20 minutes

THE MACAROON MIXTURE: Preheat the oven to 120°C/240°F/gas 1. Process the 350 g/12 oz icing sugar and ground almonds for 1 minute at medium speed in a food processor, then sift. Follow the method for Chocolate Macaroons (opposite) until the egg whites are stiffly beaten with all the icing sugar. Mix the food colouring into the pistachio paste, soften with a little beaten egg white, then mix into the rest of the egg whites without overworking. Shower the dry ingredients from a height onto the pistachio-flavoured egg whites, folding them in with a skimmer. Mix gently until the mixture is very slightly runny and completely homogeneous.

PIPING AND COOKING THE MACAROONS: Pipe ninety 2.5 cm/1 in balls of mixture onto the greaseproof paper. Cook for 20 minutes, following the method for Chocolate Macaroons.

PRESENTATION: Pile the pistachio macaroons in a pyramid on a plate.

SPECIAL EQUIPMENT:

Four 60 × 40 cm/24 × 16
    in baking sheets
2 sheets of greaseproof paper
Piping bag with a plain
    1 cm/½ in nozzle

CHOCOLATE MACAROONS
Macarons chocolat

THE NAME 'MACAROON' DERIVES FROM THE VENETIAN MACARONE, MEANING
A FINE PASTE.

INGREDIENTS:

DRY INGREDIENTS

500 g/1 lb 2 oz icing
sugar, plus an extra
75 g/ 3 oz

50 g/2 oz unsweetened
cocoa powder

275 g/10 oz ground
almonds

250 g/9 oz fresh egg whites

15 g/½ oz powdered egg
white

Makes 110

Preparation time: 25
minutes

Cooking time: 10 minutes

THE DRY INGREDIENTS: Put the 500 g/1 lb 2 oz icing sugar, the cocoa and ground almonds in a food processor and process at medium speed for 1 minute, then sift coarsely onto a sheet of greaseproof paper. Keep at room temperature.

THE EGG WHITES: Beat the fresh egg whites in an electric mixer until half-risen, then add the 75 g/3 oz icing sugar and beat until stiff. Immediately add the powdered egg white and continue to beat for another 3 minutes.

Meanwhile, preheat the oven to 250°C/500°F/gas 10.

Sprinkle the dry ingredients onto the egg whites and fold in delicately with a slotted spoon to make a perfectly smooth, very slightly runny paste.

PIPING THE MACAROONS: Pipe the mixture on to the 2 sheets of paper to make one hundred and ten 2.5 cm/1 in balls.

COOKING THE MACAROONS: Carefully slide the paper onto two baking sheets and double up each sheet on another one (hence the need for four baking sheets). Place in the very hot oven, immediately reduce the temperature to 150°C/300°F/gas 2, and cook for 10 minutes.

As soon as the macaroons come out of the oven, run a trickle of cold water between the greaseproof paper and the baking sheet so that the macaroons can be detached more easily (this is not necessary with silicone paper). Leave them like this for 10 minutes, then carefully lift off the macaroons and assemble them in pairs, pressing them together very lightly.

PRESENTATION: Pile the macaroons in a pyramid on a plate and serve them alone or with other petits fours.

SPECIAL EQUIPMENT:

2 sheets of greaseproof or
silicone paper

Four 60 × 40 cm/
24 × 16 in baking sheets

Piping bag with a plain
1 cm/½ in nozzle

NOTES:

Ideally, the macaroons should be cooked in a convection fan oven.

Do not be put off by the large quantities in this recipe. It is difficult to prepare macaroons successfully in smaller quantities. They freeze well for a couple of weeks; peel them off the paper, stick them together and immediately arrange them on a tray, wrap in clingfilm and freeze. To serve, leave the clingfilm over the macaroons until they are completely defrosted so that they remain shiny and do not lose their lustre. They will also keep well for several days in an airtight container. Store at room temperature in a very dry place.

CANNELÉS
Les Cannelés

CANNELÉS, A CLASSICAL SPECIALITY FROM BORDEAUX, ARE QUITE UNLIKE ANY OTHER PETITS FOURS; THEY ARE CRUNCHY ON THE OUTSIDE AND SOFT IN THE CENTRE, WITH A MOST DELICIOUS FLAVOUR. THEY ARE NOT EXACTLY LIGHT — BUT EVEN THE MOST BEAUTIFUL GIRL IN THE WORLD DOESN'T HAVE EVERYTHING! BOTH MY BROTHER AND I LOVE THEM; THE RECIPE WAS GENEROUSLY DONATED BY MY FRIEND MANUEL LOPEZ FROM THE PATISSERIE LOPEZ IN LIBOURNE.

INGREDIENTS:

250 ml/9 fl oz unsweetened condensed milk, or
350 ml/ 12 fl oz full cream sweetened condensed milk

540 g/1¼ lbs caster sugar (or 440 g/1 lb if using sweetened condensed milk)

240 g/9 oz flour

3 whole eggs, plus 2 extra yolks

75 ml/3 fl oz rum

600 ml/1 pint water

60 g/2 oz butter

60 g/2 oz full fat powdered milk

Makes 36
Preparation time: 15 minutes, plus at least 24 hours chilling
Cooking time: about 55 minutes

THE CANNELÉ MIXTURE: Combine the condensed milk, sugar (if using sweetened condensed milk, use only 440 g/1 lb sugar), flour, whole eggs and yolks and the rum in a large bowl and mix with a spatula.

Put the water, butter and powdered milk into a saucepan and bring to the boil, whisking continuously. Pour the boiling liquid onto the egg and condensed milk mixture, still whisking all the time. Mix thoroughly until very smooth, then pass through a conical strainer and leave to cool completely. Transfer the mixture to an airtight container and refrigerate for at least 24 hours.

Preheat the oven to 200°C/400°F/gas 6.

GREASING THE MOULDS: In a saucepan, melt the beeswax over very low heat, then mix in the oil. Warm the moulds in the oven for a few seconds. Lightly brush the insides of the moulds with the beeswax and oil mixture, then place them upside-down on a cooling rack for about 5 minutes, until the wax has set. Arrange the moulds on a chilled baking sheet.

BAKING THE CANNELÉS: Give the cannelé mixture a good whisk, then fill the moulds to within 2 mm/¹⁄₁₂ in of the top. Bake in the oven for 30 minutes, then turn the baking sheet through 180° and bake for another 20–25 minutes, until the cannelés are deeply coloured. Immediately unmould them onto a cooling rack.

PRESENTATION: Serve the cannelés just warm, arranging them on a plate lined with a doily. They can be served with other petits fours, but are delicious on their own.

SPECIAL EQUIPMENT:

36 cannelé or croquette moulds, 4.5 cm/1¾ in diam., 4.5 cm/1¾ in deep

Equal small quantities of groundnut oil and beeswax, for greasing the moulds

NOTE:

The uncooked mixture will keep in the fridge for 4 or 5 days, which allows you to bake the cannelés as and when you want them.

PIPED ALMOND PETITS FOURS

Petits fours pochés aux amandes

INGREDIENTS:

150 g/5 oz marzipan, made
  with 50% almonds
15 g/½ oz egg white
13 whole blanched almonds
30 ml/2 tablespoons Sorbet
  Syrup (page 144),
  (optional)

Makes 26
Preparation time: 15
  minutes
Cooking time: 4 minutes,
  plus 8 hours resting

PREPARING THE PETITS FOURS: Put the marzipan and egg white on the work surface and work together with the palm of your hand. Place in the piping bag and pipe onto the baking sheet into the shape of thirteen commas and thirteen teardrops, 2.5 cm/1 in long. Place an almond on each teardrop. Leave on the baking sheet for about 8 hours at a temperature of 30°–35°C/86°–95°F, so that a crust forms on the surface.

COOKING THE PETITS FOURS: Preheat the oven to 230°C/450°F/gas 8 for 20 minutes before cooking the petits fours, then bake for 4 minutes. As soon as they come out of the oven, run a little cold water between the paper and the baking sheet, and brush the petits fours with sorbet syrup if you wish. It will give them a sheen, but also sweeten them a little. After 5 minutes, remove the petits fours one by one and place on a wire rack.

PRESENTATION: Arrange the petits fours on a plate or platter, alone or mixed with other varieties.

SPECIAL EQUIPMENT:
Piping bag with a fluted
  1 cm/½ in nozzle
Baking sheet lined with
  silicone or greaseproof
  paper

NOTE:
These easy-to-make petits
fours will keep well at room
temperature for 3 days.

LITTLE LEMON CAKES
Petits cakes citron

INGREDIENTS:

1 egg

A small pinch of salt

85 g/3 oz caster sugar

Zest of ½ lemon, very finely grated

40 ml/1½ fl oz double cream

25 g/1 oz butter, melted and cooled

70 g/2½ oz flour, mixed with 1 g/¹⁄₃₀ oz fresh yeast

LEMON ICING:

70 g/2½ oz icing sugar, sifted and mixed with the juice of ⅓ lemon

Makes 20
Preparation time: 15 minutes
Cooking time: 5 minutes

MAKING THE CAKES: Preheat the oven to 200°C/400°F/gas 6.

Put the egg, salt, caster sugar and lemon zest in a bowl and work lightly with a whisk. Add the cream, then the flour and yeast mixture and mix until smooth, then add the butter.

Cover the bowl with clingfilm and leave the mixture to rest at room temperature for 30 minutes. Fill the piping bag with the mixture and pipe it into the moulds. Bake in the preheated oven for 5 minutes. Unmould the cakes onto a cooling rack as soon as they are cooked. Using a pastry brush, coat them lightly with lemon icing and return them to the oven for 15 seconds. Put them back on the rack until completely cold.

PRESENTATION: Serve the cakes alone or with other petits fours.

SPECIAL EQUIPMENT:

20 small moulds, 4.5 cm/ 1¾ in at the top, 2.5 cm/1 in at the base, 1 cm/½ in deep

Piping bag with a plain 1 cm/½ in nozzle

NOTE:

These refreshing little cakes will keep in an airtight container for 3 days.

LITTLE SULTANA CUPS
Friands de sultanas en caissettes

INGREDIENTS:

250 g/9 oz tant pour tant (equal quantities of ground almonds and sugar sifted together)

1 egg, plus 2 extra yolks

100 g/4 oz butter, melted and cooled

35 g/1¼ oz moist sultanas

35 g/1¼ oz flour, sifted

3 egg whites

A pinch of caster sugar

Icing sugar for dusting

Makes 50
Preparation time: 20 minutes
Cooking time: 7 minutes

MAKING THE LITTLE CUPS: Preheat the oven to 200°C/400°F/gas 6.

In the electric mixer, beat the *tant pour tant*, egg and yolks with the paddle whisk until the mixture becomes pale and has a runny ribbon consistency. Fold in the melted butter with a spatula. Roll the sultanas in the flour and mix them and the flour into the mixture.

In the electric mixer, beat the egg whites with a pinch of caster sugar until very stiff. Fold them gently into the mixture with a spatula. As soon as the mixture is homogeneous, put it into a piping bag without a nozzle and fill the paper cases two-thirds full. Double up two baking sheets and arrange the filled cases on them. Bake in the preheated oven for 7 minutes, then immediately transfer the sultana cups to a cooling rack.

PRESENTATION: Dust the cups lightly with icing sugar and serve with other petits fours.

SPECIAL EQUIPMENT:

Electric mixer with a paddle whisk

50 round paper sweet cases, 2.5 cm/1 in diam., 2 cm/¾ in deep

NOTE:

If you prefer, omit the sultanas and pop a cherry or raspberry in eau-de-vie on top of the mixture just before baking.

The baked sultana cups can be frozen for up to a week in an airtight container.

CHAPTER TWELVE

DECORATION AND SUGARWORK

The craft of decoration and sugarwork deserves an entire tome to do it justice. Artwork in pâtisserie is more diverse, complex and imaginative than in any other area of cooking, yet it is relatively simple and enormously pleasurable to master the skills involved. Once you have done so, you will be delighted with the decorative effects you can achieve.

Decorative techniques include COOKED SUGAR, which can be poured, pulled, blown and made into rock, ball and spun sugar; PASTILLAGE for moulding, assembling models, collage and as soft paste for piping; CHOCOLATE AND MARZIPAN can be sculpted, modelled and moulded into flowers and other shapes. PIPED DECORATIONS include decorative writing and ornamentations made with piped Buttercream or Decorative Choux Paste. PAINTING WITH A BRUSH is done primarily on Pastillage or Marzipan, using food colouring or chocolate.

Aniseed Parfait (see recipe page 72) with spun sugar caramel

ROYAL ICING
Glace royale

NUMEROUS DESSERTS CAN BE DECORATED WITH A PIPING OF THIS ICING,
EITHER PLAIN OR TINTED WITH FOOD COLOURINGS.

INGREDIENTS:
50 g/2 oz egg whites
250 g/9 oz icing sugar,
    sifted
Juice of ¼ lemon, strained

Preparation time: 5 minutes

Put the egg whites in the bowl of an electric mixer and whisk at low speed, adding the sifted sugar a little at a time, then the lemon juice. Whisk until the mixture is firm and slightly risen; the icing is ready when it forms a very straight, fine point whichever way up you hold the whisk. If it is too thick to form a point, add a touch more egg white. If it is too thin, so that the point flops over when you hold it upwards, add a little more icing sugar.

NOTE:
Royal icing is best used immediately, but it will keep well in the fridge for several days. Store in an airtight container or a bowl covered with clingfilm to prevent a crust from forming.

SPUN SUGAR CARAMEL
Sucre décor fourchette

DRIZZLE THIS SUGAR OVER LIGHTLY-OILED HEMISPHERICAL MOULDS TO MAKE
SUGAR CAGES TO PLACE OVER AN ICE CREAM OR SURPRISE DESSERT. THIS
ATTRACTIVE DECORATION IS SIMPLICITY ITSELF TO MAKE (SEE PHOTO OPPOSITE).

INGREDIENTS:
80 ml/3 fl oz water
200 g/7 oz caster sugar
60 g/2 oz liquid glucose
Food colourings, according to
    taste

Makes about 350 g/12 oz

MAKING THE CARAMEL: In the pan, gently heat the water, sugar and glucose. As soon as the syrup comes to the boil, wash down the inside of the pan with a pastry brush dipped in cold water. Add a few drops of food colouring, put in the thermometer and cook until the sugar reaches 155°C/311°F. Take the pan off the heat and leave the sugar to cool for 3 minutes.

MAKING THE DECORATION: Place the Silpat or silicone paper on a baking sheet. Dip the prongs of a fork into the sugar and let it drizzle off the fork into lines or criss-crosses, to make the pattern you require. Repeat the operation to make as many decorations as you need. When they are cold, use them to decorate your dessert.

SPECIAL EQUIPMENT:
Copper sugar pan, or a small heavy-based stainless steel saucepan
Sugar thermometer
A sheet of Silpat or silicone paper

SPUN SUGAR
Sucre filé

THIS DELICATE, BRILLIANT SUGARWORK IS EXTREMELY SIMPLE TO ACHIEVE AND ADDS AN AIR OF GREAT
FESTIVITY TO A DESSERT. SINCE IT IS VERY PLIABLE, IT CAN BE FORMED INTO ALL SORTS OF ATTRACTIVE SHAPES
(SEE ICED MELON SURPRISE, PAGE 146), AND CAN ALSO BE USED TO MAKE THE PISTILS FOR SUGAR FLOWERS.

INGREDIENTS:
90 ml/3 fl oz water
250 g/9 oz sugar
65 g/2½ oz liquid glucose
1 tablespoon groundnut oil
 or pure vaseline, for
 greasing

Preparation time: 15
 minutes

SPECIAL EQUIPMENT:
Copper sugar pan, or a
 heavy-based stainless steel
 saucepan
Sugar thermometer
2 forks, or a small whisk
 with the wires all cut to
 the same length

NOTE:
Spun sugar is very sensitive
to moisture, so it is
important not to work in a
humid atmosphere.

COOKING THE SUGAR: Pour the water into the pan and add the sugar. Stir with a spatula, then place over low heat until the sugar has completely dissolved. As soon as it begins to bubble, skim the surface. Do this several times, taking care to rinse the skimmer in a bowl of very clean water each time.

Wash down the inside of the pan with a scrupulously clean pastry brush dipped in cold water to prevent the formation of sugar crystals. These could fall back into the pan during cooking and make the sugar grainy, which might cause it to form lumps as you spin it.

Now add the glucose, partially cover the pan with a lid and cook the sugar over high heat. Put in the sugar thermometer and stop cooking when the temperature reaches 152°C/305°F. Leave the sugar to bubble down and cool for 2 minutes. It is vitally important that it is at the correct temperature and consistency; if it is too hot or too thin, it will fall in little drops and not form threads; if too cold, it will be too thick to spin.

PREPARING THE WORK SURFACE: Protect the surface with several sheets of greaseproof paper. Lay a lightly oiled broom handle between two chairs or stools, or simply use an oiled rolling pin, holding one end carefully in your hand.

SPINNING THE SUGAR: Dip the prongs of the forks or the ends of the whisk into the sugar and flick them rapidly back and forth above the broom handle or rolling pin. The sugar will run down and spread and spin into threads on either side. When all the sugar has run off, repeat the operation and continue until the handle or rolling pin is fairly well covered with sugar threads (see photo, left). Do not overfill it.

Collect up all the sugar threads and place them on a lightly-oiled baking sheet if you intend to use them quickly, or store in an airtight container if you want to keep them for a few days. Place some silica gel, quicklime or carbide in the bottom of the container and cover it with foil before putting in the spun sugar.

PASTILLAGE

EXPERIENCE IS NOT IMPORTANT WHEN MAKING PASTILLAGE, BUT PRACTICE MAKES PERFECT WHEN IT COMES TO MOULDING AND CUTTING OUT SHAPES. PASTILLAGE LOOKS LOVELY PAINTED WITH FOOD COLOURINGS, BUT CAN ALSO BE LEFT WHITE.

INGREDIENTS:

500 g / 1 lb 2 oz icing sugar, sifted

50 g / 2 oz cornflour or potato flour, sifted, plus extra for the work surface

1 egg white

1 soup spoon water

2 gelatine leaves, soaked in cold water for 20 minutes and well drained

Juice of ½ lemon, strained

Food colourings (optional)

Makes about 650 g / 1½ lbs

Preparation time: 10 minutes

Drying time: 24—48 hours, depending on the thickness

MAKING THE PASTILLAGE: Put the icing sugar and cornflour or potato flour on a very smooth work surface and make a well.

Heat the egg white and water slightly in a bain-marie, stirring with your fingertips to stop it coagulating. Remove from the bain-marie, add the prepared gelatine and stir until completely dissolved.

Still stirring with your fingertips, pour this mixture into the centre of the well, add the lemon juice and mix, gradually drawing the icing sugar and flour into the centre to make a firm but malleable paste. If it is too soft, add a little more icing sugar; if too firm, add another drop of lukewarm water. Add any food colourings at this stage. Immediately wrap the pastillage in clingfilm to prevent it from drying out or cracking.

MOULDING THE PASTILLAGE: This must be done on a very smooth work surface (such as marble or formica), dusted with cornflour or potato flour. Roll out the pastillage to the appropriate size and thickness, and cut out your desired shapes, using stencils if you wish.

DRYING THE PASTILLAGE: Immediately transfer the cut shapes to a very smooth baking sheet lined with greaseproof paper and leave to dry at room temperature for 24—48 hours. Turn the pieces over when nearly dry to ensure that the underside is also dry; well-dried pastillage is much stronger. Once the pastillage is completely dry, you can polish the surface with very fine glass paper to achieve a porcelain-smooth finish.

PRESENTATION: You could shape several pieces to make one large model (eg: a house), sticking them together with royal icing (page 181) piped from a paper cone. A painted medallion makes a wonderful presentation for a child's birthday cake (see photo opposite).

SPECIAL EQUIPMENT:

A very smooth pâtisserie rolling pin, preferably plastic

1 or more very sharp knives

NOTE:

Do not keep pastillage for too long after shaping, as it dries out quickly and will crack. It is best used immediately after kneading, but it can be kept in the fridge, tightly wrapped in clingfilm, for 24 hours.

Pastillage seal and painted medallions

BUBBLE SUGAR
Sucre bullé

THIS MODERN SUGARWORK DECORATION WILL AMAZE THE UNINITIATED. IT IS RATHER TEMPERAMENTAL; SOMETIMES IT MAKES LARGE BUBBLES, SOMETIMES SMALL ONES. TO DATE WE HAVE NO IDEA WHY IT CHANGES, BUT BOTH RESULTS ARE EQUALLY EFFECTIVE .

INGREDIENTS:

500 g/1 lb 2 oz caster sugar

150 g/5 oz liquid glucose

200 ml/7 fl oz water

A few drops of food colouring, according to taste

Makes about 850 g/1¾ lbs

COOKING THE SUGAR: Follow the method for Spun Sugar Caramel (page 181). When the sugar temperature reaches 158°C/316°F, pour it immediately in small quantities and as thinly as possible onto the sheet of Silpat or greaseproof paper and, holding the sheet by the corners, tilt it to make the sugar run, but do not tap it. Take great care that the sugar does not run off the sheet, as it could burn your fingers.

When the sugar has cooled, peel it off the Silpat. It does not matter if it breaks into different-sized pieces; it will look even more attractive.

PRESENTATION: Arrange the thin sheets of bubble sugar on the serving plates to enhance the visual effect of your dessert.

SPECIAL EQUIPMENT:

Sugar thermometer

A sheet of Silpat or thick best quality greaseproof paper

POURED SUGAR
Sucre coulé

POURED SUGAR MODELS ARE THE STARS OF DECORATIVE SUGARWORK AND ARE SIMPLICITY ITSELF TO MAKE. AN ATTRACTIVE MODEL ON A STAND WILL TAKE ONLY HALF AN HOUR.

INGREDIENTS:

500 g/1 lb 2 oz sugar lumps

200 ml/7 fl oz water

125 g/4 oz liquid glucose

Food colourings, as required

A little groundnut oil

PREPARING THE TEMPLATE FOR THE MODEL: Lay the sheet of Silpat or foil on the work surface and on it roll out the modelling paste. The larger the model you intend to make, the thicker the paste should be. Using a stencil, cut out the shapes needed for your model with the tip of a very sharp knife (see the fish, right), or use confectioner's rulers to make an outline. The base for the model can be any shape, but it must be large enough to give adequate support and stability. Lightly brush the inside edges of the paste or rulers with oil.

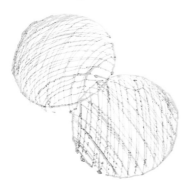

184

COOKING THE SUGAR: Cook the sugar as for Spun Sugar Caramel (page 181). Put in the thermometer and cook until the temperature reaches 140°C/284°F. Add the food colourings you require and heat to 156°C/312°F. Take the pan off the heat and let the sugar bubble down for 2 minutes. It is now ready to use without delay.

Pour the sugar in a steady stream into the template or rulers. Prick any air bubbles with the tip of a fine knife. Leave the sugar to cool for about 20 minutes, then lift off the modelling paste or rulers. If you wish, pipe on decorations with royal icing (page 181). Peel off the Silpat or foil and assemble your model.

SPECIAL EQUIPMENT:
Copper sugar pan, or a heavy-based stainless steel saucepan
Sugar thermometer
Modelling paste (eg: plasticine), or metal confectioner's rulers
A sheet of Silpat or foil
Stencils of your chosen shape

PULLED SUGAR
Sucre tiré

ANY KIND OF SUGARWORK DEMANDS CARE AND PATIENCE. COOKED SUGAR IS VERY HOT, SO BE CAREFUL NOT TO BURN YOURSELF. PRACTICE MAKES PERFECT, BUT THE ESSENTIAL QUALITIES NEEDED FOR SUGARWORK ARE LOVE AND THE DESIRE TO PRODUCE A BEAUTIFUL OBJECT, SENTIMENTS WHICH I HAVE FELT SINCE THE AGE OF SIXTEEN.

INGREDIENTS:
600 g/1¼ lbs fondant
400 g/14 oz liquid glucose
Food colourings, as required (optional)

Makes 1 kg/2¼ lbs

In the pan, gently heat the fondant and glucose to boiling point. Skim the surface and wash down the inside of the pan with a pastry brush dipped in cold water. Increase the heat, put in the thermometer and cook to 145°C/293°F. Add your chosen food colouring or leave the mixture plain for a white colour. Take the pan off the heat.

Leave the sugar to bubble down for 2 minutes, then pour it onto the Silpat or marble. As soon as the sugar begins to harden at the edges, use a palette knife or triangular metal scraper to fold them into the middle; do this four or five times. After a few minutes, the sugar will become malleable. Hold one end of the sugar and, using your fingertips, pull the mass outwards without squeezing, then fold it back onto itself and repeat about 25 times, until it becomes very glossy and smooth. After a few folds, as the sugar becomes less hot, it will hold better. Roll it up into a ball; it is now ready to use.

Place the pulled sugar under a sugar lamp or near the open oven door. Using your thumb, pull off small pieces to shape into flower petals or leaves, to make beautiful sugar roses, for example (see photo, left).

SPECIAL EQUIPMENT:
Copper sugar pan, or a heavy-based stainless steel saucepan
Sugar thermometer
A sheet of Silpat, or a marble slab lightly greased with pure vaseline

NOTES:
This fondant-based recipe is easier to work than the classic pure sugar and glucose recipe.

Pulled sugar flowers will keep well in a dry airtight container lined with silica gel, carbide or quicklime, covered with foil.

*Page 184, left: Spun Sugar Caramel cages:
Right: Bubble Sugar behind Poured Sugar fish*

Left: Pulled Sugar roses and leaves: Right: Marzipan roses, stems and leaves

DECORATING CHOCOLATE
Cacao décor

THIS SHINY CHOCOLATE IS USED FOR WRITING AND CREATING DECORATIVE
PATTERNS AND EFFECTS.

INGREDIENTS:
100 g/4 oz caster sugar
60 g/2 oz liquid glucose
100 ml/4 fl oz water
150 g/5 oz cocoa paste,
  finely chopped (for
  stockists, see page 190)

Makes about 350 g/12 oz
Preparation time: 5 minutes

Boil the sugar with the glucose and water to make a syrup, then cool to 50°C/122°F. Strain it through a conical strainer onto the cocoa paste. Whisk until homogeneous and very smooth, but take care not to overwork the mixture, or it will lose its elasticity and brilliance. The decorating chocolate is now ready to use for piping or writing.

SPECIAL EQUIPMENT:
Copper sugar pan, or a
  heavy-based stainless steel
  saucepan
Sugar thermometer

NOTE:
Decorating chocolate can be
kept in an airtight container
in the fridge for 2 weeks.
Spoon out as much as you
need and heat in a bowl in a
bain-marie or for a few
seconds in the microwave

Left: Decorating Chocolate
runouts

CHOCOLATE GLAZE
Glaçage chocolat

THIS GLAZE WILL GIVE YOUR CHOCOLATE DESSERTS AND GATEAUX A
BEAUTIFUL SHINY FINISH.

INGREDIENTS:
250 ml/9 fl oz Sorbet
  Syrup (page 144)
120 g/4 oz bitter or plain
  chocolate couverture or
  best quality cooking
  chocolate, chopped
40 g/1½ oz unsweetened
  cocoa powder, sifted

Makes about 400 g/14 oz
Preparation time: 10
  minutes

In a bowl set in a bain-marie over medium heat, heat the chocolate to 40°F/104°F. Heat the syrup with the cocoa, whisking continuously. When it reaches 50°C/122°F, pour it into the melted chocolate, still whisking just until the glaze becomes smooth and shiny. It is now ready to use.

NOTE:
The glaze will keep in an
airtight container in the
fridge for up to a week.
Reheat it in a bain-marie or
microwave oven for a few
seconds before using, taking
care not to heat it to more
than 40°C/104°F or to
overwork it.

Right: Chocolate Fans atop
Chocolate Glaze

DECORATIVE CHOUX PASTE
Pâte à choux à décor

INGREDIENTS:
35 g / 1¼ oz butter, diced
50 ml / 2 fl oz water
50 ml / 2 fl oz milk
A pinch of salt
60 g / 2 oz flour
2 size 3 eggs

Makes about 150 g / 5 oz
Preparation time: 20
   minutes
Cooking time: 6–10
   minutes, depending on the
   size of the decorations

COOKING THE PASTE: Preheat the oven to 160°C / 320°F / gas 2–3.
   Combine the butter, water, milk and salt in a saucepan and bring to the boil over high heat. Take off the heat and mix in the flour with a whisk to make a very smooth paste. Return the pan to the heat and stir with a spatula to dry out the paste for 30 seconds.
   Beat in the eggs one by one, then rub the paste through a very fine sieve into a bowl, using a plastic scraper.

PIPING THE PASTE: Pipe the choux paste into your chosen pattern directly onto the Silpat or paper. Bake in the preheated oven for 6–10 minutes, until lightly browned. For raised shapes, such as shells, pipe and bake the shapes flat, then mould them around an appropriately shaped mould as soon as they come out of the oven.

SPECIAL EQUIPMENT:
Piping bag with a plain
   2–3mm / ¹⁄₁₂–⅛ in nozzle,
   or a paper piping cone
Silpat or silicone paper

NOTE:
This choux paste will keep
for a week in a dry, airtight
container.

Clockwise from top left:
Decorative Choux Paste
shooting star: Tulip Paste
ribbon: Decorative Choux
Paste run-outs: Puff Pastry
palm trees

NOUGATINE

ALTHOUGH I NORMALLY MAKE NOUGATINE WITH NIBBED ALMONDS, FLAKED
ALMONDS CAN ALSO BE USED, AND WILL LOOK BETTER IF YOU ARE
MAKING A LARGE PRESENTATION PIECE.

INGREDIENTS:

500 g / 1 lb 2 oz nibbed or
flaked almonds
660 g / 1 lb 6 oz caster
sugar
60 g / 2 oz butter (optional)
2 tablespoons groundnut oil

Makes 1.2 kg / 2¾ lbs
Preparation time: 25
minutes

COOKING THE NOUGATINE: Preheat the oven to 180°C/350°F/gas 4.

Spread the almonds over a baking tray and toast in the oven until lightly browned. Cook the sugar in the pan over low heat, stirring gently and continously with a spatula, until it dissolves to a light golden caramel. Add the almonds and stir over low heat for 1 minute, then stir in the butter until completely absorbed (this is not essential, but will give the nougatine an added sheen). Pour the nougatine onto an oiled baking sheet.

SHAPING THE NOUGATINE:
Place the baking sheet towards the front of the warm oven, leaving the oven door half-open. The warmth will keep the nougatine malleable. Work with one small piece at a time, of a size appropriate to the shape you want. Roll

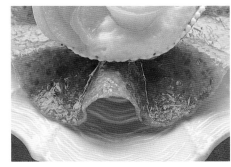

out each piece on a warm, lightly oiled baking sheet or lightly oiled marble surface. It is essential to work quickly, since the nougatine rapidly becomes brittle. If you have a microwave oven, heat the nougatine for only a few seconds to soften it. Alternatively, place a sugar lamp just far enough away from the nougatine to keep the mass warm while you mould the individual pieces.

Roll the nougatine into the appropriate thickness for your desired shape, but never thicker than 3 mm/⅛ in. Quickly cut out your chosen shapes using the cutters or the blade or heel of a chef's knife.

To mould the nougatine, drape it very rapidly over the mould so that it follows the shape and contours. Leave until completely cold before removing from the mould.

SPECIAL EQUIPMENT:

Copper sugar pan, or a
heavy-based saucepan
Pastry cutters, dessert rings
or a chef's knife (have
these ready to hand before
you start making the
nougatine)
Heavy rolling pin
1 or 2 lightly-oiled baking
sheets
Sugar lamp or microwave
oven (optional)

NOTES:

Like all sugar-based
confectionery, nougatine
should be stored well away
from any humidity. In damp
conditions, it will keep for at
most 2 days. 1 teaspoon
Nougasec (see page 190 for
stockist) added to the sugar
will keep the nougatine dry
for at least a week.

Nougatine Basket with
Yellow Peaches (see recipe
page 76)

SPECIALIST EQUIPMENT AND FOOD SUPPLIERS

CANNELÉ MOULDS: (Cannelé cuivre lunch, ref. 342)
Bordeaux Machines Sarl
45 rue Camille Flammarion
33100 Bordeaux, France
Tel: 56.86.93.99
   and **M.O.R.A.** (see opposite)

KOUGLOF MOULDS: (Moules kouglof no. 0 uni-9cm,
ref. 16100)
Poterie Siegfried-Burger et fils
10 rue de la Montagne
67200 Soufflenheim, France
Tel: 88.86.60.55
Fax: 88.86.69.97

SILPAT, RODOïDE PLASTIC AND SMALL PASTRY
EQUIPMENT:
Matfer/Cookware Française
5 Priory Close
Bishop's Waltham
Southampton SO3 1AP
Tel/Fax: 0329 287168
They also supply gold leaf and couverture

Bake-o-Glide
Falcon Products
Scott House
43 Scott Avenue
Baxenden
Accrington
Lancashire BB5 2XA
Tel: 0254 237386
   Bake-o-Glide is less expensive than Silpat. It comes in
three qualities: chocolate grade, sugar grade and standard
for baking.

SUGARWORK: All equipment needed for sugarwork,
cooking and baking, including Nougasec is available from
Déco-Relief
Allée de Bonvaux
21241 Talant-Dijon, France
Tel: 80.56.42.38
Fax: 80.58.17.99
   and **M.O.R.A.**
13 rue de Montmartre
75001 Paris, France
Tel: 1.45.08.19.24
Fax: 1.45.08.49.05

COUVERTURE, COCOA PASTE, COCOA BUTTER AND
ALL TYPES OF CHOCOLATE:
The Chocolate Society
Norwood Bottom Farm
Norwood Bottom, near Otley
West Yorkshire LS21 2RA
Tel: 0943 851101
Fax: 0943 468199

   At The Waterside Inn, I use Valrhona for the finest
quality couverture.
Chocolaterie Valrhona
BP 40
26600 Tain l'Hermitage
France
Tel: 75.07.90.90
Fax: 75.08.05.17
   It is also available from many delicatessens and by mail
order from:
Porter's Specialist Food Merchants
Bar Lane
Roecliffe
Boroughbridge
North Yorkshire YO5 9LS

INDEX